We Need to
talk about
Money

Also by the author

Little Black Book
Whites: On Race and Other Falsehoods

We Need to
talk about
Money.

Otegha Uwagba

4th ESTATE · *London*

4th Estate
An imprint of HarperCollins*Publishers*
1 London Bridge Street
London SE1 9GF

www.4thEstate.co.uk

HarperCollins*Publishers*
1st Floor, Watermarque Building, Ringsend Road
Dublin 4, Ireland

First published in Great Britain in 2021 by 4th Estate

1

A catalogue record for this book is available from the British Library

ISBN 978-0-00-835038-3 (hardback)
ISBN 978-0-00-835039-0 (trade paperback)

All names used throughout this book have been changed.
Any similarities are purely coincidental.

Printed and bound in CPI Group (UK) Ltd, Croydon

MIX
Paper from
responsible sources
FSC™ C007454

This book is produced from independently certified FSC paper
to ensure responsible forest management

Find out more about HarperCollins and the environment at
www.harpercollins.co.uk/green

For anyone who has ever felt overlooked or underpaid.
Who has gone to bed at night worrying about money,
and woken up in the morning still feeling sick with dread.
Who has felt bad or uncertain or despondent about their
financial future. Who has convinced themselves
that things are never going to get better.

This book is for you.

CONTENTS

Chapter 1

SCHOLARSHIP KID

I arrived in London on a rainy September morning, goose-pimple pricked flesh buried deep under a thick scarf and woollen tights, eyes wide in disbelief at the relentless greyness of it all. Then, and now, London seemed to me a city inexplicably enamoured of the colour grey, and determined to celebrate it in every one of its joyless permutations. Everywhere I looked, there it was glaring back at me, this never-ending parade of grey. Grey buildings, grey skies, grey streets. Grey everything.

September 1995. In the time-honoured tradition of countless immigrants before them, my parents had packed up their lives in Nigeria and come to the UK with their young family in tow – me, aged 5, and my two older sisters, S. and C., who were 8 and 9 years old. Given how young I was when we arrived, most of what I know of those early months are things my parents have since told me, as my own memories have mostly faded into a patch-work of half-remembered fragments: a pattern, a taste, a smell. My sisters, my mother and I came first, with my dad only able to join us a while later – which meant that for the first six months my mother had the unenviable task of making ends meet while single-handedly raising three young children, and trying to figure out an unfamiliar and at times unforgiving system. The four of us

1

spent those first few months crowded into a one-bedroom council flat with faded rose-pink carpet that had been worn to grey in the spots where a thousand footsteps had trodden before. Though we didn't exactly depend on the kindness of strangers, we certainly benefited from it – that pink-carpeted lodging came courtesy of an older cousin, who had readily vacated his own flat to crash at a friend's, so that we could make use of his place while we found our feet. It was this cousin too, who stepped in to look after me and C. one evening, after S. had suffered an asthma attack so severe that my mother had raced with her to the nearest emergency room. She returned home hours later, exhausted, to find a freshly-made lasagne waiting for her, and two well-fed daughters oblivious to the drama of her evening. Then there was the office admin who took pity on my mother having to ferry each of us to different primary schools while we waited for places to become available for all three of us at the same school, slyly bumping us up the waiting list so that within a few months my mother only had to make one drop-off before going to work, instead of three.

Eventually we found a place of our own, the five of us taking up residence in a slightly bigger council flat a few miles from where we'd initially settled. Money was still tight, but with the specific brand of resourcefulness seemingly innate to immigrant families on a budget, over the years we made that little rented flat our own. My meticulously house-proud mother turned fabrics bought at the local market into sweeping floor-to-ceiling curtains, and filled every corner of the flat with a cornucopia of carefully maintained plants. Meanwhile my father was enlisted to paint our bathroom an encouraging shade of sunshine yellow and put up shelves in the pastel pink bedroom I shared with S. (C., being the oldest, had a room to herself.) Bit by bit we accumulated the various souvenirs of family life, until eventually every surface was filled with ceramics and decorative mugs and the gap-toothed school photos that my parents insisted on buying each year. I still remember the collective pride when we could finally afford to have our carpets replaced with wood laminate flooring, which, my mother pointedly informed us all, would be *much* easier to clean.

It's always tricky to make firm assertions about how much money is 'enough', given what a subjective benchmark that is, but the simple fact is that in those early years we did not have enough. Only in adulthood did my father reveal to me his anguish over the time he'd realised my parents couldn't afford a new pair of school shoes to replace the ones I'd outgrown, prompting me to cheerfully inform them that we were 'poor as church mice!' (a notion I'm sure held far more excitement for me than it did for them, rendered in my child's imagination with a touch of Dickensian romance).

Even still, my childhood felt plentiful – rich, even. During the summer holidays my sisters and I would play outside for hours, hopscotching across cracks in the pavement and swinging from the branches of the overgrown willow that stood stoically in the middle of our estate, seemingly resigned to its fate as a makeshift climbing frame. We'd take it in turns to ride the pink bike our parents had bought us and count out our pennies for corner shop excursions, working out how many Maoams our funds could stretch to on the way there, and singing the jingle from the TV ad on the way back. When the weather turned cool and autumn set in, I'd rush home from school, impatient for the straight-from-the-oven sausage rolls and sugary cups of tea I knew were waiting for me, to be consumed while watching *The Animals of Farthing Wood*. There was the joy, verging on mania, that ensued

3

when I opened a carefully wrapped package one Christmas morning to find the *Spiceworld* cassette tape, the casing of which was promptly broken in the melee that followed. The family holiday taken in a caravan by the sea, where one night we simply ordered a Chinese takeaway and listened to the rain lashing down outside, sleepy and sated from the tang of hoi sin.

Young and oblivious, I never noticed the drug dealers loitering on the stairwell leading up to our flat that my father assures me were a regular late-night fixture. I was 10 when Damilola Taylor, a Nigerian boy the same age as me, was stabbed and killed on a Peckham estate in an act of such violent obscenity that it dominated the headlines for months afterwards. One child, killed by two others, Danny and Ricky Preddie: all three of their names would become shorthand for the perils of council estate life. Even at that young age I noticed how that news story in particular seemed to commandeer my parents' attention, temporarily suspending conversation whenever it appeared on the seven o'clock news, but it's only now that I'm older that I've begun to fully understand why. Like mine, Damilola's parents had left Nigeria for the UK in search of the fabled 'better life', only to have their child cruelly snatched from them on a housing estate not two miles from ours. The image splashed across nightly news bulletins and newspaper pages for months after Damilola's death – a school photo in which he could be seen smiling sweetly out at the camera – could easily have been one from my family's mantelpiece.

Still, things slowly improved for us over the years, my parents working tirelessly to make our lives more comfortable. I was 10 when we were finally able to afford a car, my dad surprising us by arriving home one afternoon and beckoning us out onto the balcony that overlooked our estate, pointing out a second-hand

Toyota that was now, unbelievably, ours. Before that, car journeys had always felt to me like a sublime luxury, given how infrequently they occurred – the occasional lift from visiting friends, or a rare minicab ride if the supermarket shop was too heavy to carry home by bus. We spent the rest of that afternoon cruising around the local area, and for months afterwards my dad was able to leverage my excitement at the novelty of having a car into getting me to help him wash it on Sunday afternoons.

My parents made sure my sisters and I always had everything we needed – and most of the things we wanted, too – from a new school bag and a fresh supply of stationery at the start of each school year, to the latest CDs and the metallic blue rollerblades that became my pride and joy. We were always – *always* – immaculately turned out, my mother viewing our personal presentation as an extension of hers, and never failing to deploy a strategic elbow nudge if ever she spotted us slouching. Under her tutelage, I took to methodically ironing a fresh shirt each morning before school, a habit I carried with me all the way to university, where it was of course swiftly jettisoned. My childhood was a revolving door of piano, violin, gymnastics and tennis lessons, all procured at low cost thanks to various community organisations that my mum had found, and all of which I unceremoniously abandoned one after the other.

But as hard as my parents tried to make money a non-issue in our lives, from an early age I sensed that it was. Little pitchers have big ears, as the saying goes. When it came to money, I couldn't help but absorb the pressure my parents were under in trying to provide for three daughters who churned through an endless cycle of new wants and needs. I noticed everything: the way my mother would grumble about the cost of fruit at the local market, going to multiple stalls to get things at a marginally lower price even if it ended up taking us twice as long; or the way she furrowed her brow if the £20 she'd topped up the gas meter with seemed to have run out more quickly than usual. Whenever I accompanied either of my parents to the supermarket for the weekly shop, I'd pay careful attention to the figure that appeared on-screen at the checkout, my eyes flicking to theirs if it seemed unexpectedly high, searching their face for a reaction. I was painfully aware of money, and how it worked, and that it was not infinite. Even though I harboured the same desire for new clothes and toys as most children, I'd feel incredibly guilty if something I wanted (or worse, needed) required my parents to spend what I deemed to be an inordinate sum of money, and so I learned to self-regulate between what I wanted and what I thought my parents could afford. I was never the child who begged for a Nintendo or an expensive pair of trainers, because I knew intuitively that those things were beyond our means.

Sometimes late at night, I'd hear my parents talking about money, the low hum of their tense conversations filtering through my bedroom wall as I strained to hear what was being said. In my presence, they'd often switch to Yoruba so that they might have otherwise private conversations publicly, and though I couldn't understand *exactly* what they were saying, it was easy enough to decipher their money worries from their body language alone. The message I absorbed was this: that money was something to be wrangled, to be twisted and stretched into place, an adversary one had to be vigilant around, lest it caught you out and put you in danger.

One of the most formative influences on our relationship with money is, unsurprisingly, the relationship our parents have with it. Most of us learn about money – or not – from our parents, inheriting their beliefs, behaviours and anxieties as surely as we inherit their genes. This is what psychologists call 'financial socialisation', the process by which we construct both our conceptual and emotional understanding of money. Perhaps you grew up in a household where money was never talked about, and to this day it remains an indecipherable mystery to you. You never learned how it worked, or about key financial concepts – no parental wisdom about budgets and saving handed down to you over the dinner table, in between lectures about chewing with your mouth closed and not playing with your food. Perhaps your parents lavished you with expensive presents and toys as a way of demonstrating their love, and now as an adult that is how you too show affection to those you hold dear, a scenario that at its best makes you a generous friend or partner, the one who always gets a round in, and at its worst makes you someone easily exploited by the people around you. Perhaps money was tight growing up, but your parents felt compelled to keep up appearances, and now your relationship with money revolves around how you appear to the outside world. You guiltily rack up thousands of pounds worth of credit card debt on expensive clothes and Instagrammable holidays, because deep down how wealthy others perceive you to be matters more to you than your financial reality. Our parents' relationships with money very often become ours, though the manifestation of those influences can at times be more oblique – think of the child from an impoverished background who grows up to be a millionaire, spending extravagantly because, finally, they can (only to be dismissed as 'nouveau riche'). In my case, the pattern was fairly linear; my parents' caution sowing the seeds for a similar wariness in me. I developed a latent anxiety around money, though that wouldn't bear fruit until many years later when I was at liberty to decide how to manage my own finances.

I was an incredibly bright child, something that might seem rather boastful to announce so unreservedly were it not a fact that would direct how the rest of my childhood played out. I'd learned to read by the age of 3, fascinated by my older sisters' mastery of what to me seemed like the coolest magic trick in the world, and demanding that my mother teach me as well. By the time I arrived in London aged 5, my schoolteachers reported to my parents that it wasn't a question of whether or not I could read, but rather which books I hadn't yet read, given how frequently I'd be presented with a book at school only to declare that I'd already read it at home. I was consistently at the top of my class, and so far advanced for my age that one particularly enterprising teacher would occasionally have me mark my classmates' work once I'd finished my own (though to be fair, this probably said more about the resource challenges she was facing than it did my intelligence).

What's more, I actually *enjoyed* learning. Loved it, in fact. I'd read news stories about child prodigies who'd sat their A levels early and wonder whether I might be able to do the same, and dreamt of the day I might be invited to take up my place at Mensa with the same enthusiasm that most children await a letter from Hogwarts. I was studious and meticulous, and smart enough to realise how smart I was, basking in the warm glow of praise from teachers and parents alike. I was probably also a little precocious.

I was lucky, too, that my parents took an active interest in my education, regarding school as just one facet of many to be deployed in their quest to ensure my sisters and I realised our full potential. While my mother taught us French and borrowed a language course from the local library so she and I could learn Spanish together, my father oversaw my education in maths, shrewdly perfecting a low-involvement/high-yield system. He'd assign me practice papers that I'd complete (while timing myself), mark (also myself, using the answers provided at the back of the book), at which point I'd report my score back to him so that I could be congratulated, before settling down to complete another paper. I never realised the extra work I did at home was to any specific end – I was nerdy enough to find pleasure in achievement for achievement's sake – but I know now that the stakes for my parents were always high. They knew that being a Black, foreign-born immigrant to the UK, my best chance of success would be to have an unimpeachable education, though they were careful never to burden me with the heaviness of that reality – instead it was simply made clear to me and my sisters that poor grades would *not* fly in our household. My parents pushed our teachers as much as they pushed us too, wary of the ease with which Black children are overlooked at school, and determined that that would not be our lot. (Countless studies have shown that Black students are more likely to be punished or excluded than their white counterparts, with teachers also tending to predict them lower grades than the ones they actually go on to achieve.)[1] A long-running family joke is that every teacher my sisters and I ever had soon learned to fear my parents, who never hesitated to write a strongly worded letter or – if the occasion called for it – make an in-person visit to the school gates if they felt some aspect of our educational needs wasn't being met. There were, unfortunately, countless such incidents.

When I was around 9 or 10 years old, a teacher caught me and some friends passing notes in class – a rare episode of misbehaviour on my part. Scribbled on various scraps of paper were a litany of childish grievances, ranging from what we perceived to be the favouritism one of our male teachers displayed towards the boys in our class, to my vehement criticism of another teacher's dishevelled appearance and 'bad coffee breath'. Along with my fellow co-conspirators, I found myself in a world of trouble, stripped of playtime privileges and forced to eat lunch in isolation for the rest of the week. All of our parents were informed.

But one teacher, Mrs Leighton, who was notorious for the apparent contempt with which she seemed to regard the children she taught, began to single me out, making sly digs and comments whenever we encountered each other. After a few days of this, my parents noticed that I was arriving home from school each afternoon increasingly despondent, and eventually they managed to prise the reason out of me. Ashamed, I tearfully recounted what had been happening – and my parents immediately swung into action. The letter below, which still shocks me to read, was drafted that very evening and addressed to my school's head teacher.

Dear Mr Levine,

The school secretary has informed us about an incident at school this week involving Otegha and some friends passing inappropriate notes. A meeting has been arranged to discuss the matter with her form teacher this coming Friday.

In the meantime, we want to bring to your attention some of Otegha's experiences at school this week:

1. On Tuesday 28th, Ms Leighton verbally assaulted Otegha, ostensibly in reaction to the incident referred to above, saying 'Your arrogant parents said we don't adequately challenge you.' This must be a direct reference to a request we made of Otegha's form teacher, Mr Stevens, many months ago (not Ms Leighton, whom we have never met before!). The request was made during the discussion of Otegha's performance, and was supposed to be part of a confidential review of her progress and academic achievements at school. We do not feel we should be penalised for making this request. Indeed, we have never been informed that said request was improper. We made that request believing that the quest to enhance the academic progress and performance of our daughter – or any other pupil at the school for that matter – should not be the trigger for unwarranted cynicism. However, it appears this is not the case, and that request has now become the catalyst for a verbal assault on Otegha, as implied by the reference to 'your arrogant parents'.

2. Later on the same day, Ms Leighton further verbally assaulted Otegha when she described her as being 'two-faced'. We believe this unsavoury remark, which later caused Otegha to burst into tears, was entirely gratuitous. As with the one referred to above, this comment was made in bad taste and as part of a premeditated agenda.

3. The next day on Wednesday 29th, and in continuation of the siege on Otegha, Ms Leighton confiscated the badge awarded to Otegha as a member of the school council. We are not aware of the capacity in which she acted thus. However, we are of the opinion that even if it was connected

to the incident Otegha was previously involved in, Ms Leighton's action was premature and her tactic intimidating. After all, the matter had neither been discussed with us nor resolved. In any case, Ms Leighton did not appoint Otegha to the school council – her classmates democratically elected her! It is reasonable to expect that, should it have been so decided, there would be a less traumatising and intimidating way of deselecting her as class president. Ms Leighton continued her verbal assault of Otegha, telling her, 'You must think you're a little goddess.'

4. The same Wednesday, just before Otegha and the rest of her classmates were due to go swimming, Ms Leighton told her she was barred from going. If Mr Stevens had not intervened, Otegha would have been bullied into submission.

We are quite ready to dismiss the reference to us as 'arrogant parents' as malicious and arrant nonsense. We consider it to be part of the hazard of parenting. However, we are unwilling to see Otegha subjected to any further verbal assault, intimidation and bullying by an adult and teacher in the person of Ms Leighton – or indeed any other teacher or member of staff. We believe that Otegha is entitled to fair treatment that is compatible with our desire for her emotional stability, well-being and safety whilst at school.

We urge you to look into this matter.

Carefully printed at the bottom of the two-page missive were both my parents' signatures, and the following morning my father hand-delivered it to the head teacher, arriving at the school office and insisting on an immediate appointment. By lunchtime, I'd been reinstated as school councillor, and Mrs Leighton never bothered me again.

Looking back on it now, it seems fairly obvious that she'd decided my parents, and by extension I, had become too 'uppity' for her liking, taking it upon herself to put us all back in our place. Unfortunately for her, she had woefully underestimated my parents' ambition for their daughters. The 'education, education, education' mantra first uttered by Tony Blair as he swept to power in 1997 could frequently be heard on my parents' lips, who were thrilled that their belief in the power of a good education had been so succinctly summarised in one of the best-known political sound bites of that era.

In a move that has since become part of our family folklore, when the time came for me to apply for secondary school, my oldest sister C. intervened on my behalf, insisting to my parents that they weren't to send me to the local state school she herself was already attending, because she didn't think I'd be sufficiently challenged. Instead she convinced them to consider sending me to a private school, pointing them in the direction of an elite and highly competitive girls' school nestled in the Barbican, attended by the daughters of bankers and barristers, and even at one point a prime minister's daughter.

Poring over the school's glossy brochure some weeks later, a burning desire to be part of it ignited in me. It looked like paradise. I flipped past pages outlining the school's dedication to academic excellence and its stellar exam results, past the breathless descriptions of its extensive facilities (a pool, tennis courts, a gym), past pictures of laughing girls by turns conducting science experiments or caught mid-action as they tore across the sports field, past all of that to the breakdown of tuition fees discreetly tucked away on its final pages: £3,000 a term. How on earth were we to afford that? I knew my family didn't have that kind of money. Tentatively, I brought it up with my parents, who told me not to worry and assured me that if I passed the entrance exams, they would 'find a way'. When I pressed, they shared their hope that perhaps I might win a scholarship, or at least a partial bursary that would enable them to make up the shortfall. But I was still worried. I had never wanted something so badly in my life, and the chances of it actually happening seemed slim to none.

Arriving for the entrance exams in late autumn, my mother tried to reassure me as we approached the imposing grey building, a concrete structure in the brutalist tradition, and on this day, it seemed, designed to intimidate.

'It doesn't matter, OK? Just go in there and do your best.'

She sensed I was nervous, my usually confident nature subdued by the gravity of the situation and the hordes of chattering girls I was convinced were smarter, better-prepared and more likely to be granted entry than I was. Handing me over to the smiling sixth-formers who'd been enlisted to help out (how old they seemed – how self-assured!), she kissed me goodbye.

The first paper, English, seemed to go OK, though afterwards I fretted that my efforts during the creative writing section had veered towards the prosaic. As we waited to be called for our second exam though, my nerves began to climb, twisting themselves into a painful knot in my stomach. By the time the maths paper came round – then my strongest subject and the one I'd been relying on to carry me through – I was in agony. I raced through the questions, finishing the paper half an hour early, but instead of using that time to go through my answers – as the teacher invigilating kept pointedly advising – I lay my head down on the desk and closed my eyes. It was the only thing that seemed to make the pain go away. Arriving to pick me up at lunchtime, my mother found me even more miserable and despondent than when she'd left me, and reluctant to talk about how I'd done. I'd messed up, and I knew it. She didn't push, and we didn't bring up the exams, or the school, again.

Months later, on a Saturday morning bright with the promise of budding spring, a pile of envelopes slid through our letter box and landed on the floor. Scooping them up, my mother immediately spotted the school's crest on one of them. As she would later tell me, in life, bad news tends to come in small envelopes, good news in large ones. She held her breath. This envelope, stamped with the school's regal insignia, was a thick brown A4. Inside, miraculously, was a formal letter of acceptance, alongside an offer of a full academic scholarship. I had somehow tested among the top 16 of the 500 or so girls who had sat the school's entrance exams, qualifying me for a scholarship that would cover the entirety of my school fees for the next seven years, right through to sixth form. My mother erupted in a display of uncontrolled joy unlike anything I'd ever seen from her before or since, yelling in disbelief, and then joy, and then disbelief again. As for me, I had no idea on that clear spring day of the extent to which my life had just been transformed.

My first day at the school saw me encounter Mary, a rather haughty girl who I would later learn was the daughter of a prominent journalist. As we filed into the main hall for our first assembly, she and I fell into polite conversation. 'Do you live in

Islington?' No. 'Hampstead?' No. 'Well, where do you live then?' Elephant and Castle. 'Where's that?' South London. She looked confused and wrinkled her nose before declaring that she'd never been south of the river.

I don't know how two 11-year-old girls got onto the subject of cleaners, but we did, and I revealed that no, my family did not have a cleaner.

'What do you mean you don't have a *cleaner*?' she asked, incredulous, as though I'd told her the house I lived in didn't have a roof, or walls.

I stared at her, unsure of how to answer. Prior to that moment it hadn't even occurred to me that having a cleaner was a thing. I didn't know anyone who did.

'We do it ourselves,' I shrugged, and turned to follow the rest of the girls into the hall.

In the weeks leading up to that first day, my mother and I had paid a visit to John Lewis, the school's official uniform supplier (having recently taken over that role from Harrods, of all places). We spent what to me seemed like a small fortune – £405 – an amount I still remember clearly all these years later. Even the shop assistant serving us protested.

'She won't need the cardigan, the jumper *and* the sweatshirt. Why don't you come back once she's been there a few weeks and you can see what she's missing, buy the rest then?' she advised.

My mother was not in the mood to be advised. Her pride in my having won a scholarship to the school outweighed her usual financial prudence and she insisted on buying every single item on the suggested uniform list, right down to the gym knickers, which I would never once wear.

My encounter with Mary was an inauspicious start, but

thankfully not an indicative one. I am one of those people who genuinely enjoyed their school days, and in many senses I was lucky – as private schools go, mine turned out to be something of an anomaly, mostly avoiding the atmosphere of social snobbery often rampant within those environments. My being there on a scholarship only marked me out as different in that I was understood to be 'one of the smart kids'. It was never something that I hid, or felt embarrassed about.

I struggle sometimes to accurately convey my class identity to others. In a society as class-obsessed as Britain, where class is so weighted with meaning and plays such an influential role in the trajectory of one's life, the definitions we rely on are surprisingly rigid. There is little room for, or appreciation of, nuance, especially in the middle of the class spectrum, where things are considerably more fluid than at its outer reaches. Rich = upper class. Comfortable = middle class. Poor = working class. And yet class is composed of so much more than the bare bones of income or occupation, both of which can change drastically overnight without really altering your fundamental class identity. So what defines your class? Is it the one you were born into, or the one you die a part of (though statistically speaking, for most people those are likely to be one and the same)? Is it your bank balance, or the newspapers you read? The job you do, or the job your parents did? Settee or sofa? Tesco's or Waitrose? It would be easy to assume that because I grew up on a council estate, I'm working class – and it's true that those experiences do tend to go hand in hand – but I've never felt that to be a narrative I could fully claim. One of the most influential thinkers on the subject of class was the twentieth-century sociologist Pierre Bourdieu, who in 1979 published his seminal text *Distinction: A Social Critique of the*

Judgement of Taste, exploring class and culture within French society. In it, he argues that class background is determined by how much 'capital' one's parents possess (capital in this sense meaning resources), breaking that down into three brackets: social capital (being well connected and having friendships with people of influence); economic capital (income, wealth, ownership); and cultural capital (having the 'right' cultural tastes, knowledge and educational credentials). Or, as the writer Eula Biss puts it, 'what you own, what you know, and who you know'.[2]

Though my family was of very modest means, living in a rented council flat on a housing estate, I also grew up in a home where the shelves were heaving with books, my illustrated encyclopaedias and *Harry Potter*s jostling for space with my parents' political biographies and copies of *Reader's Digest*. Radio 4's never-ending reel of documentaries provided the background noise to our days, and weekends were spent on visits to museums and galleries, whether I liked it or not (which, often, I did not). Perhaps most importantly, I was raised by two degree-educated parents, which statistically speaking means I was almost certain to end up going to university myself. Indeed, I was probably 10 or 11 before I even realised that going to university wasn't compulsory, such was the party line in our home. I grew up in an environment with an abundance of cultural capital – we just didn't have a lot of *actual* capital, in the more traditional sense of the word. To describe myself as *either* working class *or* middle class, as the established categorisations invite us to do, has always felt too simplistic. In my upbringing at least, I straddle the two.

And despite how different our backgrounds were, my day-to-day life wasn't all that different from those of the girls I went to school with. By the time I was a teenager my parents had worked their way up to what I think most people would define as the lower middle class, and financially our situation had improved markedly in the decade since we'd arrived in London. We weren't rich by any means, but my parents could now afford to spoil us a little, which they did, dispensing crisp £20 notes whenever I wanted to go to the cinema with my friends. My mother – ever the aesthete – indulged our love of fashion with regular forays to Oxford Street, where my sisters and I would spend hours carefully perusing the aisles of H&M and New Look, returning home laden with bags. We were able to travel, going on holiday to visit family friends in France and Switzerland, and once, Canada. My parents were always keen to make sure I could keep up with my friends, so while I wasn't the first in my year group to get a mobile phone, I wasn't the last, either.

Sometime around Year 8, sleepovers began to hold the sort of social currency that only teenage girls can fully understand, the question of whether or not one is invited and the ceremony of hosting becoming a high-stakes political drama. After I'd been to a few, my parents suggested (or perhaps I asked) that I host one of my own. And so it was that on a Friday afternoon a few weeks later, a group of six of my closest friends excitedly collected by the lockers, aglow with the quiet smugness of girls who have, on that occasion, been anointed. We were chaperoned by my mother to the then *very* cool Hard Rock Cafe for dinner, before all seven of us crowded into the living room of our little flat for the night. My parents, eager for my first-ever sleepover to be a success, had done their bit – stocking the fridge with copious snacks and then largely staying out of our way, a far cry from the over-interfering helicopter parents I'd sometimes encounter at my friends' houses. As such, it was widely regarded as one of the better sleepovers of my friendship group, and I floated into school the following Monday high on the success of it.

By any standards, then, I had plenty – but there was no getting around the fact that many of my friends had so much more. I socialised with girls blissfully free (it seemed to me) of the near-constant stream of financial calculations whirring at the back of my mind, girls who always seemed to be sporting whatever must-have item was currently trending – an iPod or a dress from Urban Outfitters, the occasional designer bag. There were two sisters who were chauffeured to and from school in a blacked-out car, commandeering separate cars on days when they'd argued. There were girls who had second, and sometimes third, homes; who lived in Georgian townhouses in central London and holidayed in Monaco. If my early childhood was when I learned what it's like to exist in the world without very much money, my teenage years were when I first began to understand what it's like to have an abundance of it.

Childhood beliefs are hard to shake, often imprinted in the psyche with the indelibility of a tattoo. Even as adults, most of us instinctively revert to the habits we formed as kids.

During sixth form, one morning my history teacher announced that there would be a class trip to Russia the following term, to help further our understanding of the Soviet Union module we were studying. Scanning the permission letter we'd been given to take home to our parents, my eyes quickly alighted on the cost of the trip. £600! Not to mention all the extras I'd need – a week's worth of spending money in a country I'd heard was ruinously expensive, and weather-appropriate clothing for the sub-zero temperatures. The letter had suggested skiwear as an ideal option, the underlying assumption being that most of us would either have access to a pile of ski clothes at home or would be happy to buy some, at not inconsiderable expense. All in all, I estimated that the trip would cost upwards of £1,000, which to 16-year-old me seemed like an unfathomable sum, and it was here that my old childhood instinct to avoid burdening my parents with money worries rose to the surface – more so because I'd decided that the trip was something of an indulgence. Though most of my class would be going, it certainly wasn't critical to my understanding of the subject, or to my grades. I assumed my parents either couldn't afford it, or that even if they *could*, it would be a strain, and I didn't want them to have to calculate where they might find the money, what they could squeeze and cut back on so that I could go on a week-long jolly around Russia. I decided to make the decision for them. I never showed them the letter.

A few months later at parents' evening, the three of us settled down to speak to my history teacher, Mr Phillips, who made cheerful conversation as he updated my parents on my progress. Everything was going well – I was a serious student, easily on track for an A in my exams. I breathed a sigh of relief, forever worried that one of my teachers might reveal to my parents that though an excellent student, I was also irritatingly unruly and prone to talking *constantly* during lessons. On more than one occasion I'd been mournfully sequestered in a lone seat at the front of the class, under a teacher's watchful gaze and away from my friends.

'I *am* disappointed you won't be coming on the Russia trip, though!' Mr Phillips exclaimed, turning to me.

Oh crap.

'What Russia trip?' my mum asked, and all three of them – my mum, my dad and Mr Phillips – turned to look at me, the latter looking especially confused. For months I'd feigned disinterest in the trip, aligning myself with the few disaffected girls in my history class who didn't want to go for reasons of their own, which was unlike me – I was an otherwise enthusiastic student, and in fact, history was my favourite subject.

Explaining why I'd kept the trip from my parents on our way home that evening, they were crestfallen, reminding me that my education was the one thing they would *never* scrimp on, the very thing they worked so hard to ensure was unassailable. They instructed me to sign up for the trip the next day, but by that point it was mere weeks away. It was too late.

Years later, I'd be sitting on the sofa with my mother watching a news segment about Russia, when out of the blue she remarked, 'you know, it still pains me that you never got to go on that Russia trip.' I looked at her, surprised. I'd barely given it a second thought, even back then, using the free time I'd had while my class was away to mess around in the school library with friends. Not for the last time, she expressed a slight guilt that perhaps our earlier financial constraints had permanently burdened me with unnecessary anxiety over money.

And yet, I felt happy and secure at school, somehow thriving in an environment that I had every reason to feel insecure in – besides being extremely well-to-do, my school was also extremely white. I was one of perhaps four Black girls in a year group of seventy. Still, I managed to form tight-knit friendships, spending most evenings on the phone giddily rehashing the day's events with girls I'd seen just hours before, convulsing in fits of hysterical laughter before reluctantly bidding each other goodbye so we could actually do some homework. I had room to explore my interests, and wrote regularly for the school magazine, turning in pious little essays on feminism and politics, and the occasional review of a school play. I was elected head girl in my final year and spent much of my time fundraising for bursaries and scholarships, feeling it important to pay forward the same good fortune that I myself had had.

Like many, my teen years were the period where I developed my early aspirations around money and work, and on that front those years left two lasting legacies. My school went to admirable lengths to foster an ardently feminist atmosphere, our teachers impressing on us early and often that women were indisputably equal to (if not better than) men, a well-meaning agenda that nonetheless meant I was ill-prepared for the injustices of the working world I'd later encounter. For all their good intentions, that early introduction to feminism didn't much prepare me for the actual reality of workplace sexism, which as a teenager I deduced would be a sort of game, where all you had to do to win was work hard. Girls vs boys. It didn't even occur to me that racism would be an issue – *that* was never discussed.

Then there was the school's proximity to the City, which meant we were subject to a steady stream of banking-focused career events – picture a gaggle of wide-eyed teenage girls being given a tour of, say, the Merrill Lynch trading floor. By the time I was 15 I could expertly reel off a list of all the major investment banks. (This was 2006, before the financial crash, when banking didn't have quite the image problem it does now.) At one careers event, a few recent alumni were invited back to give talks about their respective industries during a lunchtime session. One had gone into investment banking at one of the big banks, and immediately our collective gaze homed in on her. She was the epitome of what we imagined a successful working woman to be – glossy and well groomed, in a smartly tailored skirt suit and vertiginous heels, self-consciously tapping away at her BlackBerry the entire time, the better to show off a comet-sized engagement ring. She seemed *impossibly* grown up, and leaving the assembly hall afterwards, several of us agreed that yes, we too wanted to work in investment banking.

It would be churlish of me to complain about my school having encouraged us to aspire to well-paid work, and I'm not. What an immense privilege as a young woman to be steered towards a financially rewarding career, and to have the paths into those industries demystified for you when so many young women experience the very opposite. Still, that focus on banking and other corporate professions only served to skew my assumptions of what the working world would be like, especially when it came to salary expectations. I imagined that by my mid-twenties I'd be pulling in a six-figure salary, and that that sort of salary was perfectly normal. By the time I left school, I'd formed two key conclusions about how my adult years would play out: that I'd necessarily grow up to make lots of money, and that climbing the career ladder as a woman would be a breeze.

Suffice to say, I was wrong on both counts.

Chapter 2

DREAMING SPIRES

The drive up to Oxford was a muted affair, my parents humming along to the radio while I sat quietly in the back, books and bedding piled high around me. Every now and then my mother would twist round to peer at me inquisitively, until eventually:

'You're very quiet! Are you nervous?' she asked, teasingly.

'No!?' I scoffed, full of teenage derision, offended at the very suggestion.

I caught her and my father exchange knowing glances as she turned back around, the two of them barely managing to suppress their smiles. Irritated, I rolled my eyes and carried on staring out of the window, watching as the landscape morphed from the grey blur of motorway to the muted gold of Oxford's cobbled streets and limestone towers, until finally the satnav announced that we'd reached our destination.

The three of us sat waiting in the car for a few moments, suddenly unsure, until at last one of the older students who'd volunteered to help out during freshers' week rapped his knuckles on the window.

'New College?' he asked.

I nodded gratefully, and together the four of us began ferrying my belongings into my new home, a room ensconced in a centuries-old gothic building that looked out onto one of Oxford's famous green quads.

I'd been waiting months for this day to arrive, and now each of my actions felt oddly charged and heavy with meaning, from the way I smoothed down my bedspread to the way I crossed my legs as I sat through that afternoon's inductions. I'd spent those dull, final few months of school daydreaming constantly about what Oxford would be like, constructing dozens of scenarios and weighing up various theories based on the scraps of information I'd managed to patch together. I was excited about the prospect of living away from home for the first time, away from rules and curfews and parental supervision, and free to cast off the bits of myself that I'd outgrown. I considered carefully what sort of impression I wanted to make, and how I'd make it – what clothes I'd wear on that crucial first day (a Breton top and brown knee-high leather boots, if you're interested), and how to decorate my room in a way that conveyed personality, eventually settling on the same mass-produced IKEA bedding as everyone else. My mission was, if not to reinvent myself entirely, then certainly to fashion a version of myself that felt fitting for this new, more grown-up phase of life. Cooler, more sophisticated, possibly even a little . . . *mysterious*. I briefly considered taking up smoking in service of this goal, eventually abandoning that idea and resolving instead to wear more black. I was enthusiastic about the prospect of boys too, after seven years at an all-girls' school where sightings of the opposite sex had been rare, and usually disappointing. I spent months cycling through the same set of questions: what sort of friends would I make? Would I be popular? Would I get a first? What would the boys be like? Would they think I was hot? Would I meet The One?

And then there were a few, slightly more serious concerns, thanks to Oxford's reputation as a bastion of privilege over-ridden with the progeny of Britain's moneyed elites. Pretty much every article I'd ever read about the university was accompanied by pictures of boys in white tie and tailcoats stumbling out of extravagant-sounding May Balls, while tweedy-looking girls with carefully backcombed hair hung off their arms. Mixed in with all the excitement was a deep anxiety that I was about to be sur-rounded by the sort of people whose definition of 'estate' only extended as far as 'country', who I'd have nothing in common with, and who'd want nothing to do with me. Desperate for reassurance, I did what any child of the digital age would do – I created an anonymous account on a popular online forum for students, posting questions about the class divide at Oxford, and whether you needed to be from a wealthy background in order to 'fully enjoy' your time there. Of course what I really wanted to know was whether or not I'd fit in, because I was 18, and that's all you really want when you're 18.

That fear, that I wouldn't be able to keep up financially, was pressing enough that over the summer I'd taken on a few waitres-sing stints with a catering company to save up some extra cash. It was deeply unglamorous work, mostly involving slinging dried-out jacket potatoes to grey-suited punters at conferences, but I was thrilled to be earning my own money, and comforted by the couple of hundred pounds I managed to earn in the weeks lead-ing up to my arrival.

To my relief, I found my footing easily, making friends quickly, and neatly sidestepping the homesickness that seemed to blight others. My fears of not fitting in with my fellow students were laid to rest early on, with student life mostly revolving around the same few bars and cheesy nightclubs, just like at any other uni. There is a certain levelling effect to being collectively laid low by 2-for-1 specials on Jägerbombs.

That's not to say Oxford's culture wasn't heavily shaped by middle-class sensibilities. To an extent, being privately educated provided me with a layer of protection against the blunt edge of the alienation I might otherwise have felt there, but if I thought going to a private school meant I already knew what privilege looked like, Oxford was about to show me otherwise. There was the kind of posh I'd grown used to – Islington mums who did their food shop at M&S and obsessed over Farrow & Ball; and then there was Oxford posh – the sort of people who had a minor aristo title and lived in manor houses that had been 'in the family' for generations. It was Oxford that really exposed me to people who existed at the true pinnacle of class and wealth in Britain, rounding out the education in the rituals and mores of the upper middle classes I'd begun at school. These were people who compared skiing destinations at pre-drinks, weighing up the merits of various resorts according to which destination was likely to have better 'powder'. People whose families had summer houses in Tuscany, and winter chalets in Verbier; who chartered private yachts for their holidays and went shooting at the weekends.

At a party during those first few weeks, I got talking to another student, the conversation eventually drying to a lull before he piped up,

'So, what school did you go to?'

I told him.

'Oh yeah, I think I've heard of that one – it's near the Barbican, right?'

'Yup. How about you, where'd you go to school?' I replied, returning the question that I'd be asked countless times in the months to come.

'Eton,' he smiled, with just a hint of self-satisfaction, and I realised that he'd only asked about my school so that he could name-drop his in response.

'Cool – I guess you already know lots of people here then?' I said. He nodded, yes, of course he did. Old Etonians were everywhere at Oxford.

I soon came to understand the significance of 'the school question', and the way that other students – mostly those who'd been privately educated – would politely ask about where you'd gone to school. Both question and answer are proxies, a fairly unsubtle way of probing into someone's background and signalling your own credentials, as well as potentially unearthing any mutual connections; I am convinced that the privately educated in Britain are only ever two degrees of separation from each other. There have been times, both at Oxford and since, when I've wielded my school's name as a shield, aware that in certain circumstances being privately educated counteracts the aspects of my identity that might otherwise mark me out as an outsider, specifically my being Black.

Even Oxford's antiquated slang, a world of bops (parties), formals (dinners), collections (mock exams) and subfusc (those famous black gowns), mirrored the traditions of the grand old public schools like Eton and Westminster, which have long maintained a similar vocabulary of colloquialisms largely indecipherable to the outside world. At Oxford, using those words quickly becomes second nature, regardless of your background – when you are there, that slang just feels like yet another Oxford quirk, devoid of any greater significance. But over the following three years my friends and I would often refer to the 'Oxford bubble', and the way in which that quaint chocolate-box city sometimes felt strangely removed from the rest of the world. Much as mastering Oxford's private language and arcane little rituals was a faint source of pride, bonding you to your fellow students in the way that mastering the social codes of any new environment tends to do, those codes also quietly reinforced the invisible walls of that bubble, doing little to quell Oxford's reputation as an establishment reserved for those from grand families – a reputation not without substance.

Despite only 7 per cent of schoolchildren in Britain attending a private school, the privately educated are grossly over-represented at Oxford, making up 38 per cent of its student body in 2019 (down from 46 per cent in the years I attended).[1] When it comes to Oxford – and Cambridge, while we're here – socio-economic diversity is not the name of the game. I soon realised that even among the state-educated students, who I hoped might offer more in the way of shared experience, most still came from comfortably middle-class families. In 2019, just 12 per cent of students admitted to Oxford were from the two most socio-economically disadvantaged groups in the UK, families whom economists define as either 'financially stretched', or living in 'urban adversity' on struggling estates like the one I grew up on.[2] Even fewer were Black or first-generation immigrants like me, and privy to that very specific experience of straddling two cultures that I always cleave to in others. (I wouldn't meet anyone like that my entire time at Oxford, which is unsurprising given that even in 2020 only 3.1 per cent of students admitted to Oxford were Black.[3]) The vast majority of students came from homes that were *at a minimum* 'comfortably off' in relation to the rest of the population, if not far, far wealthier: affluent families who lived the kind of lifestyles most of us associate with the one per cent. Little wonder that Oxford is embedded in the public consciousness as a symbol of social inequality.

Still, for all the students who arrived at Oxford clearly hell-bent on acting out their *Brideshead* fantasies, hosting port and cheese parties during freshers' week and donning black tie at every conceivable opportunity, most came across as fairly normal. The signifiers of wealth that reminded me of the disparities between us were usually more subtle, as I found hanging out in a friend's room one evening when he pulled out his laptop.

'Is that a MacBook?' I asked, as breezily as I could.

As far as I was concerned, MacBooks were for millionaires. I was astonished that someone my age – a *student* – actually owned one, but I'd soon grow accustomed to seeing row upon row of sleek grey MacBooks in the college library, that tell-tale glowing logo winking back at me as my own bulky laptop whirred so loudly that sometimes it seemed as if it were about to take flight.

The girls I'd met during freshers' week ended up being the friends who would see me through my three years at Oxford, and beyond. Though they were broadly middle class, and in some cases incredibly affluent, I had found a gang of girls with whom I could truly be myself, as raucous and vulnerable and slobby as that was. Within weeks we'd fallen into an easy rhythm of constant texting and silly nicknames, and dissolving into hysterics over nothing at all. We moved en masse, congregating in each other's rooms to get ready before nights out, and swapping clothes with such frequency that it was easy to forget what belonged to whom. I might lend a favourite dress or a pair of shoes to one friend only to bump into another slyly wearing it a couple of weeks later.

My student days were a few years before the resurgence of feminism in popular culture that started to build in the mid-2010s, but even then we were a staunchly feminist bunch. It came naturally to us to analyse our experiences through the lens of feminism; we were quick to point out sexism, and to voice our discontent with the many small injustices and gendered double standards we encountered on a daily basis. This was the pre-#MeToo era, when 'lad culture' at British universities was at its peak, and all manner of dubious male behaviour was blithely dismissed as 'banter'. Websites like LADBible and UNILAD reigned supreme, trading in viral memes and video clips that spoke to their largely male audiences. Even after UNILAD was forced to issue a sheepish apology for publishing an article describing rape as 'surprise sex' and encouraging its loyal lad following to commit sexual assault by reminding them that '85 per cent of rape cases go unreported', the tone of its output didn't change drastically.[4] I'd heard that surprise sex 'joke' from a few of my laddier male friends more times than I care to remember. Meanwhile, the phenomenally popular TV show *The Inbetweeners* – for all its well-observed humour about the indignities of teenage life – also revelled in crude laddisms, gifting young men a vocabulary of objectionable phrases. It wasn't at all unusual for the otherwise well-mannered boys I knew to drop references to 'gash' or 'clunge' (both synonyms for female genitalia) in the middle of a conversation, behaviour that we girls were under pressure to either laugh off or emulate. Nobody wanted to seem uptight. It was always 'just banter'.

Girls were talked about as though they were prey, to be coaxed or tricked into bed, with or without the aid of alcohol. University was the first time I encountered the concept of 'sharking' – the practice of older (mostly male) second and third years looking for naïve freshers to hook up with in their early weeks, behaviour that in hindsight seems to be very obviously predatory but at the time was totally acceptable. As recently as 2012, Oxford's student newspaper, *Cherwell*, published an explainer describing sharking thus: '*No matter how much you try to withstand the temptation to shark, the excitement of the new "fresh meat" coming into college is all too overwhelming. So whether you are abusing your position as Freshers' Week President or acting the role of over-friendly college parent/grandparent (sounds creepy but it happens – I can testify), you are guaranteed to get a bit more nookie than you did in freshers' week.*'[5]

Midway through my third year, Sky Sports' long-time football commentator Richard Keys became embroiled in a scandal after misogynistic comments he'd made off-air about a former girlfriend of the footballer Jamie Redknapp were leaked to the public. His use of the phrase 'hanging out the back of it' to refer to sex was quickly adopted by the boys in college, even as Keys lost his job. His explanation for his behaviour? Banter, of course.

In short, casual misogyny and sexism were endemic, though even now the part of me conditioned to brush these things off as 'just a bit of banter' wonders if I'm not being a bit heavy-handed in describing these incidents as such. I don't even really blame the boys I studied with – there was never any real malice in their jokes and, to my knowledge, few ever actually crossed the line. These were young men simply aping the prevailing model of masculinity, as dictated by lads' mags and reality TV.

And though Oxford was far from the only university home to these retrograde dynamics, its old-fashionedness lent everything a veneer of respectability, offering the rose-tinted cover of history and tradition. By the time I arrived, the infamous Bullingdon Club had mostly lost the social cachet it once had, tainted by association with a series of criminally uncool Tory politicians, and the prospect of membership potentially earning you a career-ruining write-up in a tabloid newspaper. But plenty of other male-only drinking societies had sprung up in its place – Oxford was still a fine place to live out your fantasies of being an old English gentleman, if you were that way inclined.

These clubs thrived on archaic traditions, their members often wearing special patterned ties and memorising Latin mottos, a real-life approximation of the old boys' club. Most only opened their doors to women for select dinners or cocktail receptions, but on these occasions we were mere chattel, invited to simper prettily and all but auctioned off to the highest bidder at the end of the night. 'The only role conferred on women in such organ-isations is sexual availability and subservience to men,' barrister and former Cambridge student Charlotte Proudman wrote in the *Guardian* in 2015 (Cambridge having a similar tradition of male-only drinking societies). 'Women are invited to events as objects of sexual desire – to be consumed and jettisoned. Women attend because it enhances their social capital, and nonconformity could be social suicide.'[6] Being invited to one of these dinners or socials was considered a compliment, even for those of us not particu-larly in thrall to the rites and rituals of Oxford life. Invitations – or lack thereof – felt like a comment on your attractive-ness, and so I wanted to be invited, even if I didn't actually want to go.

A few weeks into my first term, a 'fit list' of the five hottest female freshers began to circulate through a college whisper network, the definitive version of which seemed to change depending on who was telling you about it. Who had created it? Nobody knew, but we all pretended not to care whether or not we were on it. My gang of girls retaliated by trying to construct our own version ranking the boys, but it was all a bit half-hearted. (The year I left Oxford, a drinking society at another college made headlines after a similar list was leaked to the press, along with emails in which its members had joked about luring female freshers to places 'with no witnesses' to properly 'welcome' them into college life.[7])

As a result I was constantly aware of my appearance, and the social capital it did or did not offer. I'd spend long hours staring at the mirror in an attempt to quantify exactly how attractive I was, all the while *willing* myself to be prettier, more conforming to the prevailing standard of what tended to be deemed 'fit' (which of course was a specific brand of attractiveness commandeered exclusively by white boarding-school girls who looked like they'd been reared on strawberries and milk). Midway through my first year, I confided to a friend that I was sure I'd grown uglier since arriving at Oxford, though I now realise it was just that I'd never before spent so much time thinking about my appearance, never before been so aware of being constantly sized up and appraised.

New College had two drinking societies, one of which was said to send out invitations to the best-looking people at New (alas, I was not considered), while the second, the Prae Prandials, supposedly only invited students who'd been privately educated – enough to score me an invitation in my second term. But wary of their notoriously booze-heavy initiation ritual, and of the aggressively public-school cohort who ran it, I declined. Part of me took pleasure in being contrary, and rejecting the invitation felt like a power move, but I was also deeply conscious of the mental effort required to play along with the brash public-school vibe of a bunch of people who clearly assumed we had far more in common than we actually did, simply because of where I'd gone to school. Often I'd leave situations like that, where I felt like I hadn't been my 'real self', feeling oddly flat, and I learned over the years simply to avoid them.

In my second year, a boy at another college who I'd been told had a crush on me invited me to his drinking society's annual dinner. I debated whether to go, knowing full well I wasn't interested in him, but this time my curiosity got the better of me (as did my friends, who eventually cajoled me into giving this would-be suitor a chance). The dinner was disappointingly dull, full of loud public-school boys in black tie getting increasingly drunk and shouting over each other. Eventually, predictably, a drinking game was initiated.

'Never have I ever . . . had SEX with . . . the girl who I've brought as my date tonight,' one of the boys roared, unsteady on his feet. Most of them, having brought their girlfriends as dates, whooped as they showily downed their drinks. Out of the corner of my eye I saw the guy who'd invited me – who I'd never so much as *kissed* – tentatively reach for his own glass, presumably to save face. 'Excuse me?' I said archly, and he smiled sheepishly, his hand dropping back to his side. *You wish*, I thought to myself.

As he walked me out of his college at the end of the evening, he stopped and leaned in optimistically, ready to claim his pound of flesh.

Oh Christ. I'd hoped to avoid this, but alas – no such luck.

Keeping my lips pressed firmly shut, I turned my head slightly as he approached, so that the kiss landed mostly on my cheek.

'Well . . . goodnight!' I said brightly, and dashed out into the street, virtually flying home so that I could dissect the entire thing with my waiting housemates, the awkwardness of the evening worth it for the hilarity of the debrief that followed.

And yet somehow, the lame boys and the drinking societies and the overwhelming whiteness of the place never came close to defining my time at Oxford. I mostly loved being there, and the last few weeks after finals were bittersweet, full of what I knew would be 'lasts' – the last night out at this club or that bar; the last time I'd venture to the library for the sole purpose of catching a glimpse of one of my many crushes; the last time I'd sit on the grass quads with my days stretching lazily out in front of me, the most urgent thing on my mind the question of what to wear to a house party that night. At the back of my mind was the knowledge that this was the last time in my life I'd ever be so young and free of obligation, that a future filled with words like 'commute' and 'line manager' was hurtling towards me faster than I was really ready for. I'd started to miss Oxford before I'd even left.

Then there was the low-level panic brought on by the slow realisation that while *I'd* spent my free time hanging out with friends and illegally streaming episodes of *Gossip Girl*, a surprising number of my year group had been quietly applying for and securing that most coveted of post-graduation tokens – a job. Panicked, I applied for a dozen or so grad schemes in management consultancy, law, finance – whatever everyone else seemed to be doing. I didn't get a single response. By the time I was ejected from my cosy student bubble, I had nothing lined up, and wasn't sure whether to keep applying for the corporate jobs that everyone else seemed to be going for, or to try and pursue something more creative. After years of clearly defined milestones – GCSEs, A levels, finals – I'd been released into society to try and cobble together some semblance of a career, tasked with finding my place in a world I knew very little about.

These were the post-recession years, where entry-level jobs were thin on the ground but unpaid internships were in ready supply. It was an anxious, stressful period, the pressure intensified by the sense that everyone except me seemed to have it all figured out, and that somehow, I was falling behind. Back at my parents' house now, I spent my days writing and rewriting my CV, sending out cover letters and trawling job boards for potential leads, all the while trying to eke out the dregs of my rapidly dwindling bank balance.

What I *really* wanted was to become a journalist, and so I applied for all of the extremely rare media grad schemes then on offer, proudly attaching cuttings from my school magazine and an interview with a Mercury Prize winner I'd conducted for Oxford's student newspaper. When an interview for a competitive scheme that I'd prepped religiously for failed to materialise into a job offer, I was devastated. By that point I'd exhausted all the entry-level journalism schemes I could find, so that one had been (to my 21-year-old eye) my last chance as far as journalism was concerned. The prospect of doing unpaid internships just didn't seem like a sustainable option, even though my parents lived in London – I didn't want to have to rely on them for money, and the idea of working for free seemed to me like a 'rich people thing', not a possibility someone like me could entertain. No – I needed to make money.

At that stage, the question of money played a bigger role in how I weighed up my future career prospects than pretty much anything else. Once I'd run out of paid opportunities to apply for, I discarded journalism as a potential career path, and by the same logic I ruled out working at a think tank or at an NGO. Those too seemed to require an indeterminate period of unpaid experience to get one's foot in the door, or expensive masters degrees that I had no idea how I'd fund.

And that's how it goes, for me and for countless others. The unpaid internships that were (and often still are) a rite of passage for the work I wanted to do – creative jobs in the arts or media – make it so that one's ability to pursue those careers is dependent not on talent or merit, but on your ability to withstand working for free for months, even years, on end. Even if I *could* have toughed out those unpaid internship years, living at home and taking on odd jobs around the sides for beer money, how long would it be until I was earning a decent salary, or got a staff job? Nothing I'd heard about journalism suggested that would be the case any time soon. More likely I'd be stuck on an endless treadmill of unpaid work and be writing for free well into my twenties, with no guarantee of a job at the end of it. I didn't feel like I had the kind of financial safety net required to take the risk of embarking on an uncertain – and probably low-paid – creative career. Playing it safe seemed like my best bet.

Instead I watched as those jobs were scooped up by the quietly affluent middle-class types I knew, even as they expressed oddly puritanical attitudes about 'selling out' and shied away from acknowledging money as a factor in their professional choices, seemingly unable or unwilling to recognise the outsized role it played in their ability to realise their ambitions. In her book

Steal as Much as You Can, which examines how Britain's artistic and cultural output came to be dominated by the upper middle classes, the journalist Nathalie Olah highlights how 'the self-righteousness that defines the liberal media [has created] a culture in which it's acceptable for them to breed contempt for poorer people who did respond to the call of social mobility in a bid to escape poverty and struggle.' It irked me in those early years, when we convened at house parties to drunkenly pick through our career-related existential crises, to occasionally hear people brag about 'not caring about the money', as though that attitude were borne of some superior values system, and not the fact that they were already quite rich.

The advantages the middle classes bring to the job market often extend far beyond their financial resources, encompassing many of the intangibles that are part and parcel of their existence. They know the right people and use the right words, qualities that tend to be identified as confidence or even intelligence, but are more often than not simply a function of class. Their upbringings ensure that they're well versed in the behavioural codes required to thrive in professional environments, and in possession of the right cultural references and 'good taste' required for success in creative ones. As sociologists Sam Friedman and Daniel Laurison point out in *The Class Ceiling*, their recent exploration of class and social mobility in Britain, this sort of cultural competency tends to be 'rooted in middle-class socialisation and inculcated disproportionately via a privileged, white, family milieu.'

I would see this first-hand a few years into my career, when the son of one of my employer's most important clients was given a three-month internship as a way of ingratiating us with his father. This despite the fact that the company didn't even have an internship programme, and that he had neither applied nor been interviewed for the position. It had simply been arranged for him: a three-month internship at one of the most influential media companies in the world. I saw too how, at least initially, my bosses simply assumed that he was a 'good fit' because of the way he spoke and how he carried himself, the full force of a lifetime of private education behind him. Even so, it eventually became painfully obvious that he simply did not have a work ethic, slinking out of the office early whenever it suited him, and dismissing the more unglamorous tasks we sometimes had to do. This was his second post-graduation internship, the first having been at the globally recognised media company where his father worked.

These are the hallmarks of privilege, that condition that dare not speak its name; the patchwork of unearned advantages, often a function of our identity, that substantially alters our experience of the world; what Friedman and Laurison call the 'hidden mechanisms that propel [the elite] forward'. Of late, the practice of 'checking your privilege' and rooting out that of others has grown into something of a cultural obsession, albeit one frequently dismissed as an example of millennial preciousness, an indictment of our inability to cope with the harsh realities of life. But given how long privilege and the role it plays in life outcomes has gone unexamined in the mainstream, it seems only right that our experiences and achievements are now threaded through its needle, and scrutinised to determine the extent to which unearned advantage – or lack thereof – has contributed to someone's appointed station in life.

In July 2018, *Forbes* magazine published a lengthy profile of reality TV star and entrepreneur Kylie Jenner, detailing the enormous success of her beauty business Kylie Cosmetics.[8] From an initial capital investment of $250,000 by Jenner herself, the company had grown into a beauty industry juggernaut then valued at $900 million.[9] In its write-up, *Forbes* christened her the world's 'youngest ever self-made billionaire', a description that provoked immediate backlash online, as social media users and other media outlets rushed to dispute *Forbes*'s assertion that Jenner – born to a wealthy white Calabasas family and granted easy access to the entertainment industry – was indeed 'self-made'. (Forbes later downgraded her estimated worth in May 2020, suggesting that the value of Kylie Cosmetics had been inflated.[10]) At the root of the outrage was *Forbes*'s failure to acknowledge the immense privilege Jenner was born into. By calling her self-made, the magazine implied a rags-to-riches ascent that couldn't be further from the truth. Jenner is as self-made as her pneumatic curves and famously voluptuous pout – that is to say, she's had a little helping hand. In fact, the entire Kardashian-Jenner clan have had their path to the top smoothed by their family's pre-existing wealth and adjacency to fame – Kourtney, Kim and Khloe's father, Robert Kardashian, was a lawyer and close friend of OJ Simpson's, who also assisted his legal team at trial; while matriarch Kris's second marriage was to the Olympic gold medal-winner Caitlyn Jenner.

What does it even mean to describe ourselves, or others, as self-made? Is that ever a realistic descriptor, given how privilege works and the fact that so many 'peculiar benefits' (as the writer Roxane Gay calls them in an essay of the same name) are embedded in our lives from birth? Jenner's is far from the only self-made success narrative that neglects to mention significant pre-existing wealth or socio-economic privilege. Contemporary culture is rotten with success stories that deliberately obscure the affluent parents who provided the initial injection of capital that allowed a business to flourish, or who quietly transferred a few hundred pounds into a bank account each month while their offspring waited for their professional endeavours to pay off. Just days after publishing its initial interview, *Forbes* was forced to issue a follow-up offering clarification on its definition of 'self-made'. 'To be clear,' it read, '*Forbes* defines "self-made" as someone who built a company or established a fortune on her own, rather than inheriting some or all of it. As long as the list member didn't inherit a business or money, she is labelled self-made. But the term is very broad, and does not adequately reflect how far some people have come and, relatively speaking, how much easier others have had it.'[11] In other words, *Forbes*'s grasp of the term didn't – wouldn't – account for privilege, even though that can be as advantageous as an actual cash inheritance.

Is the term 'self-made' really as broad as *Forbes* claimed, or had the magazine simply misapplied it in its eagerness to shoehorn Jenner's ascent into a media narrative we've come to expect – that of the preternaturally young entrepreneur bootstrapping his or her way to success; or the promising young creative periodically christened 'the voice of a generation', who increasingly hails only from the upper-middle-class backgrounds that allow the kind of financial freedom required to make it through the early years of penury. (One thinks specifically of *Fleabag*'s creator Phoebe Waller-Bridge, descended from nobility and privately educated; and across the pond millennial marmite Lena Dunham, the highly networked daughter of affluent Manhattan artists.)

These sleights of hand are a polite subterfuge endemic among the creative class: the failure to mention the parent who just so happens to be a titan of industry, or the circumstances that allowed you to move to an expensive city on a minimum wage salary. At my most generous, I interpret these omissions as an indicator of shame, which as I often have to remind myself, spares no one when it comes to money, not even the rich. In this cultural moment, when unprecedented levels of economic inequality have triggered a generalised class rage, and anti-billionaire sentiment is no longer fringe or radical; when democratic socialism has ascended to mainstream status on the back of the Corbyn–Sanders–Ocasio-Cortez trifecta, and 'eat the rich' has become a frequent, even pedestrian, social media refrain, it is embarrassing – almost indecent – to appear to be a silver spooner. So people downplay the help they've had and the privileges they enjoy. Family histories are rewritten, middle-class roots dropped, accents adjusted and working-class affectations adopted. To admit one's privilege is to risk diminishing the legitimacy and significance of your achievements, and to have others think your successes have been handed to you, particularly as the word 'privileged' has shifted from a relatively neutral assessment of socio-economic status to something verging on an insult, easy shorthand for the entitled cluelessness of the coddled rich. 'We tend to believe that accusations of privilege imply we have it easy,' Roxane Gay writes in *Peculiar Benefits*, 'and because life is hard for nearly everyone, we resent hearing that.'

This semantic shift means there's often a defensiveness that accompanies privilege, where those who have a lot of it are reluctant to admit or even consider how great a role it has played in their lives. Instead they say things like, 'yes, I went to a private school, but I also worked really hard to get where I am', betraying a fundamental misunderstanding of what an immense advantage a private education is, a nearly absurd tipping of the scales in one's favour that makes itself known again and again over the course of a lifetime, and one that means the reverse formulation ('yes, I worked really hard, but I also went to a private school') is probably more accurate. That obliviousness to one's own good fortune is mentioned in *The Class Ceiling* when, having interviewed hundreds of people from a range of different backgrounds, Friedman and Laurison recall finding that 'those from upper-middle-class backgrounds tended to narrate their career progression, and that of those around them, mostly in terms of "merit", as the result of talent and, most importantly, hard work . . . [they] almost never questioned the legitimacy of their own success.'

In a recent article published by the *Guardian*, the novelist Lynn Steger Strong unveiled what she called the 'dirty secret' of the publishing industry: that writing does not usually pay well (unless you are very, very successful), and that most full-time writers are in some way cocooned by the soft cushion of privilege and tend to have another source of income that sustains them, whether that is a trust fund or a well-earning partner.[12] (This deceit is, I think, particularly true of writers, who are perhaps under more pressure than other creative workers to appear to live 'the life of the mind', dreamily philosophising into Moleskines, unencumbered by pedestrian issues such as invoices, or tax.) 'There are ramifications, I think, of no one mentioning the source of this freedom when they have it,' Steger Strong concludes. 'There is the perpetuation of an illusion that makes an unsustainable life choice appear sustainable, that makes the specific achievements of particular individuals seem more remunerative than they actually are.' Similarly, Friedman and Laurison worry in *The Class Ceiling* that the downplaying of parental financial support 'means that the true value of the Bank of Mum and Dad goes largely unspoken in professional life, and its distorting influence on individual trajectories remains hidden from public view.'

These observations cut right to the heart of why rooting out privilege has become such a widespread social practice, particularly among the millennial media commentariat where it's developed into something of a blood sport. Spend enough time on Twitter and you'll soon become used to onlookers resentfully pointing out a 'too nice' apartment, or a suspiciously fast career trajectory – perhaps you'll even become one of them.

In covering up the helping hand they have had, there is often a pretence among the middle classes that professional success and the financial rewards that follow from it are more or less a meritocracy. For those of us who know otherwise it's maddening when we see through that obfuscation, especially as these falsehoods aren't without consequence. By painting an inaccurate picture of the ease of professional success, those with privilege give others a false impression of their own prospects – the 'perpetuation of an illusion' that Steger Strong writes about. It also denies the ways in which one individual's privilege might compound others' lack thereof, how being able to accept a six-month unpaid internship perpetuates a system that penalises those who cannot.

In the evasiveness that sometimes surrounds privilege, there is often an appeal to the right of privacy – and it's certainly true that no one *owes* honesty about his or her privilege to anyone else. How much better, though, if more people were able to see that honesty for what it is: a moral imperative, and the social tax payable on their good fortune.

Chapter 3

'PLEASE SIR, CAN I HAVE SOME MORE?'

'Yeah, and once you're finished with those boxes, come and find me. I need to talk you through how the post works and all that *crap*,' Brian finished, emphasising the word 'crap' to indicate how entirely beyond – or beneath – him any tasks that might be thought of as 'office admin' were.

'OK, cool! Will do.'

Brian – my new boss – looked me up and down doubtfully, taking in my outfit, specifically my newly purchased espadrille wedge heels.

'Are you gonna be able to manage in those shoes?'

'Yeah, of course!' I replied cheerfully. 'I basically live in heels anyway.' (A lie.) 'All good!'

He grunted a dismissal, and I wobbled off to complete my morning's work, methodically flattening a stack of empty cardboard boxes before ferrying them downstairs to the rubbish chute at the back of the building with all the diligence of a surgeon operating on a newborn baby.

It was my first week at my first job after graduating. I'd managed to find a temp role as a receptionist for a small marketing agency, and in the manner of most graduates entering the world of work for the first time, I was determined to shine. I imagined every task to be *the* defining task against which my performance would be judged and, potentially, found lacking. *Did she stack the boxes flat enough? Tear them apart too loudly? Too slowly?* Things that would eventually dissolve into the minutiae of working life seemed gravely important in those early weeks, and I resolved that no one would find fault with *my* box-crushing technique.

Naturally, there was more to the job than simply stacking cardboard boxes. As promised, Brian did indeed teach me how to handle the post, which I did twice a day, in between answering the phones and signing for couriers and nipping to the shops whenever we ran out of milk. As first jobs go, it was a pretty cushy set-up, though with typical youthful naïveté I failed to realise that at the time. I found office life to be a crashing disappointment, a world away from the vision of pencil skirts and pitch meetings I'd cobbled together from an adolescence spent gorging on Nancy Meyers films. Oh, how I resented that unglamorous office, and my unglamorous colleagues! How I hated commuting each morning, squeezing onto trains full of dead-eyed office workers, knowing that I was now one of them. I found the unspoken rules that required me to initiate small talk with people whose weekend activities I was largely uninterested in ridiculous. Where were the high-stakes deals? The witty repartee? The handsome male colleague with whom I was supposed to develop a tense but sexually charged rivalry, before we inevitably warmed to each other after an evening spent working late and fell head over heels in love?

The only thing that helped to soothe the bitter sting of my new reality was the fact that I had plenty of downtime, which – combined with a conveniently positioned computer screen – meant I could browse the Internet for hours on end. I alternated between messaging friends on Facebook to tell them how 'fucking BORED' I was, and idly poring over the careers of people far more successful than I could ever hope to be. I was paid £250 a week, which rose to £400 as the months went by and I – in typical Type A fashion – proved myself both conscientious and reliable, and my employers proved themselves to be astonishingly decent, adjusting my wages without having to be asked. That was the first and last time that would ever happen in my career.

Of course, it was the morning with the cardboard boxes that would later go on to be immortalised in an article in *The Times* documenting the plight of four 'bright, brainy, keen – and unemployed' millennials, who, having graduated into a recession, found that the utopia we'd been promised all our lives was actually more of a mirage. Responding to a friend's Facebook plea scouting for people willing to speak to a journalist for an article on graduate unemployment, I imagined myself issuing a rousing polemic, a blistering address indicting the greedy bankers and spineless politicians who had landed my generation in this hopeless situation: saddled with mountains of student debt and forced to work for free for baby boomers who bragged incessantly about how much harder things had been in their day. Secretly, I also thought that perhaps the ensuing article (which, after all, was set to run in a national newspaper) might somehow wind up being the thing that transformed my fortunes, entertaining an absurd fantasy that a high-powered media exec somewhere would see my unsmiling face glaring out at them over their morning coffee and think 'Ah! This plucky young lady seems like she'd make a *fine* journalist. I think perhaps I'll contact *The Times* and offer her a job!' What a brilliant story that would make in years to come, when people asked me how I'd got my first big break!

Needless to say, no such offer materialised, and to this day my friends still trot out the now infamous line about my having to 'crush boxes in her wedge heels', a detail the journalist had inexplicably latched on to. My parents, I think, saw the article as a cry for help. Even worse than the interview itself were the accompanying photos – we'd been shot in a studio with unfathomably harsh lighting, holding signs across our chests displaying our respective qualifications, and instructed not to smile. Looking at them in print, they resembled a series of police mugshots (which I suppose was the intended effect), the four of us imbued with an air of resentful criminality. 'PPE. OXFORD. TEMPING.' my sign bellowed, as though a temp job is the worst possible fate that could befall a recent graduate, and not, in fact, a divine stroke of luck. The only upside to the whole episode was that I later managed to secure a week's worth of work experience at *The Times*, having cornered a long-standing columnist I'd spotted at the photo shoot and guilt-tripping him into giving me his email address.

Years later I actually bumped into one of my fellow 'gilded graduates' at a house party, spotting him across the room and instantly recognising him from the photo that had sat next to mine, pointedly captioned 'ENGLISH DEGREE. REDUNDANT'. I approached, tapping him lightly on the shoulder.

'Heeey . . . this is gonna sound kinda weird but – I think we were both featured in an article in *The Times* a couple of years ago? About, er . . . graduate unemployment?' I smiled, weakly.

As opening lines go it wasn't my *best* work, and I tailed off with the sudden realisation that this might not actually be the person I thought it was.

'Oh yeah! Fuck! I thought I recognised you. God, that was awful wasn't it! What are you doing now?' he asked, and we fell into an animated conversation during which we both bitterly agreed that being interviewed for that feature had been 'the worst fucking decision' of our lives, given that our respective mugshots were now the first thing that came up whenever anyone Googled us. (Thankfully, only one of those photos still remains on the Internet – bad luck Orlando.) The irony of my actually *having* a job at the time the article was published was entirely lost on me, and few of my colleagues mentioned reading it when I strolled into work the following Monday. I imagine they secretly thought me an entitled snob, having correctly guessed that my agreeing to be featured in the piece was symptomatic of how little I cared for my current job, and having also sniffed out my private education within weeks of my joining the company. It would be years before I'd learn to downplay the tell-tale signs of private education, so that people wouldn't jump to conclusions about my background or world view. Those who themselves had gone to private schools would blithely assume I was 'one of them', co-opting me into a collegiate atmosphere of public-school chumminess that I wanted no part in, while those who had been educated at state schools would feel instantly alienated, regarding me with narrow-eyed suspicion until I'd proven my credentials. Truth be told I *didn't* really see what I was doing as a 'proper' job. I'd only ever intended it to be a layover, a financially necessary stepping stone on my way to the dazzling career I knew would surely soon materialise. And yet I ended up working there for nearly two years, begrudgingly accepting a permanent role as an account executive that was offered to me after five months of covering reception.

I say 'begrudgingly' because my initial salary of £24,000 – though in hindsight *very* respectable – was far from the six-figure salary 15 year-old me had envisioned, and some way off the salaries my friends with corporate jobs were on. Dismayed, I ran the salary offer past a friend who'd recently started working at an investment bank (where graduate starting salaries were around the £40,000 mark). I can still recall the exact cadence of the awkward pause before she enthusiastically reassured me that a salary of £24,000 was 'actually pretty good!' That I was in any way disappointed with that sum is perhaps telling of how warped my expectations had become on account first of all of my schooling, and later the promises made by the corporate milk round at Oxford.

Still, once I'd adjusted my expectations, I quickly came to appreciate my good fortune. Here I was, not a year out of university and being paid good money for reasonably interesting work. At £24,000, I was at the upper end of the range for average graduate salaries in the UK at that time. I found earning a regular wage liberating, and relished the monthly replenishing of my bank account. This was the first time I'd received substantial amounts of money with any regularity, my only previous sources of income having been a modest allowance from my parents, the odd holiday job, and the triannual blessing of my student loan payments. At last, I felt like a proper grown-up. I could now afford to eat a Pret sandwich every day, so I did, entirely failing to understand why some of my co-workers went to the bother of bringing in a packed lunch. I met friends after work for drinks or dinner, where those of us with jobs would bitch endlessly about our colleagues, while those who were still scrabbling around in the thankless mire of job-hunting quietly seethed at our ingratitude, counting out the exact change for their main meals (no starter) when the bill came. My office was all too conveniently located near Oxford Street, which made it easier than ever to indulge my lifelong love of shopping, so I bought myself expensive cashmere jumpers and a shiny new MacBook, and splurged on *those* Russell & Bromley penny loafers that every Alexa Chung wannabe was wearing circa 2012.

And, because I have never not worried about money, I saved.

The thing about growing up in a house where money is a source of stress is that you carry those feelings with you forever. Watching your parents trying to conceal their panic over an unexpectedly high gas bill, or performing the mental gymnastics required to make the numbers add up each month – that leaves a mark. Those memories lie dormant under the skin, waiting to be triggered by what are often the most innocuous of circumstances, a toxic Pavlovian response. For as long as I can remember, I've harboured a deep-seated anxiety about money that occasionally dissipates depending on my current financial situation, but never fully goes away. Unlike the majority of my school and university friends who grew up in comfortably middle-class households, I grew up painfully aware that my family didn't have an endless supply of money. Though we never actually 'ran out' – we were never in dire straits, or unable to afford basic needs – I was always fearful about what series of events might conspire to tip us over the precipice and into financial destitution, a fear made infinitely worse by not knowing what was waiting for us at the bottom of that cliff.

If you grow up in a household where money is tight, things tend to go one of two ways. One is that you develop a scarcity mindset, forever operating under the underlying fear that you'll never have 'enough' money, your thoughts and actions stemming from a feeling of lack. People with scarcity mindsets tend to focus on the short term as opposed to planning for the future, often making poor financial decisions as a result. In fact, having a scarcity mindset is a consistently reliable symptom of poverty (as opposed to its cause, though conservative governments all over the world would have you believe otherwise. The myth of the 'feckless poor' who bring financial hardship upon themselves by blowing their paltry wages on cigarettes and widescreen TVs is exactly that – a myth.) So say you have a scarcity mindset and you get a sudden windfall – an unexpected tax rebate, for example, or maybe even just your monthly wages. Relieved to finally actually have some cash, the bitter taste of being barrel-scrapingly skint still fresh in your mouth, you spend it all at once, worried that if you don't spend it now, it'll disappear anyway, sucked up by the never-ending cycle of Oyster card payments and council tax bills that seem to constitute modern life. You don't save – you spend.

Or you could end up like me, a money vigilant. According to psychologist Brad Klontz, a pioneer in the field of financial therapy, most of us operate according to one of four key 'money scripts': money avoidance, where you believe that money is inherently bad and that people who are concerned with it are simply greedy; money worship, where you convince yourself that having more money would solve all of your problems; money status, where you equate your self-worth with your net worth; and money vigilance, where you're generally pretty careful with money, to the point of developing a nervousness around making sure you have enough saved in case of emergency. These money scripts are typically unconscious and developed in childhood, but nonetheless they play a crucial role in shaping your financial behaviour as an adult.

Though I recognise elements of all four of those scripts in myself (as I imagine you might too), by far the one I most closely identify with is money vigilance – which also happens to be the only script *not* associated with poor financial health. The deep-seated fear of financial destitution I'd inherited from childhood meant it never occurred to me to squander my entire salary, as so many young adults do when they first start earning money. I always anticipated leaner times ahead – so I saved, starting with that very first box-crushing pay cheque of £250. Each week I would religiously transfer between £100 and £150 into a separate savings account, a habit admittedly only made possible by being able to live at home with my parents, and so avoiding London's exorbitant rents. On the rare occasions I dipped into my savings pot, I would make a note of the *exact* amount I'd withdrawn and tighten my belt for as long as it took to pay myself back. Fairly quickly I built up a nest egg of several thousands of pounds.

Those first few years in full-time employment also brought with them my first few salary negotiations. Not long after I went from receptionist to account exec, I realised that I was doing far more than my job description actually required of me, winning favour with clients, taking the lead on key accounts and operating at a level on a par with colleagues two or three rungs senior to me. Call it youthful braggadocio, or call it the fact of my natural confidence not having yet been dampened by corporate culture (studies have shown that on average it takes a company around two years to rob women of the confidence and ambition they initially enter the workplace with[1]), but feeling particularly bold one afternoon, I impulsively asked my boss Brian if we could have a chat.

'Sure, how about 4.30 this afternoon. Can you book a room?'

'Of course,' I replied, slightly caught off guard by how quickly my casual request had morphed into a Serious Meeting. I spent the intervening hours frantically Googling various iterations of 'how to ask for a pay rise', making a careful note of all my successes over the preceding months as instructed, and measuring my performance against that of other colleagues. A few hours later, I sat opposite Brian and stated my case, asking for a pay rise of £4,000 (which would bring my salary to £28,000), and an accompanying promotion from account executive to senior account executive. Quickly agreeing to the promotion, Brian countered with an offer of £27,000, but I stood my ground, stubbornly reiterating my reasons, and we went back and forth for a while.

'Fine. Let's call it £27,500 then,' he said eventually, glancing at his watch. I agreed, careful to hide my pleasure under a veneer of serene professionalism. It felt important not to gush or seem overly effusive, lest he think agreeing to give me a pay rise constituted some sort of personal favour. *I deserve this salary*, I thought to myself, and I wanted him to know that I knew that.

A few hours later Brian sent me an email. Somewhat unbelievably, he'd reconsidered our conversation and decided to bump my salary up to £28,000 as I'd requested – meaning that aged 21 I was already earning more than the average UK salary of £26,500. Of course I was elated, but even with that victory under my belt, I still had to be cajoled by a friend into meeting her for a celebratory glass of champagne that evening. I was determined to keep my spending exactly as it had been before, funnelling the additional £4,000 I'd be earning straight into my savings account. While my friend's (perfectly understandable) logic was that there was no point in working hard enough to secure a pay rise if I didn't allow myself to then reap the rewards, my attitude lay at the opposite end of the spectrum: why would I spend more money when I'd been getting by just fine on what I had before? The way I saw it, these extra funds were easy pickings – I could save even more money without having to adjust my lifestyle, and for the most part that was what I did.

Unfortunately, not all my salary negotiations would prove to be as straightforward – or as successful – as that initial episode.

My escape route from that first job finally presented itself in the form of two weeks of work experience at an advertising agency, which by that stage I'd latched on to as my chosen profession, based almost entirely on a few seasons of the hit TV show *Mad Men*. Paying little attention to the show's depiction of rampant sexism and its borderline alcoholic protagonists, I focused instead on breaking into an industry I imagined would provide me with the excitement I was so badly craving.

I took ten days of annual leave to undertake a mini-internship of sorts, lying to my then colleagues that I was going on holiday. Instead, I was secretly commuting to an office just a few miles away in the hope that once I was physically in the building, opportunity might present itself. Upon arriving and once again finding myself with more downtime than any sentient being should ever really be confronted with, I made it my mission to network as aggressively as I possibly could during those two weeks, trawling the company's personnel directory to track down its head of HR so I could make my case. My strategy paid off – though that agency didn't offer me a job, their head of HR introduced me to the person who would eventually secure me my first job in advertising.

A few weeks after that clandestine work experience, I found myself sitting opposite a recruiter called Emily in a train station Starbucks, nursing a lukewarm cup of coffee as we discussed my current salary and expectations.

'Well, right now I'm on £28,000,' I said confidently. 'So—'

'Hmmm. That's quite *high*,' Emily interjected, 'for someone at your level. Would you be prepared to take a pay cut?' she continued. 'If it came to it, that is.'

Eager to please – and desperate to break into a shiny new world that now seemed so tantalisingly close – I rolled over instantly.

'Well, I'm still living with my parents so, like, I don't *need* a high salary. What's that gonna buy me, an extra pair of shoes a month?' I said, converting my potential loss of earnings into the only real currency I understood, and at pains to convey how unimportant money was to me lest I came across as greedy.

'Great!' she said, her eyes lighting up. 'Send over your CV, and we'll get to work.'

I should, at this point, explain why Emily might have been eager to dampen my salary expectations, given that generally speaking recruiters work on commission, and the higher the agreed salary for a candidate they've put forward, the more they stand to earn if and when that person is hired. But, as I've since realised, recruiters work for their clients (i.e. the companies doing the hiring), not for you. They might well be briefed by said clients to operate within a particular salary range for prospective candidates, and so their financial goals won't always necessarily 100 per cent align with yours.

Of course it's possible that a candidate's salary expectations are unreasonably high, and recruiters are well placed to advise on that, given their knowledge of the market. At £28,000, I probably *was* at the upper end of the account executive salary range – but by this point I had nearly two years' experience, and Emily had agreed it made sense for me to go for account manager positions, a role for which £28,000 and above is perfectly reasonable. Although recruiters should try to secure you the highest possible salary they can, the savviest recruiters will realise that a successfully placed candidate on a slightly lower salary is better than failing to close the deal and not getting paid their commission at all. I suspect that's the category that Emily fell into, given what happened next.

After meeting her, I decided to increase my chances by also signing up with another recruiter, Jodie – so now I had two different recruitment agencies going to bat for me. Sure enough within a few weeks I'd interviewed, and then received job offers, at two of the leading ad agencies in London, with each offer having been secured by my (now competing) recruiters. The offer that had come via Emily's efforts was from AMV, who would match my current salary of £28,000. Jodie's client, Saatchi & Saatchi – having caught wind of AMV's offer, which I'd judiciously inflated to £29,000 when probed – had countered with a salary of £30,000. I told Jodie I'd need a day or two to think things over, and then immediately rang Emily.

'Can we not use the Saatchi & Saatchi offer as leverage?' I asked. 'Y'know, try and get AMV to match their offer? I definitely *prefer* AMV – they're hands down the better agency, so I'll probably accept their offer even if they can't match. And obviously I don't want to taint their goodwill or anything like that, I do really want to work there.'

'Well yes, *exactly*,' Emily responded encouragingly, no doubt eager to stop her commission from slipping away. 'They're such a *nice* bunch there, and like you say, you wouldn't want to taint their goodwill. And you know, after tax an extra £2,000 a year really doesn't boil down to that much a month anyway. But I can certainly put the question to them!' she chirped.

Had I known then what I know now about the impact those initial salaries have on one's overall lifetime earnings, I'd probably have pushed much harder over that supposedly insignificant £2,000. Starting salaries tend to act as an anchor for your future earnings, setting the benchmark for subsequent negotiations and offers, given that on-the-job pay rises are usually calculated by taking into account your existing pay. Even when it comes to starting a new job with an entirely different company, prospective employers often base their offers on your current salary – so a figure that may have once been insignificant can snowball into a cumulative effect that follows you around for the rest of your life. By failing to negotiate those early salaries, you stand to lose out on far greater sums over the course of your career. Though I'd come out of the gate strong by securing a good starting salary at my first job, rather than pressing home my advantage and keeping that momentum going into the next role, I'd fumbled the ball, too inexperienced to properly leverage what was actually a uniquely advantageous position.

Unsurprisingly, given that I'd pretty much confirmed that AMV had my loyalty regardless of salary, they held fast at their initial offer of £28,000. *Tant pis*, as my mother is fond of saying – it could have been worse. At that point, I was just thrilled to have finally landed my dream job. Here, at last, were the pencil skirts and pitch meetings of my fevered imagination, or so I thought.

That in years to come I would grow to dread the 10 p.m. finishes and tepid boxes of takeaway that are the hallmark of ad agency life, eventually defaulting to a uniform of baggy jumpers and jeans with holes in them, was at that point unbeknownst to me.

At last, I thought, I had my foot in the door.

At last, I had made it.

I never quite hit my stride at AMV. There were a few moments when I felt I'd begun to ease into it and that I'd managed to get the measure of the place, but the truth is I never did. For the first time in my life, I found myself socially adrift, the ability to slot into almost any social scenario that I've always taken for granted suddenly challenged. Success at AMV seemed to be predicated on one's ability to master the art of office politicking, and to position yourself *just so*: building relationships with the 'right' people, and thus being sufficiently visible within the company; having 'good chat' and being just the right level of drunk at office socials (and heaven forbid you didn't attend enough of them). It was an inscrutable alchemy of oddly gendered behaviour and forced camaraderie, the ultimate aim of which seemed to be being described as 'a legend'. I shrunk into myself entirely.

In many ways AMV's culture was similar to Oxford's, but at least at uni I'd been able to carve out my own friendship group and dip in and out of certain social dynamics safe in the knowledge that they couldn't really affect my grades – but at work, where your 'grades' are partly based on social status, that's much harder to do. I never really bonded with my managers, or attained the kind of 'golden girl' status crucial for advancement at a company where progress seemed to be contingent on senior leadership regarding you as the sort of person they'd have been 'mates' with at uni – and I know I wouldn't have been friends with any of them (though God knows I tried to force it). The company culture was cliquey and hierarchical, and could at times be incredibly savage.

On one occasion, my colleagues and I were informed that a new account exec would be joining our team the following week, her name and bio circulated via email as a heads-up so that we could make her feel welcome on her first day. It must have been a slow afternoon, the kind where everyone's just counting down the hours until they can call it a day, and so someone decided to look her up on Facebook. Soon our entire team was crowded round one monitor as we scrolled through her pictures, trying to suss her out. There were photos of her at festivals, hanging out with friends, out partying. Nothing unusual except – unlucky for her – she was young, very pretty and often wore clothes showing off her figure. The claws came out.

'She doesn't look very bright,' someone commented.

'She looks like a bit of a slag if you ask me,' someone else piped up, and everyone laughed, shocked but also secretly delighted. I think I laughed along too, happy for once to shake off the constant feeling I had of being an outsider by momentarily transferring that status to someone else. I felt a little uneasy too, knowing deep down that this was textbook sexism at play.

I don't know whether her fate was sealed from the start or whether she really wasn't cut out for the job, as was quickly concluded. I never worked directly with her. But within six months she'd been let go, though not before her confidence had been slowly eroded by consistently damning feedback and various 'interventions' by the people managing her. Though I was senior to her, we were around the same age, and she came to me for advice on a few occasions. I offered what little guidance I could, but in truth I was also far too preoccupied with my own problems at the company to offer any meaningful support, and I worried that being too closely associated with her might taint my own fairly mediocre reputation.

Part of how I'd rationalised accepting AMV's lower salary offer to myself was by clinging to the belief that once I was in the door, I'd probably end up getting a pay rise pretty quickly anyway. Given my experiences up until that point, that seemed entirely possible, if not likely. In reality, I would remain on the same salary I'd joined the company on for the entirety of my two-year stint there. Although I've always been pretty forthright about asking for more money when I think I deserve it, I sensed that securing a pay rise at AMV was highly unlikely. I still think I was correct about that – I didn't have the necessary social capital to make that request, or a sponsor who might advocate for me to senior management.

Personal disposition notwithstanding, women have to deal with all manner of obstruction when it comes to pay negotiation, particularly in the form of social norms. We are often judged negatively (and even penalised) for having the temerity to ask for more money. In a 2005 Harvard-led study, rather ominously titled 'Sometimes it Does Hurt to Ask', researchers found that women encounter more social resistance than men do when attempting to negotiate for higher compensation.[2] Indeed, they are penalised more harshly for even *initiating* negotiation conversations, regardless of outcome. This despite the fact that the participants in this particular study were all university students – in other words, a young, well-educated and supposedly progressive demographic. Notably, men's willingness to work with women who negotiated dropped significantly, due to said women being perceived as 'less nice' and too 'demanding'. The findings from this Harvard study have since been backed up by numerous others, including a survey of 34,000 employees conducted by the leading global consultancy firm McKinsey in 2016, which found that women who negotiate pay rises or promotions are 30 per cent more likely than their male counterparts to receive feedback that they are 'intimidating' or 'too aggressive', and are 67 per cent more likely than women who don't negotiate at all to receive such negative feedback.[3] For a long time, my argument when persuading friends, and indeed myself, to negotiate more aggressively on salary or fee has been: 'Well, what do you have to lose?' Not nothing, as it turns out.

Still, most women already intuitively know this stuff. We don't need a research project to tell us that when women assert themselves and ask for more – whether more money, more respect, more credit, or any one of those interchangeable synonyms for 'power' – that behaviour contradicts the stereotypically 'feminine' traits men and women alike have been conditioned to believe we should display: docility, agreeableness, subservience. And woe betide if you're Black as well, given how frequently Black women's assertiveness is coded as aggression. Most of us live in societies where power is perceived to be the natural domain of men, where it is expected – even encouraged – that men actively seek out power. Women who subvert these expectations are, by contrast, problematic, posing a threat to a reigning order heavily skewed in favour of men (who all too often see our gains as happening at their expense). By negotiating pay, we violate what society deems to be 'normal' female behaviour, and there are few things more threatening than a woman who operates outside the bounds of normality. No wonder that so many of us have internalised these norms, subconsciously (and at times, consciously) adjusting our behaviour and expectations to protect the male ego, whether in our personal lives with family members and romantic partners, or in our professional lives as we skirt around a temperamental boss. The aim of the game is to avoid emasculation – and it feels important to emphasise that the female proclivity to strive for likeability isn't a desire merely borne of vanity, or a symptom of the kind of innate weakness in the female psyche that Victorian patricians were so fond of assigning us. It is a survival tactic, an evolutionary mechanism honed over millennia to improve our chances of success, using guile and smiles to more easily make our way through a hostile world.

If we leave the workplace and enter the romantic arena, men's discomfort with women who exhibit financial assertiveness remains evident in the way they react to high-earning partners. A 2016 research paper published in Sweden found that women whose earnings overtake their male partners during the course of their marriage – thereby shifting the division of earnings away from the norm of male dominance – are more likely to divorce.[4] And ultimately that's what it all comes down to: the *norm* of male dominance, and the converse expectation of female subordinance. The constant expectation that we are to reduce ourselves, contracting our desires and ambitions to be small enough to take up only the spaces left for us by men, pouring ourselves quietly and without complaint into the cracks between their egos, expectations and pride. Is there any more damning evidence of male fragility than the fact that men with female partners who out-earn them are more likely to cheat, as sociologist Christin Munsch discovered in 2014?[5]

Yet when the writer Ashley C. Ford wrote an article for women's media platform Refinery29 in 2017, suggesting that many millennial women who are the breadwinners in male-female relationships feel conflict or even shame about that (Ford interviewed 130 such women),[6] I watched as the feminist Twitter-sphere burst into flame with pithy declarations of 'can't relate' and 'could never be me', scores of women expressing disbelief at the article's rather 'un-woke' findings. Such was the intensity of the online reaction that Ford eventually addressed it with a tweet that read, 'I just want to say that whether you agree with these women or not . . . this is what they said.' As is the case with many of the studies I've cited, Ford's research merely confirmed what most women already intuitively know to be true – that for women, financial success can be romantic napalm, no matter how woke the object of their affection purports to be.

I had my own encounter with one such entanglement about a year after my first book was published, when it began to be translated into other languages and my Italian publisher flew me to Milan for a press tour. Throwing caution to the wind, I decided to invite along a guy with whom I'd been engaged in an improbable long-distance romance over the preceding few months. An Australian living in Melbourne, we had met over a brief work-related coffee when he'd been in London two years earlier, our first encounter occurring somewhat inauspiciously on the day Donald Trump was elected president of the United States. In a truly twenty-first-century courtship, we ended up staying in touch via Twitter and WhatsApp, and eventually through daily phone calls and Skypes, our relationship progress-ing as the months went by from professional acquaintance to genuine friendship, before blossoming into something verging on romance. We spoke constantly, long meandering conversations that sometimes went on for hours. I'd wake up to the messages he'd sent overnight, or he'd call on his drive home from work to tell me about his day, and I'd float through the rest of mine, storing it all up so I could tell him about it later. Our WhatsApp history became a logbook of feelings, filled with rambling voice notes and too many emojis and photos – so many photos! His adorable dog, my holiday selfies, photos from our desks taken when either of us was working late. He'd tell me stories about his friends, adding casually, 'You'll meet them when you come to Melbourne,' as though it were inevitable that I one day would. Eventually, after shyly circling the fact for months, we admitted to each other that, yes, there was something here, each revealing that – rather inconveniently given the distance and the ten-hour time difference, and the fact we'd actually only met once – we'd developed feelings for each other. We speculated about the next time he might need to visit London for work, or the likelihood of me somehow ending up in Melbourne. When we realised that he'd be in Italy for a wedding at the same time as my upcoming book tour, it felt like a sign from the universe. We decided to coordinate our trips so that he could come along to my events in Milan, before travelling to Rome to spend a few days together. It seemed like the perfect low-stakes way of testing the waters without either one of us having to make the gesture of purposely flying to Melbourne or London, and all the pressure that would add.

'Are you sure you're OK with me dragging you around all these press events though?' I asked, as the trip drew closer. 'You could always just skip that bit and we could meet up afterwards? It might be a bit boring for you . . .'

'No, I wanna see you in action!' he replied. 'I can just take loads of photos in the background, like some terrible Instagram boyfriend.'

And yet, despite all the promise and planning and the months of anticipation, the trip turned out to be an unmitigated disaster, and it quickly became clear that our much-hyped reunion was to be utterly devoid of any semblance of romance. The Australian (as I'd taken to calling him) seemed to have undergone an in-flight personality transplant, and right from the start things felt oddly tense. When I showed him the hotel my publishers had put me up in, he raised his eyebrows. 'Wow. Nice hotel,' he remarked, but something about the way he said it made me feel instantly embarrassed. 'Yeah, it's a bit much,' I replied, laughing apologetically.

The press events he'd been so keen to attend now seemed to bore him. Arriving early for a panel discussion I was taking part in, I suggested he sit up front, pointing out a seat that had been reserved for him. 'Nah, I'm good,' came the response. Instead he stood at the back of the room for the duration of the event, looking back stony-faced whenever I caught his eye. I beamed into the audience, secretly hoping for the ground to open up and claim me as its own.

Over dinner afterwards, he asked how I felt about my success as a writer being partially predicated on my attractiveness, a reference to the fact that the event compere had sweetly introduced me to the audience as *bellissima*. His delivery made it sound like an accusation, and it was the only real comment he had to offer on the event, where I'd spoken at length about my book to an auditorium packed with people, in a country that was not my own.

'You know a lot of women would be quite offended by that comment,' I replied even-handedly, continuing, 'but I'm going to take it as a compliment,' though I knew it hadn't been intended as one.

It was all such a stark contrast to the romance of our previous conversations, and I tried repeatedly to get to the bottom of things.

'Have I done something to upset you?' I asked. 'I feel like you don't even want to be here.'

Each time the answer was the same – 'No' – but he remained painfully aloof the entire trip, which prompted bouts of confused tears from me and yet more cool indifference from him. I later described it to friends as like being on a bad date that went on for three days instead of three hours, his sourness even more pronounced given how sharply it contrasted with the intense beauty of Rome in late summer. It just didn't make any sense. As we parted ways I told him never to contact me again, and burst into exhausted sobs on the phone to one of my best friends, Tommy.

Back in London, I phoned another friend, Jenny, and recounted the entire trip to her in all its excruciating misery. After she'd expressed an appropriate amount of shock ('Oh my God, are you *kidding* me'), and offered up the requisite condolences ('What an absolute DICK'), she paused for a while, before declaring,

'He's a burger.'

'A what?'

'A burger.'

'Mmm . . . I'm not sure I follow.'

'You know – like in *Sex and the City*. Remember Carrie's

awful boyfriend Berger? The one who can't handle her success, and flips out at her when she buys him that really expensive Prada shirt.'

Ah yes – Jack Berger. He of the flagging writing career (and inexplicable Hamptons summerhouse), who'd bristled in the face of Carrie's professional success, eventually dumping her by way of Post-it note. The similarities *were* there. It had been my first time travelling abroad to promote a book, and I'd been entirely unprepared for what a spectacular fuss my Italian publishers would make of me, putting me up in that plush hotel and ferrying me around in a chauffeur-driven Mercedes, while fans I was surprised even existed queued up to have their books signed after a sold-out event. Not to mention that I was a debut author, and not exactly a famous one at that. It had all come as a massive surprise, and clearly not just to me. Such obvious evidence of my professional success was in stark contrast to The Australian's own situation at the time. The business he'd spent years building with friends was in the process of going under, and he was trying to figure out what his next move would be.

I thought, too, about how weird he'd been about the money side of the trip, and all the little red flags I'd conveniently brushed aside because I was so besotted. For convenience's sake (and because I am A Planner), I'd found and paid for our Airbnb in Rome. Though I'd never asked him to pay his share, it had bothered me that he hadn't even offered, and that when I'd asked him to book our train tickets from Milan to Rome, he'd come up with a lame excuse about his credit card not working. I ended up paying for those too. (Eventually, towards the end of the trip, I'd casually asked him if he could PayPal me his share of our Airbnb bill, and he'd dragged his feet over it, waiting until I'd reminded him a few times before finally doing it, and parsimoniously making deductions for a round of drinks he'd paid for.)

Now that I thought about it, he'd grumbled about the price of *everything*, vetoing anywhere he deemed 'kinda fancy' – restaurants, bars, the botanical gardens we'd walked forty minutes in the sweltering heat to find, only to discover that there was an €8 admission fee to enter (which he didn't want to pay). On our final night, instead of having a drink at a cute bar a friend had recommended, we bought a few bottles of beer from a local supermarket and drank them sitting on the Spanish Steps, which is forbidden and meant we had to hide our drinks every time one of the security guards on patrol walked past. I felt dismayed. It was as though he hadn't planned on spending any money on the trip, which made me wonder whether he'd secretly been hoping for me to foot the bill entirely.

'But he's always been so supportive of my work!' I protested to Jenny. 'That's one of the things I really like about him. He even bought copies of my book for some of his girl friends.'

'Well, yes,' she replied with the sage air of a Buddhist monk who has finally worked out the meaning of life and is now going to patiently explain it to you, a moron. 'It's easy to be supportive from a distance, but it sounds like when he was actually confronted with your success up close, he just couldn't handle it. Your Instagrams looked great though!'

Lying in bed that night, I thought back to The Australian's refusal to sit in the audience at the panel discussion, and of the forced smile he'd flashed me the next morning as I was being mic'ed up ahead of a TV appearance on a major news network; the muted praise for my meticulously put-together outfits (perhaps the bitterest pill to swallow, for I am nothing if not well-dressed).

Jenny was right. I'd fallen for a Berger.

Of course, it's not just men who behave strangely where women and money are concerned – judgement about money transcends gender. But where men's attitudes often veer towards viewing financially empowered women as overly entitled or as some form of threat, the female version of the internal dialogue around women and money very often tends towards shame. There is a specific cadence of judginess we reserve for other women's money choices – be that in relation to personal spending, or how they handle money within their relationships – and sisterhood very often goes out of the window. And why not? It's virtually impossible to avoid internalising the message that woman + money = bad when our culture is so rife with it. In a 2018 linguistic analysis study of personal finance articles published in the UK, semioticians found huge discrepancies in the way the media speaks to men and women about money, with women overwhelmingly characterised as 'splurgers' with poor judgement, and articles for female readerships portraying finances as a complex minefield too complicated for our tiny brains to handle.[7] These articles – often published by women's media outlets – are riddled with what the study refers to as 'guilt language'; guilt over money, or sex, or ambition being one of the patriarchy's sharpest and best-concealed tools.

Take the concept of the money diary, an editorial format first popularised by Refinery29, in which anonymous people (usually women) give detailed accounts of their expenditure over the course of a week, documenting their income and outgoings down to the penny. From salaries and student loan payments to sex toys and weed, nothing goes unaccounted for. These money diaries are often responsible for delivering digital media platforms their highest traffic numbers, but the diarists themselves are often critiqued, mocked and taken to task in the comments over their spending choices, with some of these occasionally garnering enough traction to briefly cross over into social media virality – furiously dissected, and then dismissed. Too spoiled. Too wasteful. Too rich. Too poor. There is a reason why money diaries are so often published anonymously – it seems we love nothing more than to judge other women's financial choices, modern-day emperors observing from our armchair thrones, ready to denounce anyone who deviates from our own personally approved money script. Sensible saver? Thumbs up. Financial assistance from your parents? Thumbs down. Ordered three takeaways in one week? Undecided (but surely that's a *bit* extravagant, no?). Cultural critic Jia Tolentino describes money diaries as 'a place where millennial women go to judge and be judged',[8] a guilty pleasure I've certainly availed myself of in the past.

When a money diarist whose account of the cost-cutting measures she'd implemented to try to claw her way onto the London property ladder went viral during the summer of 2018, I was part of the online pile-on that transpired. Like many, I felt the numbers she'd outlined just didn't add up, and I tweeted as much. Although my comments were light-hearted – in contrast to much of the genuine vitriol that emerged – the fact is I too was judging her, this woman who earned nearly £70,000 a year, and whose idea of 'cutting back' involved spending £80 a week on a (vegetarian!) food shop and paying £830 a month for a 'cheap' house share. Never mind that she'd also cancelled an expensive gym membership and started socialising less, and was clearly trying to save up without compromising too heavily on her quality of life. I merely focused on what (in my opinion) she was doing wrong. What a blinkered, spoiled fool, I thought disapprovingly, feeling that if she was *truly* serious about saving, she needed to buckle her belt several notches tighter. As is so often the case when it comes to our perceptions of others' financial behaviour, my reaction to her spending habits said far more about me than it did about her, in this case exposing my own rather self-flagellating attitude towards money: 'Saving up should hurt, or you aren't doing it right. If it isn't painful, then you aren't saving hard enough.'

More broadly, the wider media characterisation of this diarist – and she ended up making headlines around the world – played into the 'avocado toast' narrative of why millennials cannot afford to buy houses, pinning it on our inability to deny ourselves small indulgences instead of focusing on the insanity of property prices. Rather than question why the housing market is structured so that someone earning a distinctly above average salary was *still* struggling to get on the property ladder, most of the subsequent reportage chose instead to focus on all the tiny ways in which this one woman was potentially mismanaging her finances. The collective reaction was akin to bullying, with photographs from the 'moaning millennial's'[9] Instagram ending up splashed across the Internet before the newspaper which had published her account stepped in to update the original article, removing her photograph and changing her name. Like I said – there's a reason why these diaries are so often published anonymously.

Would I have judged the diary as harshly had it been written by a man? I like to think so, though of course the best reaction would have been for me to not judge the diarist at all. But I doubt it would even have come to my attention in the first place had the diarist been male (and, indeed, money diaries written by men are few and very far between). The tenor of the outrage had an undertone of 'look at this silly woman mishandling her finances' to it that I find it difficult to imagine would have been replicated were 'she' a 'he'.

Given the risk of penalty or censure when women *do* speak openly about money, in particular desiring it, it's a wonder any of us do. I suspect the scarcity of honest accounts of one's financial ambitions is the reason a 2018 *New York Times* article[10] by the bestselling author Jessica Knoll was sent to me no less than four times by various friends in the days after its publication. Under the headline 'I Want to Be Rich and I'm Not Sorry', Knoll unapologetically describes her desire for 'advances that make my husband gasp and fat royalty cheques twice a year', and the strategic career choices she's made that have turned those desires into reality. Even the headline – blunt, uncomplicated, entirely unsentimental – feels at odds with how women are generally conditioned to speak about money. 'Success, for me, is synonymous with making money,' Knoll writes, an attitude I also share, but often feel the need to temper by pointing to all the other things I value *besides* money, lest I come across as too materialistic or too accepting of capitalist ideology.

In an interview with *The Hollywood Reporter* a few months before Knoll's piece was published, *Grey's Anatomy* star Ellen Pompeo matter-of-factly outlined exactly how she'd managed to secure a $20 million-a-year salary, a figure that made her the highest paid actress on prime time TV.[11] The interview stood out to me not only because of its transparency – rare in Hollywood discussions of pay – but also because of the bullishness of

Pompeo's tone, and her obvious unwillingness to conform to the cultural expectation whereby women are socialised to feel shame over desiring money. Here was a woman entirely aware of her value to the TV network that employed her, and willing to openly leverage that position to get the best deal possible. *Grey's Anatomy* is a multibillion-dollar franchise for Disney, and as the show's titular character, Meredith Grey, Pompeo is essential to its continued success, even more so after the producers killed off her love interest of eleven seasons, Derek Shepherd.

Clearly Knoll and Pompeo are women unafraid to ask for more – but they're also both wealthy enough to employ a phalanx of agents, lawyers, managers and business advisers to negotiate on their behalf.

What about the rest of us? How do ordinary women ask?

The received wisdom has long been that when it comes to pay rises, we don't. Or rather, that we don't ask for them as often as men do. We are supposedly too timid or too self-deprecating to march into boardrooms and demand the same amounts that men do, and as a result we end up being paid less. It's a narrative promoted by even the most well-meaning of spokespersons, and on the surface it makes sense. The idea that women don't ask for pay rises in the same way men do is seductively plausible, and fits in neatly with deeply ingrained stereotypes around so-called 'feminine' personality traits.

It is also, quite simply, not true.

In a recent study titled 'Do Women Ask?', published in the economics journal *Industrial Relations* and using data collected from more than 4,600 Australian workers, researchers were surprised to find that women actually *do* ask for pay rises as often as men – we're just more likely to be turned down.[12] Having expected to find confirmation of long-established theories around women's reluctance to negotiate, analysis instead showed that propensity to negotiate is roughly equal for men and women. When I shared this conclusion on social media a few years ago, I was inundated with responses from women eager to share their stories of having asked for pay rises only to be denied. One woman told me about the time her boss had responded to her request for more pay by telling her that it was 'inelegant', a choice of word that seems very obviously gendered. Another told of being threatened with a demotion simply for having asked.

The findings from the 'Do Women Ask?' study challenge the commonly accepted wisdom on this topic, not to mention the findings of other well-known studies, specifically those of the economics professor Linda Babcock and her fellow academic Sara Laschever. In 2003, the duo co-authored an era-defining book called *Women Don't Ask*, the general thrust of which is probably fairly obvious from its title. Their book and the studies underpinning it[13] have been cited ever since as evidence of women's reticence to ask for more in the workplace, and have no doubt introduced a degree of confirmation bias into the research studies and more informal analyses that have occurred since. (It's worth noting that neither Babcock nor Laschever have suggested that women's supposed reluctance to negotiate stems from innate 'feminine' qualities, as others have. Rather, they believe it to be a learned trait inculcated by external social forces.[14])

But – unlike in other studies carried out on this topic – the researchers on the more recent 'Do Women Ask?' study had access to data detailed enough to account for a crucial fact: that women are far more likely than men to work in low-skilled hourly wage jobs or part-time roles where salary negotiation isn't necessarily possible. Previous studies that have reached the 'women don't ask' conclusion often failed to take into account the fact that certain types of jobs and industries are dominated by one gender, focusing instead on the *overall* number of men or women who had reported salary negotiations, which – given the number of women who do jobs with 'non-negotiable' salaries – skewed their findings considerably. This recent study, on the other hand, found that when comparing men and women who do similar jobs (and jobs where there are genuine opportunities for salary negotiation), women actually ask for pay rises at the same rate as men. Those findings have subsequently been reinforced by others, including two separate studies[15] by McKinsey, the most recent of which, published in September 2018,[16] surveyed 64,000 workers in North America and found that women actually negotiate for pay rises at a slightly *higher* rate of 31 per cent to men's 29 per cent.

Depressing as it is to have confirmation that women are more likely to be denied pay rises than men, it's somehow also grimly satisfying to have a robust challenge to the notion that women are mostly to blame for wage inequality as a result of our actions, or lack thereof. To buy into the narrative that women don't ask is to assign blame for a situation outside our control, while simultaneously eliding a more unpalatable and frankly depressing truth – that we are often systematically cheated out of our fair share. The term 'gaslighting', taken from the 1944 film *Gaslight*[17] starring Ingrid Bergman, means to manipulate someone's perception of reality, deliberately making them question what they know to be true. Denying women's requests when they *do* negotiate while also promoting the idea that the gender pay gap is down to their reluctance to do so is an exemplary form of gaslighting. So too with the clichéd stereotype of the frivolous woman who spends all her money on clothes, or the notion that women are inherently bad with money, which not only wilfully ignores the documented reality of female expenditure, but acts as a cover for all of the proven structural reasons why women have less money than men. The idea that we don't ask is a convenient narrative, but it's also incorrect. When it comes to women and negotiation, rumours of our reluctance have been greatly exaggerated.

And, as I came to the end of my time at AMV and started a new job, I was about to learn just how bad this kind of workplace gaslighting could get.

Chapter 4

BOYS' CLUB

By my second day at Vice, I already knew I'd made a mistake.

That morning my new boss, Jamie, had suggested we have lunch together so he could bring me up to speed on the projects I'd be working on. As lunchtime approached and my colleagues began to slope out in twos and threes, I waited for him to make the first move. He did not. Eventually, emboldened by the pangs of hunger beginning to make their presence known, I went over to his desk.

'Hey! Do you wanna go grab lunch soon?' I asked, as casually as I could.

Jamie looked up from his laptop and sighed, visibly stressed.

'Yeah . . . I actually don't think I'm gonna be able to do lunch today – sorry. I'm just completely slammed right now, it's nuts,' he said, looking apologetic. 'But why don't we do lunch or something tomorrow?'

'Oh, yeah, of course – no worries,' I replied sympathetically. 'Hope it's not too mad!'

I returned to my desk, hoping that one of my new colleagues might suggest we go for lunch together. But no one did, instead studiously avoiding eye contact with me as they picked out their usual lunch buddies. Eventually, bored and hungry, I headed out on my own, doing a loop of the surrounding streets before buying a sandwich to eat at my desk. *Like a loser*, I thought, the words popping unbidden into my head as I walked back towards the office.

To my surprise, I spotted Jamie walking towards me, accompanied by a few of the guys who sat on the desks next to mine, all of them cracking jokes and laughing loudly. They avoided my gaze until we were almost level – quite the feat given we were the only ones on the narrow street leading to the office – but I smiled brightly as we passed each other, raising a hand in acknowledgement. They smiled back and kept walking.

Maybe he's just going to pick up something to eat at his desk, I thought. *Nothing wrong with that.*

About an hour later the group returned, their conversations interrupting the strangely tense quiet of the office as they settled back into their desks for the afternoon.

'It's just quite *different* from AMV,' I said later that evening, relaying the day's events to my housemate Lydia. 'We always made such a big effort welcoming new people there, like, taking them for a team lunch or something on their first day. I don't know – the fact he bailed on me to go for "lunch with the boys" just feels a bit . . . off.'

'You're reading way too much into it,' Lydia replied, trying to reassure me. 'Honestly – there's, like, a million and one reasons why he might have changed his mind. Don't overthink it.'

'Yeah . . . yeah, you're probably right,' I conceded.

Unfortunately for me, my instincts would turn out to be completely spot on.

I probably should have seen it coming. There'd been plenty of warning signs along the way, an embarrassment of them now that I think about it. I'd just chosen to ignore them.

Even before joining Vice I'd been unimpressed by the way the company had conducted its interview process, which had veered uncomfortably close to the 'haphazard' end of the 'relaxed' spectrum. I'd sat through two vague, unstructured interviews where I'd been asked questions like what kind of pizza I'd be and why (though, for my sins, I have blocked out whatever hastily attempted witticism I offered up in reply). There'd been last-minute interview cancellations, and for some reason the job title I was eventually offered was completely different from the one I'd actually applied for. In the past I'd turned down job offers based on impressions I'd formed after sloppily conducted interviews, reasoning that a company's handling of that process is likely to be indicative of its day-to-day culture. But for Vice – cool, zeitgeisty, everyone-wants-to-work-there Vice – I'd been willing to make an exception.

It didn't help that in the nearly two years since joining AMV, I'd slowly grown to hate working there, feeling increasingly alienated by its cliquey atmosphere, and stifled by my lack of progression. I had tried to compartmentalise my unhappiness by finding things to occupy me outside of work, applying for and being accepted onto an Arts Council-funded writing programme that I tentatively hoped might be my route into a writing career. Within weeks, I'd had to drop out when it became clear that my consistently leaving the office by 5.30 p.m. every other Monday to get to the workshop on time just wasn't realistic.

At what would end up being my final performance review with AMV, my boss informed me that she found my ambition 'hard to manage', as though the ambition of a 23-year-old woman is something to be tempered instead of nurtured. Dissolving into embarrassed tears, I vowed to be more of a 'team player', unquestioningly accepting that it was me who was the problem. Not long after that review, I was abruptly parachuted onto a different account as a way of resolving a personality clash with a fellow team member, having been identified as the source of conflict by the head of our team. Given that this new account was responsible for marketing one of our clients to a largely West African market, I'd initially imagined that my being Nigerian might prove to be an advantage, given my innate cultural understanding of our target audience. Instead my days became focused on navigating the constant barrage of low-level racism from my new all-male, all-white team, with the fact that our account necessarily involved engaging with African culture providing ample opportunity for my colleagues to expose the depths of their bigotry. This was at the height of the Ebola crisis in West Africa, so jokes about Nigerians having Ebola and 'eating rats' were dropped into meetings as casually as comments about the weather. The colleagues in various African agencies we partnered with were discussed as if they were morons, their efforts largely dismissed. To make matters worse, I was not only the youngest person on the team, but also the only person of colour and the only woman. I had no idea how to even begin challenging my colleagues' racism, didn't even know if I could call it that, and – still reeling from my performance review – I didn't want to appear difficult by asking to switch teams, nor did I want to be accused of 'playing the race card' if I made a formal complaint. Instead, I simply grew more and more withdrawn, eventually realising that the only solution was for me to find a new job. By the time Vice came knocking, I'd have taken a job as a canary in a coal mine.

As I weighed up whether or not to accept Vice's offer, I decided to confide in Lucy, a colleague whose kindness and work ethic I admired, and who I viewed as something of an informal mentor. I could see from her expression that she *wanted* to be encouraging about Vice, given she knew how deeply unhappy I'd become at AMV, but even still – she seemed hesitant to give me the green light I was so clearly seeking.

'I just haven't heard *great* things about the vibe there. I think it's a bit of a snake pit,' she said gently. 'But if you're really that unhappy here . . .' she tailed off.

That evening I went online to do more research, scrolling through page after page of search results as I tried to build up an accurate picture of what working at Vice would be like, and whether or not I should take the job. Alongside dozens of articles breathlessly proclaiming the company to be the future of journalism, peppered with memorable sound bites from its larger-than-life then-CEO Shane Smith, there was also a small but persistent undercurrent of reports that presented a damning picture of its company culture. Most notable was a Gawker article published only months before, under the headline 'Working at Vice Media Is Not as Cool as it Seems'.[1] In the article Gawker asserted that Vice was a 'less than ideal employer', having spoken to several employees to build an image of the company that was far from enticing: abysmally low pay, undervalued and overworked employees, and questionable editorial standards that involved changing content to suit advertisers.

Well, maybe that's just the New York office, I thought, moments before unearthing a similarly acerbic takedown of Vice's London outpost, also by Gawker.[2]

Oh for fuck's sake.

'Shitty pay, stressful work, and a "boy's club" [sic] atmosphere that's not so fun if you're not one of the boys,' it read. One anonymous employee had given an account suggesting that in order to survive at Vice one had to be 'cutthroat, a liar, totally out for yourself and ready to reinvent yourself at a moments [sic] notice.'

They're probably just jealous, I reasoned. After all, Vice was a brand that had grown exponentially in the early 2010s, succeeding where many other media companies seemed to be failing. As the self-professed enfant terrible of new media, it was certainly true that many long-standing media outlets quietly resented Vice's success, regarding its bombastic style of gonzo reporting with a mixture of suspicion and scorn, while simultaneously trying to figure out how they could emulate the magic that had brought advertising and investment dollars pouring into Vice's much-hyped 'war chest'.[3] That Vice's competitors – new and old media alike – were looking for chinks in its armour turned out to be the line of defence Vice itself would adopt, publishing a riposte pithily titled 'Fuck You and Fuck Your Garbage Click-Bait "Journalism"' that characterised Gawker's articles as a 'smear job' and cited the company's 'obvious and embarrassing emotional vendetta against [Vice], its success, and its senior management'.[4]

Wary of getting bogged down in the he said/he said of New York media rivalries, I turned to Glassdoor, a website where current and former employees can submit reviews of companies they've worked for, sort of like a TripAdvisor for the workplace. To my dismay, page after page of anonymous employee reviews told of a toxic working environment characterised by long hours, low morale and low pay. Everything at Vice seemed low in fact, except for its staff turnover, which was described by turns as 'unusually high' and 'insane'. One reviewer described the company as 'a hipster sweatshop that would make Aldous Huxley roll in his grave'.

I kept scrolling.

'The company is so deeply dysfunctional to the core that even if you love your co-workers it's hard to shake the bad stuff,' another review read, a comment that somewhat bafflingly had been listed as one of the 'pros' of working at Vice.

Under the pros section of yet another review, one former employee had simply written: 'You're allowed to work indoors.'

There were comments, too, about the supposed boys' club culture. I clicked on one.

'While Vice purports to be growing up and including women more, it's actually not a good place to work for women. The boys' club culture is embedded in everything – even some of the women are sexist.'

Click.

'Highly misogynistic environment.'

Click.

'People at Vice seem depressed, even paranoid.'

Click.

'You will hate yourself for being there.'

They're probably all just disgruntled employees, I thought. *Lots and lots of . . . disgruntled employees.*

(Dear reader, a word of advice: if ever you apply for a job and find that a company has left an army's worth of disgruntled employees in its wake, I suggest you run as fast as you can in the other direction and never look back.)

That I decided to join Vice despite the mountain of evidence advising otherwise is testament to the fact that desperation is a terrible position from which to make good decisions – and by that point I was truly *desperate* to leave AMV. I was also still in my early twenties, with a fairly limited experience of the working world. The scope of just how bad a workplace could be was entirely beyond the boundaries of my imagination, and I told myself that Vice couldn't possibly be *that* bad. In the end the thing that swung it for me was my re-emerging desire to pursue a career in journalism. Though I'd been hired to work within Vice's in-house ad agency, I hoped that simply being inside the building might be the foothold I needed to turn my hand to writing.

Anyway, I reasoned, *it's the Internet. Everyone complains on the Internet. That's what it's there for.*

So I did it. I took the job.

Very quickly it became clear that I had indeed entered a boys' club, in which I was far from welcome. If I was in any doubt about my chances of progressing at Vice while also being in possession of a vagina, I was soon forcefully disavowed of those illusions. The lad culture I'd been warned about was impossible to ignore, and though I'd encountered that sort of environment in the past, Vice was somehow far, far worse, on account of the unspoken party line: *this is what you signed up for, so suck it up.* A few weeks after joining Vice, I went for a drink with some of my new colleagues, including Lily and Rosa, two women who'd both been at the company for a couple of years, and Adrian, a member of senior management. A few drinks in, Lily and Rosa began to berate Adrian over what they (rightly) perceived to be the company's ingrained sexism, which they felt was holding them back from ascending to senior management themselves. Sensing their frustration, Adrian didn't attempt to deny what they said was true. Instead, he deflected. 'I know – and it sucks but . . . that's just how it is here,' he said. 'It *is* changing,' he continued philosophically, 'but these things take time, y'know?' It struck me then how odd it was that he should feign powerlessness, as though he himself were not in a position to effect drastic and immediate change.

I sipped my drink quietly, knowing it wasn't my place to weigh in given how new I was to the company. Turning the conversation over in my mind later that evening though, as well as being dismayed, I also felt strangely energised. I was tough, wasn't I? Brian, my boss at my first job, had once called me 'bolshy', on account of my ability to corral difficult colleagues. He'd intended it as a compliment (though goodness knows it was a heavily gendered one), and my directness had been part of why I'd done so well there. Outside of work I was regarded by friends as someone not easily intimidated, who always spoke their mind. Though AMV had badly knocked my confidence, I felt certain I could resurrect my natural take-no-shit approach and rise up through the ranks at Vice. I could picture the story already – a whip-smart female media exec who, against all odds, had risen to the top of a notoriously male-dominated company. The narrative my school had instilled in me of workplace sexism as a system to be gamed, something you could simply work your way through by being clever and hard-working enough, once again came to the fore.

When several of the senior guys on my team went on a lads' trip to Vienna one weekend, I felt Rosa and Lily bristle as the guys trooped out of the office on a Friday afternoon, overnight bags flung over their shoulders, bearing an expression I recognised all too well from seven years at an all-girls' school – the sheepish-yet-smug smile of the select few who've been invited to the popular girl's sleepover. I left work a few hours later feeling strangely despondent. Although I had zero desire to spend my weekend listening to techno music and ingesting my body weight in ketamine, it was screamingly obvious to me that the trip – which as far as I was aware no women in the office had been invited on – was a pseudo team-bonding exercise, one that would undoubtedly have a knock-on effect on day-to-day office dynamics. It was the hipster equivalent of visiting a strip club with your male colleagues.

For a while, I also had the uneasy sensation of being an object of curiosity, a feeling which finally made sense when a few weeks in I rocked up at the Old Blue Last, the grimy Shoreditch boozer Vice had owned for some years. We were there to mark the fact that a mid-tier grime artist had dropped by the office, grime music inexplicably being the genre of choice for the company's predominantly white, middle-class employees. I looked around. This was the largest number of Vice staffers I'd seen all together since I'd joined, and it was glaringly obvious that something was missing.

'Where are all the women?' I asked my boss pointedly.

'We're working on that,' he laughed self-consciously. 'That's why we hired you!'

I raised my eyebrows. It was a terrible joke. I didn't even bother pointing out the other glaringly obvious absence in the room.

As I stood awkwardly in a circle, politely nodding along to in-jokes I didn't really get, one of my colleagues – Sean – nudged me.

'Oi Otegha, listen to this.'

I perked up, pleased to finally be included in the conversation. Sean stood with his legs apart, and then with the practised motion of someone who'd performed this trick many times before, began to jerk his hips vigorously from side to side.

'Can you hear that?' he said, looking me in the eye. 'That's my balls slapping against my thighs!' he added, dissolving into fits of laughter. Everyone else followed suit.

It was quite possibly the most vulgar joke I'd ever encountered in a professional setting, and I felt utterly repulsed – but I also didn't want to come across as prudish, so I laughed it off, pulling a face and changing the subject. But again, I felt deflated. Not long after, I made my excuses and went home.

I noticed early on that there was a stark divide between the 'OG' Vice staffers – those who'd been there at least a couple of years and spoke longingly about the good old days before the company had been taken over by 'suits' – and recent hires like me, who'd been brought in from more traditional ad agencies and had different (read: higher) expectations of how an office should operate. It felt no different from misty-eyed pensioners who talk longingly about the glory days of empire or bemoan the rise of political correctness, except here the target of opprobrium seemed to be the expectation of fairly basic standards of professionalism. Having come from a well-established advertising agency which – for all its flaws – ran a pretty tight ship when it came to the actual work, I was entirely unprepared for Vice's considerably more 'relaxed' way of working. Still, I tried desperately to drink the company Kool-Aid those first few weeks, nodding along as my Nathan Barley-esque colleagues skulked around in scuffed Reeboks and ironic Slayer hoodies, while salivating over how 'lucky' we were to be working at Vice and rhapsodising about their 'vision' for the company's future.

By the time I'd been there a month though, I'd stopped pretending to myself that I was happy in my new job. Far from galvanising me into action as I'd initially thought it might, the sense that my gender was holding me back in all-too-tangible ways – and the feeling of exclusion which accompanied that – had bubbled over into burning resentment. At an early one-on-one, Jamie had asked me to 'babysit' a new project so that another of my (white, male) colleagues would be free to do the more substantive creative development. Never mind that this colleague was actually my junior, Jamie saw him as something of a wunderkind on account of a fabled intellect that I myself never once observed.

'I just need you to send calendar invites, keep track of meetings . . . stuff like that. Basically just keep things running smoothly.' He smiled, careful to frame this arrangement as an indicator of his faith in me by referring to me as 'a safe pair of hands'. I saw through it immediately and refused, appalled at being shunted into what was evidently a secretarial role so that Jamie's star student might be free to shine.

My parents did not *leave Lagos for this*, I thought to myself, quietly furious.

A flicker of irritation flashed across Jamie's face, his carefully laid plans unravelling. He hadn't counted on my reading between the lines of his proposal, much less saying no. That evening I messaged my friend Tommy, who also worked in advertising, and could therefore be trusted to fully understand the weird political machinations of my job.

Me: I'm pretty sure I'm going to quit Vice after this weekend.
Tommy: Why??
Me: I'm just feeling really irritated about work.
Furious, actually.

I was having lunch with that guy Danny earlier
And he mentioned that he's getting a promotion
Tommy: OK . . .
Me: But then he was like 'Oh yeah, well at least I hope it
    actually happens, we were all pretty coked up when
    it came about'
Tommy: Christ
Me: Yup
    And it turns out that long-ass bender they all went on
    last week is when he got offered the promotion
    Which is just so frustrating
    They have all these socials and stuff and obviously I'm
    not invited
    But that's clearly how you get ahead here
    It's so annoying, it feels like a gender thing as well
    And I feel like I'm not being considered for projects as
    a result

And it was true. I was often left out of after-work forays to the pub, occasionally plucking up the courage to invite myself along if I got wind of an outing (though doing that was so excruciating I could only bear to do it occasionally). When I *did* go, I'd wonder why the hell I'd been so eager to join, smiling thinly as I listened to a male colleague bragging about 'doing coke off a stripper's tits before being frogmarched to a cashpoint' by what he referred to as 'two huge Black guys', and watching as he got a congratulatory fist bump from another (senior, white, male) colleague.

As far as I could tell, Lily was the only woman who seemed to have penetrated the company's boys' club, a feat she'd achieved by making a clear effort to distance herself from the other women on our team, displaying a palpable spikiness towards us all. The concept of sisterhood didn't seem to be one Lily was familiar with, and yet even she wasn't immune to the ingrained sexism that seemed to define women's trajectories at Vice. Once, in the midst of a team restructure, Jamie had confided in me that he didn't feel he could promote either Lily or Rosa – who were both level pegging in terms of seniority, and both overdue for promotion – to head up our team for fear of 'upsetting' the other, the unspoken subtext being that as two women they were necessarily in competition with each other. So he did what was to him the logical thing, holding them both back and stunting both their careers. I began to understand the quiet fury I'd observed Lily and Rosa level at Adrian at those drinks some months earlier.

When a few months after joining, I received an email from Jamie casually informing me that my notice period had – without consultation – been increased from one month to two, I pushed back. At the time, I positioned it as simply a matter of principle, rather than an indication of my commitment to the company, but looking back I think on some level I knew that my days at Vice were numbered. My notice period didn't feel like an abstract concept to be properly considered at some misty point years down the line, but a very real – and very pressing – concern. We settled on six weeks. Around the same time, I also passed my probation period, a cheery email from HR landing in my inbox informing me that I was now a bona fide Vice staffer. My heart sank, and I messaged Tommy.

Me: I know I should be thrilled but honestly, I'm just completely exhausted.

> Emotionally, physically, mentally
> I think Vice is going to break me

To compound my misery, actually *working* at Vice was proving incredibly stressful. Staying late quickly became the norm, and I expended huge amounts of energy getting what felt like the most basic of tasks accomplished as a result of the chronic apathy many of my colleagues seemed to radiate. Some evenings I'd be so exhausted that I'd fall asleep fully clothed on my bed as soon as I arrived home from work, waking up at 5 or 6 a.m. after a horrendous night's half-sleep, and have to do it all over again. Other days, I'd end up skipping lunch, unable to find even fifteen minutes to spare in the chaos of my day. I'd make up for it in the evenings with comically large bowls of pasta that my housemates began to use as a way of gauging how badly my day had gone.

Me: I feel like I'm trapped in a nightmare
My entire life feels in complete disarray
I feel so sad about where I've ended up
And really mad at myself for not having made different decisions
I want to quit so much
Tommy: You're being too hard on yourself
And I really think you should leave. You're clearly very unhappy there
Me: I know but I don't want to make a rash decision that messes up my career
I feel like I need to stick it out here for at least a year, otherwise it'll look bad on my CV

> Plus I need the money. I can't move back home with
> my parents

Predictably, my perpetual anxiety about money reared its ugly head. I had moved out of my parents' house two years earlier, renting a series of flats with friends, strangers and semi-strangers, largely because living at home with my parents post-university had seriously strained our at times fraught relationship. Though my parents would have gladly had me back, I didn't want to go back – a mixture of pride, dread at the prospect of losing my independence, and anxiety about returning to the tension that had driven me out in the first place. At that point, moving back home genuinely *didn't* feel like an option, but the idea of handing in my notice without a job lined up and just 'hoping for the best' work-wise – as a few of my friends were suggesting – wasn't something I could contemplate while I still had £650 a month in rent to cover. So back and forth I went for the next few months, resolving to quit one day only to call it off the next. My predicament felt insurmountable and I existed in a constant fug, alternating between panic and despair, and contemplating my next career move with a level of intensity that I can now see it didn't warrant. Everything in my life felt heavy, and hard, and once again my sense of desperation short-circuited my ability to think rationally about my situation. I began concocting increasingly ridiculous ideas about how I could possibly avoid a job I hated without having to pluck up the courage to actually resign.

> **Me**: God this sounds so terrible but I've even been
> wondering whether someone close to me dying might
> get me some time off work

Hypothetically speaking, obviously

Or like, maybe I could make up that I'm pregnant or something

Tommy: What would you do when everyone wanted to meet your baby?

Me: I don't know. Let's cross that bridge when we get to it

Tommy: Lol. How's your day been?

Me: Terrible. I had a panic attack this morning :(

Tommy: Oh wow . . . Are you OK?

Me: Yeah, fine. Nothing like constant stress and impossible expectations to get your blood pumping! I just don't understand how I've got here I feel so defeated, and I'm literally on the edge of tears the whole time

Tommy: Quit

Me: I can't

For a while, I toyed with the idea of running away to Paris to become an au pair, imagining that a year strolling through the Marais and eating bonbons in charming little cafés might be the balm for my wounded spirits, and giving little consideration to what being an au pair actually involved. I even went so far as to set up a profile on a website dedicated to matching English students with French host families, sending my mother a bio packed with lies ('I find children tend to warm to me very quickly') that she dutifully translated without so much as a raised eyebrow, though I imagine it took considerable self-restraint not to question whether I'd really thought the whole thing through.

When I ran the idea past Tommy, he was rather more prosaic.

Me: So I'm thinking of quitting at the end of August
[five months after I'd joined Vice] to go and au pair for
a bit, in Paris
Thinking that might give me a bit of breathing room
to maybe do some writing
Thoughts?
Tommy: Are you even good with children?
I imagine you just gobbling them up
Boiling them in a stew
Me: I hate you

Perhaps the most significant effect Vice had on me was in relation to my confidence, what little of it I had left now replaced with near pathological self-doubt. Whenever a project I was managing involved strategic or creative input, Jamie would advise me to 'get [insert male colleague's name here] involved if you need a brain on this project', delivering his advice with a smile so benign that I realised he wasn't even aware of how condescending he was being. He thought he was being helpful.

'If you need a brain.'

God, how I hated that phrase.

Does he not think. I have A FUCKING. Brain! I'd huff angrily down the phone to Tommy, who'd laugh sympathetically while trying to placate me.

But over time the insinuation that I wasn't up to the task began to stick. Maybe I *wasn't* smart enough to be working there. I began pre-empting Jamie's 'helpful suggestions' by avoiding the thornier aspects of the projects I was involved with, pre-emptively referring them to one of the so-called 'brains' I worked with, which probably did little to improve Jamie's opinion of my capabilities. I'd often hear other colleagues' intelligence described in reverent tones, on account of their ability to optimise banner ads or come up with silly puns or some other dubious measure of genius that was imbued with the same weight as having found a cure for cancer. I never once heard that term applied to any of the women I worked with.

Early one morning before work, a now familiar sense of dread settling in the pit of my stomach, I texted Tommy.

Me: I just feel like a real dummy
I'm worried Jamie thinks I exaggerated my capabilities when I was applying for the job
Which obviously I didn't
But I feel like every time I try to stretch myself and try to do some creative or strategic thinking, it just goes horribly wrong
Like maybe I should just admit to myself that I'm not actually that smart

Despite the many incongruous scenarios I've found myself in over the years – a council estate kid at an elite private school; a Black student at a predominantly white university – working at Vice is without doubt the period in my life where I have felt most out of place. As the months wore on, my imposter syndrome intensified to almost unbearable levels, which is in many ways completely unremarkable. Prevailing narratives about 'imposter syndrome' often frame it as largely a mental barrier, something you can lean into or out of and overcome through personal endeavour, pathologising it to the point of medical disorder (the clue is in the name: 'syndrome'). Few consider how the homogenous cultures and institutionalised discrimination present in many workplaces conspire to exclude those of us whose identities might reasonably be described as 'marginalised' – women, ethnic minorities, the working class. Often we feel like interlopers because we actually are.

Eventually I began to realise that I wasn't, and would never be, the right fit for Vice, no matter how hard I tried. Not smart enough (or so I thought), not white enough, and definitely, *definitely* not male enough.

It all ended with the rat. Or rather the rats, because there were definitely a few of them, although thankfully I only ever came face to face with one, perched bold and beady-eyed atop my kitchen counter. Of all the places one might ideally hope to encounter a rat, I'm going to go out on a limb and suggest that kitchen counter is fairly low on that list.

We locked eyes, the rat and I, and for a second both of us were still. Then I screamed, making a sound I hadn't even realised I was capable of making, and the rat scurried off to wherever the fuck he'd come from. I too scurried off into my housemate's bedroom, sobbing and shaken, and insisting that she let me spend the night in her bed.

It turns out that the only thing more powerful than my pride is my fear of rodents. A few weeks later I moved back home with my parents in what was to be a temporary measure while I looked for a new flat. Thankfully the rat sighting had also coincided with the end of my lease, which unsurprisingly my housemates and I chose not to renew.

At the same time, things at Vice reached new lows. Most evenings I'd call Tommy after work, walking home in the early autumn sun and just sobbing down the phone to him.

'I can't spend another six months doing this. Just lurching from crisis to crisis, shitty conversation to shitty conversation . . . I physically *cannot* do it anymore.'

Even though I'd only moved back home to avoid my unwanted four-legged housemate, the reality of no longer being burdened by rent meant that for the first time in months I allowed myself to fully reckon with how intensely unhappy Vice was making me.

A few days later, I messaged Tommy again.

Me: I did it
    I handed in my notice
    I don't know if I've made the right decision though
    I don't think I've ever felt this sad about my life before, or so lost about what I should do next
    And I feel like whatever decision I make next will be a mistake

As I left work that evening I got a call from a friend who'd just found out they'd been offered a job in New York, complete with a six-figure salary and generous benefits package. Meanwhile, I was staring into the abyss of impending unemployment and what I thought was certain career suicide. I felt sick with regret. At a party I went to later that night, I bounced around telling anyone who'd listen what I'd done, radiating an intense, febrile energy and overcompensating for my uncertainty with a forced nonchalance. Then I got home, and the fear truly set in.

I spent the rest of the weekend drafting an email rescinding my resignation, resolving to swallow my pride and send it to Jamie the following week. But then Monday went by, and then Tuesday, and somehow, I just couldn't bring myself to send it. As word got out that I was leaving and colleagues began asking me what I was doing next, I'd smile mysteriously and trill 'We'll see!', because the truth was I had absolutely no idea. More than one person soberly told me that they thought I was 'making a mistake', which did nothing for my nerves. Increasingly worried about the fact I didn't have another job lined up, when Jamie asked if I'd be willing to stay on a little longer than my contracted six-week notice period to see out a few projects, I agreed, glad to have a little extra time to figure out my next move, and an extra pay cheque or two to add to my savings. At the same time, I began tightening my belt, switching my daily Pret almond croissant for a new diet of cold milk and rolled oats (so basically gruel), and at last coming to appreciate the money-saving benefits of bringing a packed lunch into work.

With the clock counting down to my last day, I met a recruiter to sound out my options. I wasn't entirely sure I wanted to continue working in advertising, but I was also panicked about finding another job with a stable salary, so I'd got in touch with her on Tommy's recommendation. Over coffee at a trendy east London co-working space, she sized up the printout of my CV I'd brought along with me, muttering under her breath, before finally she sat back and looked at me.

'So, salary-wise, I'm guessing you're on about £40k or so?'

I looked at her in shock.

'Uh . . . not quite.'

She looked at me enquiringly, waiting for me to volunteer a piece of information I usually kept fiercely guarded.

'I'm on £32,000 at the moment.'

Now it was her turn to look shocked, though she quickly composed her face, a seasoned professional.

'I see! Well, given your level of experience, and the role you're currently doing . . .'

She looked back at my CV.

'Yes, that's quite a bit lower than what I'd expect you to be on. But on the plus side, that means you can expect a nice big jump with your next job!' she finished cheerily.

I left our meeting reeling, completely devastated. Walking back to work I mentally calculated how much money I'd theoretically lost out on, the only balm being that I'd been at Vice for a relatively brief period and so the salary differential hadn't had time to accumulate into a truly wounding amount. Back at my desk, I looked over at my colleague Jack, who did the same job as me and had joined at around the same time I had – Jack, who'd recently bought a two-bedroom flat in Hackney with his girlfriend, and was now planning his wedding; Jack who with his Red Wing boots and side gig as a DJ had slotted in easily with the rest of the (white) guys in the office – and I knew with a sudden clarity that he had to be earning far, far more than me. I felt deeply embarrassed. Boys' club or not, ultimately it was up to me to make sure I was being properly compensated at work. *How* had I let this happen? I'd tried to negotiate the initial salary offer of £32,000 I'd been offered with the job but had been denied for vague reasons – but even still, the research I'd done online had led me to believe that £32,000 was smack bang in the middle of the salary range for my job.

That evening I called Tommy to tell him what I'd found out, and his response surprised me.

'How did you *not* know that was below the market rate?' he asked, incredulous.

'I mean it's Vice so I knew it was a *bit* lower than the norm,' I replied. 'But I thought it was maybe £2,000 or £3,000 less. But £8,000? At a minimum?'

For days afterwards, I thought about Tommy's question. How *had* I not known?

The answer was that I'd always kept my salary to myself, adopting a 'don't ask don't tell' policy in the years following graduation. Around friends who I knew were earning more than I was (those in corporate jobs – banking, law, management consultancy), I felt slightly embarrassed about my comparatively low salary; around those who were either unemployed or doing low-paid waitressing jobs while they attended law school or studied for master's programmes, I felt awkward about my relative affluence – so I didn't share my salary with them, either. Instead, I'd developed a somewhat sanctimonious attitude, adopting the view that you shouldn't share your salary with anyone you weren't contractually obliged to – so your employer, your spouse or your bank.

And look where that's got you, I thought, furious at myself.

I messaged Tommy a few days later.

Me: I've completely changed my mind about the whole salary thing by the way
Tommy: What do you mean?
Me: Well you know how I always refuse to tell anyone my salary

Tommy: Yeah I've always thought you make too big
a deal of that
Me: Well ANYWAY
I'm gonna message all the girls tomorrow
Not asking to know their salaries, but just encouraging
them to discuss them with their peers at work
Because I think asymmetry of information is why this
happens, especially for women
Tommy: Yeah that's a good idea

Given that workplace sexism tends to go hand in hand with gender pay gaps, it will surprise absolutely no one to learn that Vice has since been accused of systematically underpaying its female employees. It certainly didn't surprise me. In February 2018, a former Vice employee, Elizabeth Rose, who had worked for two years at the company's New York and LA offices, filed a lawsuit against the company claiming they had systematically discriminated against female employees by paying them far less than their male counterparts for doing the same work, after she discovered internal documents revealing the salaries of thirty-five Vice employees.[5] Ms Rose's case developed into a class action lawsuit involving 675 women, and was eventually resolved in March 2019, with Vice agreeing a nearly $2 million settlement.[6] Though I'd suspected the company's deeply ingrained gender bias was at least partly responsible for my lower salary, I'd had no way of knowing that for sure, and for years I'd carried the bitterness and shame of that fact with me.

Still, discovering how badly I was being underpaid was the final insult. Even though I was leaving, I still nursed a burning fury over the many injustices and slights I'd endured, and continued to endure, though the target of my anger wasn't Vice alone.

Me: I feel so angry at myself
    I always seem to end up in these situations
    In crap jobs I don't like
    With crap managers who treat me as though I'm stupid
    I'm so fed up just thinking about all of the fucking
    hours I've poured into this place
    And all the times I've gone above and beyond
    Yet the idiots who fuck around shoving coke up their
    noses and swinging their dicks around get all the
    rewards
    Literally fuck Jamie, fuck this stupid place, fuck their
    stupid shitty 'content' and their shit jokes, and their
    shitty obsession with heavy metal.
    Fuck ALL of them.

Tommy replied.

Tommy: Heavy metal??
Me: Yeah
    Heavy metal is 'cool' again apparently
    That and trance

Ignoring the momentary distraction, I returned to my theme.

Me: Fuck this fucking bullshit
    Fuck all of it
    And FUCK Vice

And so it was that in a torrent of expletives, my time at Vice finally, mercifully, came to an end. It had been a brief but impactful experience, completely eviscerating my sense of self and giving me eight of the unhappiest months of my life in return. During my final few weeks at the company I barely showered, finding the effort required to make myself look presentable for work each day to be entirely beyond me. Even though I was finally leaving, I was still plagued by constant sadness and a deep sense of despair about my future, both of which took me years to shake off.

Just as those Glassdoor reviews had predicted, I was now depressed, paranoid – and much as I hated the company, I hated myself even more for being there.

My experience at Vice, though extreme, is far from unique. In a 2019 Cambridge University study, 74 per cent of female employees[7] surveyed spoke of their workplace culture making it more challenging for women to advance in their careers than men. As part of their research, the authors asked participants to rank a list of the most common career challenges, a list that will, for most women, read like a checklist of an average week at work: informal networks geared towards male team members (like men-only sports teams – or lads' trips to European capital cities); women being judged negatively when they behave in the same way as men ('being seen as competent but not likeable, branded as aggressive or bossy for behaviour that would be described as assertive in men'); being interrupted in meetings or not getting due credit for their contributions; men having better and more frequent access to senior leaders (which improves their chances of sponsorship by those who matter, hastening their progress up the career ladder); and benevolent sexism – behaviour that might be well intentioned, but nonetheless hampers our career prospects, such as downgrading a woman returning from maternity leave to the 'mommy track' and giving her less challenging assignments on the assumption that her priorities have now shifted. Notably, the researchers found employees believed female colleagues also perpetuate many of these harmful behaviours, concluding that 'the majority of women think female managers judge the same behaviour differently according to gender too'.

Speaking to female friends about their own experiences of workplace sexism, I'm dismayed but unsurprised by the similarities, regardless of age, seniority or industry. There is the friend whose male colleagues used to jokingly refer to the only two female employees in the company as Girl 1 and Girl 2; the brand consultant who had to laugh off flirtatious texts sent to her by her (much older) client in the middle of the night lest she be seen as a spoilsport or, worse, lose his business. The friend whose female boss used to criticise her physical appearance, instructing her to wear more make-up and heels ahead of client presentations. The photographer whose employer hired an older male colleague to work alongside her as a 'good influence' because they'd deemed her 'overly passionate', as though she were a flighty horse that needed taming. The friend who, when fundraising for a new business, was asked by a straight-faced potential investor 'can women make money?'

'What did you say??' I texted her.

'He's one of the most powerful people in our industry,' came the response.

On 23rd December 2017, two years after I'd left Vice and as the #MeToo movement was sweeping across the world, the *New York Times* finally broke a story it had been working on for months. In it, the Pulitzer Prize-winning business journalist Emily Steel reported a culture of sexual harassment and gender bias at Vice, documenting a series of alleged sexual harassment cases involving (often very senior) male members of staff and younger, more junior female colleagues; four of these cases had led to sizeable cash settlements. The article described 'a top-down ethos of male entitlement' that had created a workplace that was 'degrading and uncomfortable for women'. One former female employee, Sandra Miller, who worked as the head of branded production, spoke on the record of 'a toxic environment where men can say the most disgusting things, joke about sex openly, and overall a toxic environment where women are treated far inferior than men'. In total Steel interviewed more than 100 current and former Vice employees, though many spoke off the record or declined to comment altogether, as a result of the rigid non-disclosure agreements they'd signed with the company.[8] Vice's then-CEO Shane Smith and co-founder Suroosh Alvi responded with a joint statement admitting to having 'failed as a company to create a safe and inclusive workplace where everyone, especially women, can feel respected and thrive,' and acknowledging that Vice's boys' club culture had 'fostered inappropriate behaviour that permeated throughout the company'.

The timing of the article – published two days before Christmas – made it feel like an extremely unconventional Christmas present, and as I watched reactions to it unfolding on Twitter, I felt a dozen different emotions at once. Colleagues I'd worked with had featured as both the accused and their alleged victims, which was unsettling to say the least. Because the article was published at the height of the #MeToo movement, it had – understandably – focused primarily on employee misconduct as it related to sexual harassment (which thankfully I'd never really experienced myself at the company), and at first I felt conflicted over whether I could really lay claim to the experiences outlined in the piece. But I also felt a sense of liberation, as though I'd finally been given licence to lift the veil of silence I'd cast over my time at Vice. Until that point, when anyone other than a close friend asked why I'd decided to leave the company after only eight months, I'd given vague non-answers about 'wanting to explore other creative projects' and changed the subject. Now, the problems I'd faced at the company were a matter of public record.

More than anything, I finally felt some sort of vindication – because up until that point I'd completely internalised the circumstances under which I'd left Vice as a failing on my part, often wondering whether things might have turned out differently had I been smarter or more strategic in how I'd navigated my time there. It took an exposé by one of the most respected newspapers in the world, the testimony of hundreds of fellow Vice alumni and a *mea culpa* from the company's founders to help me realise that there was very little I could have done differently to change my experience.

Chapter 5

THE RIGHT TYPE OF BLACK

Human beings are fundamentally lazy creatures. We are built that way by design, the laziness hardwired into our systems, a relic from our caveman days when conserving energy was a matter of life and death. And because we are lazy, we like to label people, to sort them into categories that fit neatly with what we already know of the world, before filing them away as quickly as possible. It makes life easier, being able to rely on shortcuts. Less thinking to do. No matter that few people fit neatly into a standard-issue box.

Take me, for instance. I am a 'good' Black person. Well-spoken. Smartly dressed. Privately educated. An Oxford graduate. Not poor. Not 'ghetto'. Basically everything society is conditioned to believe that Black people are not. My accent – the cut-glass received pronunciation typical of the middle classes – opens doors usually cordoned off to Black women who actually sound like they grew up in south London. I am palatably Black, and as a result people – particularly white people – often struggle to figure out where to place me. They hear my accent, or find out where I went to school, or pick up on any number of cues they usually associate with whiteness, but then they look at me and I'm . . .

Black. Sometimes I swear I can literally *hear* the cogs spinning as their brains struggle to compute, the mental effort of digesting the contradictions I present written across their faces. Even the mere fact of my presence in certain spaces can sometimes be a source of confusion.

A few years ago, I found myself at a publishing party, a fairly grand affair held in the gardens of a world-famous museum. Plates of sashimi and truffle-topped canapés circulated among clusters of minor celebrities, while a handful of retired politicians mingled with the aura of newly freed prisoners. Queuing at the bar, I stood next to a man who looked to be in his sixties or so, wearing the tweed blazer and unkempt eyebrows that are the uniform of men of a certain demographic.

'Where are the margaritas? Have they run out of margaritas? I heard a rumour they've run out of margaritas,' he asked of no one in particular, craning his neck to see if the bar had indeed run out of frozen margaritas.

'Let's hope not – they're the only reason I showed up tonight!' I joked.

A beat, and then:

'And *where* did you get that accent from?' he turned to me, beaming.

I froze.

'Sorry?'

'Well, you just have the most *delightful* way of speaking,' he continued, leaning in enthusiastically to appraise me, a scientist examining a rare new species.

'I mean you and I seem to have pretty much the same acce—'

'Yes I know, but *I* went to one of those very *grand* public schools,' he smiled apologetically, attempting to cover up his

111

evident pride in that fact with a thin (and wholly unconvincing) veneer of faux modesty, clearly aware that these days such extreme privilege is no longer viewed as something to be proud of, while also volunteering information of his schooling at the earliest possible opportunity. Then followed the usual: personal questions ('*Your name, where does that come from?*'), irrelevant trivia ('*I do so love Kenyan music*'), talk of 'Rhodesia'. Eventually, I managed to shake him off and return to the party, irritated at having walked into such an obvious ambush.

I have always been one of very few Black people in majority white environments, first at school and then at university, so microaggressions are sadly nothing new – but I was still surprised, when I first started working, to find that aspect of my identity to be a genuine issue. Conversations about the challenges women face at work play out frequently enough in public forums that even at the very start of my career, it was always immediately clear to me whenever gender was an issue. I'd read enough copies of *Glamour* as a teenager to be able to sniff out a patronising comment or double standard a mile off, even when I couldn't necessarily do anything about it. But, in the absence of any glaring instances of overt racism, the challenges I've experienced because of my skin colour haven't always been as (forgive the pun) black and white. It took me far longer to suss out the ways race presents a barrier for me at work, partly because for a long time I didn't want to believe that it did.

One thing it didn't take me long to figure out is that being Black in the workplace is – among other things – an exercise in biting your tongue. Biting your tongue when someone misspells your name, or decides to assign you an anglicised nickname because 'Well, Otegha doesn't exactly roll off the tongue, does it!' Biting your tongue when HR makes a point of including photos of you on the company website, when the only other Black person you've ever seen in the office is a cleaner. Biting your tongue when your white colleagues make confident statements about 'the Black community' when you are likely the only Black person they've ever interacted with in any meaningful capacity. Biting your tongue when these same colleagues make jokes about lesbians and gingers and little people, until one day you realise with a jolt that they probably do the same thing about Black people when you're not in the room.

A few months after joining AMV I was invited to one of the company's welcome dinners, which were hosted every few months to give the latest batch of new employees a chance to mingle with members of senior management. On this particular occasion, the company's MD, Robert, the most typical of public school stereotypes, moved around between courses to make sure he spoke to as many people as possible. Sometime between the main course and dessert, I found him sitting close by, conducting an animated discussion about an ongoing cricket test match with a few of the guys sitting around him. Perhaps spotting that I hadn't said anything for a while, he attempted to draw me into their conversation, asking for my prediction on who was likely to win the game overall.

'Oh! Er . . . I don't actually know. I don't really know that much about cricket if I'm honest,' I offered, sheepishly.

'Right – well, this conversation's not going to make much sense to you then, is it?' he responded sharply, turning back to the trio of male colleagues he'd been chatting to, one of whom he'd later take under his wing as a mentee. I was mortified – my one chance to make a good impression and I'd blown it. It didn't occur to me until many years later just how little chance I'd stood of engaging with him in any meaningful sense, and not just because I don't understand how cricket works. In *The Class Ceiling*, Friedman and Laurison analyse the formation of sponsor relationships with senior colleagues. These relationships are a potent combination of advice, mentorship and said colleagues actively advocating on your behalf to the powers that be; securing a sponsor is often crucial (though not essential) to progressing in certain 'elite' professions, of which advertising is one. But Friedman and Laurison also caution that these relationships are 'rarely established on the basis of work performance. Instead they are almost always forged, in the first instance at least, on cultural affinity, on sharing humour, interests and tastes.' They also emphasise the role that 'homophily' plays in career advancement, a term they define as 'the tendency among decision-makers to favour those who are, in various ways, like themselves'. In short: like attracts like. Middle-class white men are more likely to hire, sponsor and promote other middle-class white men, because they share a deep cultural affinity. Friedman and Laurison's analysis is primarily conducted with class in mind (though they certainly acknowledge the importance of race throughout *The Class Ceiling*), but it's not a huge leap of the imagination to imagine how those dynamics might also apply to race, not least because white people are more likely to belong to a higher class background than Black people. Men like Robert just didn't see themselves in me, my skin colour rendering me near invisible to him while at the same time making me hyper-visible to tweed-wearing gentlemen at publishing soirees.

That women's experiences of gender discrimination vary according to their race is a central tenet of intersectional feminist theory. A term first coined in 1989 by the Black feminist scholar Kimberlé Crenshaw, 'intersectionality' takes its name from the idea that different modes of oppression – in this case racism and sexism – necessarily intersect with one another, altering women's experiences of each form of oppression, so that they differ from the experiences of women subject to only one or the other. Crenshaw, a law professor who developed her theory after observing how discrimination lawsuits brought by Black women against their employers played out in court, argued that Black women often suffer discrimination that doesn't fit neatly into the category of *either* racism *or* sexism, but rather is a combination of both. In her words:

> Black women can experience discrimination in ways that
> are both similar to and different from those experienced
> by white women and Black men. Black women
> sometimes experience discrimination in ways similar
> to white women's experiences; sometimes they share
> very similar experiences with Black men. Yet often they
> experience double-discrimination – the combined effects
> of practices which discriminate on the basis of race,
> and on the basis of sex. *And sometimes, they experience*
> *discrimination as Black women – not the sum of race and*
> *sex discrimination, but as Black women.*[1] [italics mine]

One of the reasons it took me a long time to fully understand the role race played in my early experiences of the workplace is that being both Black *and* female, it's impossible to isolate the biases I face due to either one of those facets of my identity. The effect is additive, but also transformative – to make a simple analogy, 1 (racism) + 1 (sexism) = #?! (an entirely different category of discrimination altogether, which actually has its own name: misogynoir, a term coined in 2010 by the Black feminist Moya Bailey). That women of colour face the double whammy of both gender *and* race bias translates to us experiencing a rather different set of career-related challenges compared to white women. We have to wrestle with whatever unconscious biases or negative stereotypes are typically ascribed to women of our race – for Latina women that might be the stereotype of the volatile, hot-headed temptress; for East Asian women it's often one of presumed submissiveness and the notion that they are lacking in leadership qualities. For Black women it is that we are inherently prone to aggression, thanks largely to the stereotype of the 'angry Black woman' that emerged from antebellum America and endures to this day. Consequently, Black women are subject to double standards, penalised for behaviour that might be praised in our white colleagues but is misread when we exhibit it – directness is perceived as hostility, assertiveness becomes 'argumentative'. During the performance review at AMV where I was advised to rein in my ambition, I was also cautioned that my demeanour sometimes came off as 'aggressive' and 'hostile', which I now understand to be a textbook critique of Black women, though at the time I simply internalised it and tried to adapt accordingly.

One Black woman who knows more than most about racialised stereotypes is tennis maestro Serena Williams. From the very start of her career Williams has had to contend with a media narrative characterising both her demeanour and physique as somehow lacking in femininity, and portraying her as an aggressive brute. Indeed, fellow tennis player Maria Sharapova, who until her retirement was frequently positioned as Williams's rival (though at twenty-three Grand Slam singles titles to Sharapova's five, Williams is arguably in a league of her own), published a memoir in 2017 in which she said of Williams, 'her physical presence is much stronger and bigger than you realise watching TV. She has thick arms and thick legs and is so intimidating and strong.' Journalist Bim Adewunmi offers an analysis of the sly insinuations in Sharapova's description, writing that it 'has nothing to do with Serena's world-straddling skill and ability. It is about setting her up as "other", as superhuman (but in the detrimental way that curls into itself and re-emerges as subhuman).' She continues, 'Sharapova painted a shorthand cultural picture we have come to understand very well, in which a dainty white lady is menaced by a hulking Black spectre.'[2]

Thanks to the prevalence of racialised stereotypes and double standards, most Black people who regularly find themselves in majority white environments are experts at code-switching, which NPR's Gene Demby (host of the popular podcast *Code Switch*, which explores the phenomenon in more detail)[3] defines as the practice of 'subtly, reflexively [changing] the way we express ourselves'. To an extent, *everyone* code-switches according to their audience. Consider the difference in tone you might adopt when hanging out at a bar with your friends, versus the way you behave at Sunday lunch with your grandparents, versus the way you conduct yourself in a meeting at work. The ability to code-switch, to adapt your mode of communication to more seamlessly blend in with different social settings, is a measure of emotional intelligence, an ability to 'read the room'. For people of colour though, code-switching escalates from mere social lubricant to professional necessity, and very often involves the suppression of one's racial identity. In their 2018 book *Slay In Your Lane*, co-authors Yomi Adegoke and Elizabeth Uviebinené explore the pressure Black women face to adjust their communication style at work, offering up more 'palatable' versions of themselves that minimise their Blackness:

> Friends tell me that they have strategically tried to find common interests with their white colleagues, by de-emphasising racial and ethnic differences to assimilate seamlessly into their work environment. They shift their body, speech and attire to counter perceived images of inferiority and stereotypes [. . .] code-switching is a coping tool used by many [Black women] to fit into white work spaces.

Adegoke and Uviebinené describe this behaviour as akin to wearing 'white face' to work, an idea pushed to its absurd but somehow plausible extreme in Boots Riley's 2018 film *Sorry to Bother You*, a dark comedy in which an African-American man adopts a 'white voice' at his telesales job and immediately sees his sales figures skyrocket, eventually being promoted to 'Power Caller'. The movie's protagonist is played by African-American actor LaKeith Stanfield, but its creators go so far as to dub his speech in the scenes where he deploys his 'white voice' with the voice of an actual white man (actor David Cross, who you might know as *Arrested Development*'s Tobias Fünke). Though much of the film is intentionally surreal, that particular message – that for Black people emulating whiteness is necessary to achieve professional success – is firmly rooted in real-world learnings. Evaluating how my words and actions might be interpreted because of my

118

skin colour and adjusting them accordingly is a facet of the Black experience so constant as to verge on the mundane.

But eventually, these things take their toll. There is a heavy mental load required in always having to consider how to make others feel more comfortable around you; in the pressure to be the very best version of yourself at all times, lest a momentary slip-up lead someone to assume the worst about Black people more generally; in avoiding playing into even positive stereotypes around your race, lest you give greater credibility to the negative ones.

Increasingly employers, particularly those keen to position themselves as forward-thinking, place considerable emphasis on 'cultural fit' when recruiting new employees. It's a fairly nebulous term that nevertheless sounds fairly benign, until you realise that – besides being an incredibly subjective measure against which to evaluate current or prospective employees – it's a requirement that also demands conformity, and rewards those who are culturally similar to what will probably be a majority white personnel, at least in the UK. Given how vocal many of these same employers have become about their commitment to diversity, demanding that employees conform to a specific cultural or social template and expecting anything other than a homogenous workforce seems like cognitive dissonance in the extreme. Dr Nicola Rollock, an academic who specialises in racial justice in education and the workplace, makes a distinction between people of colour who are perceived as either 'racially palatable' or 'racially salient',[4] explaining the difference thus:

> Institutions regard people of colour who minimise
> or downplay their racial identity – that is they are
> seen as *racially palatable* – as more likely to fit in

with organisational culture and norms. Conversely, institutions are less likely to see those who embrace their racial identity or who foreground issues of race – who are therefore seen as *racially salient* – as complementing their organisational culture.

I'm self-aware enough to realise that I actually am perceived as racially palatable by many institutions and individuals but – private education or not – as a Black woman I was never going to share the same depth of cultural affinity as a group of cricket-obsessed and fairly posh white men. Ultimately, having a private education or the 'right' kind of accent doesn't make me any less Black, and statistically speaking that means I'm likely to be paid less than my white counterparts even when my qualifications outrank theirs. Researchers at the social mobility-focused think tank Resolution Foundation found that all things being equal (for example, age, qualifications, region and levels of experience), Black female graduates earn on average 9 per cent less than white ones, while Black non-graduate women earn 6 per cent less than their white counterparts.[5] Indeed, among female graduates, Black women actually face the biggest pay penalty of all ethnicities, a differential that equates to more than £3,000 a year for full-time workers. Even my name puts me at a disadvantage, thanks to the prevalence of name bias – the statistically proven phenomenon where people with 'unusual' (read: ethnic) names are more likely to be discriminated against by recruiters and other institutional gatekeepers. In a 2003 study where identical CVs were submitted for job applications under 'Black-sounding' and 'white-sounding' names, the latter were 50 per cent more likely to be called for interview.[6] Every time I go to fill out an application or have to send a cold email, I think about that statistic. A name like mine is an instant giveaway, a subconscious repellent even for the left-leaning liberals who imagine themselves to be open of mind and heart, and yet made up the core participants of a more recent study that came to a similar conclusion in 2015.[7]

And, even though I began this chapter by theorising about being the right kind of Black, as a dark-skinned Black woman I am in the eyes of some very much a less-than-ideal version of Blackness. Among many communities of colour, there exists an often-unspoken prejudice against darker-skinned members known as colourism, a cultural parameter that – as with most beauty standards – tends to weigh more heavily on women than it does on men. For Black people, colourism and the practice of skin colour stratification has its roots in the slave trade, where light-skinned Black slaves were frequently born to enslaved women who had been raped by their white slave masters. Children born of those circumstances would usually themselves become slaves, though they were often given preferential treatment – kept as 'house niggers' instead of 'field niggers' – thus instituting a hierarchy of skin tone among Black Americans that has been passed down through the generations.

Even after the abolition of slavery, light-skinned Black Americans had greater access to economic and social opportunities than their dark-skinned counterparts. Colourism wasn't just practised by white America – it was (and is) also upheld within the Black community, an insidious form of internalised racism. During the Jim Crow era (after the abolition of slavery and before the civil rights movement of the 1950s onwards), entry to certain Black churches was predicated on being able to pass the 'paper bag test', that is, having a skin tone lighter than that of the brown paper bags typically found in American grocery stores. At some historically Black colleges and universities, a preference for lighter skin was an unspoken part of the admissions criteria. Having 'good hair' – i.e. the looser curls characteristic of mixed-race individuals or those with Caucasian heritage somewhere in their bloodline, as opposed to the tightly coiled texture that is my own birthright – is another dimension of colourism that places some Black people on a higher ranking than others, again thanks to associations with whiteness and Eurocentric standards of beauty. Indeed, many of the African-American churches that excluded dark-skinned Black people from their congregations had a practice of hanging a comb on a piece of string at their entrances, the message being that if your hair was too coarse – i.e. too Black – for the comb to pass through easily, then you were also too Black to grace their parish. Jesus surely wept.

As with much of African-American culture, these social norms have been exported to Black communities all over the world, from Lagos to London, by way of films, magazines, beauty campaigns and music videos. The presence of colourism also extends far beyond those of African descent – within most communities of colour, from Asia to Latin America, preferential treatment has long been predicated on proximity to whiteness, the dark shadow of colonialism firmly in place long after its official cessation. In nearly every corner of the planet, being darker-skinned tends to relegate you to the bottom of whatever formal or informal caste system is in place.

Research examining the effects of colourism in more quantifiable terms consistently turns up depressing, if fairly unsurprising, results. A 2007 study conducted using data from the National Survey of Black Americans found that the darker their skin tone, the less Black workers earn with researchers specifically citing favourable treatment of lighter-skinned workers as the source of those wage differences.[8] In fact, the wage gap between white workers and light-skinned Black workers was deemed to be so small as to be statistically insignificant – the wage gap between light-skinned Black and dark-skinned Black workers was where the real disparity lay. (Though the study was carried out using data from male workers, it seems reasonable to assume a similar correlation between skin tone and wages for women as well, especially given that darker skin is more stigmatised in women than it is in men.) A more recent study examining the effects of skin tone on job prospects for American workers found that recruiters uniformly assess light-skinned Black (and Hispanic) interviewees as being more intelligent than their identically qualified darker-skinned counterparts.[9] Darker-skinned Black women like me can look forward to a lifetime of our skin tone negatively affecting all aspects of our lives, from our earning power to the education opportunities available to us – we are three times more likely to be suspended from school than our light-skinned peers,[10] more likely to marry partners with lower levels of education, and in fact less likely to get married at all.[11] But these statistics only confirm what society has already made clear to me over the years. To be a dark-skinned Black woman is to be seen as less desirable, less hireable, less intelligent and ultimately less valuable than my light-skinned counterparts, and nowhere is that more evident than in industries where one's appearance is an explicit part of the job description.

In recent years an uptick in the number of Black models, singers, actresses and media personalities given prime billing within mainstream culture has been held aloft as evidence of the diversifying of female beauty standards – and yet the (few) Black women granted access to these hallowed spaces almost always tend to be light-skinned or biracial. For Black women working in the entertainment industry, proximity to whiteness is very often a predicator of success. Take, for example, September 2018, a month heralded as a landmark for diversity in the fashion industry thanks to the presence of Black women on the covers of several major magazines in a month deemed to be the most important of the fashion industry calendar. Even then, the faces featured on the covers of the most prestigious titles – British *Vogue*, *Vogue* US, *Elle* UK, US *Marie Claire* – were all light-skinned Black women sporting the looser curls and Eurocentric features more readily accepted by mainstream media: Rihanna, Beyoncé, the model Slick Woods, and actress Zendaya. Reading the dozens of articles breathlessly hyping those images as a sign of progress, I wanted to join in their excitement, but it was hard to ignore the elephant in the room: that none of those women even came within a whisper of my skin tone. It felt like erasure to be celebrating those covers as an achievement for Black representation, and yet no one seemed to be pointing out the obvious.

Among Black women in the music industry, it is the Beyoncés and Rihannas, the Cardi Bs and Nicki Minajs who tend to thrive on the global stage – all hugely talented women, of course – but also all women who benefit from a heavy dose of 'light skin privilege'. In the UK, the lack of visibility of dark-skinned Black women – even within urban music genres such as grime and R&B – is endemic, with the spotlight largely falling on biracial or light-skinned Black women with 'good hair' and enough Blackness to make them credible as urban artists without offending or alienating the white mainstream; think of rising stars Mabel, Jorja Smith and Stefflon Don. Cultural gatekeepers often look to biracial or light-skinned Black women as a way of satisfying the pressure to engage more diverse talent, happy to be able to tick the 'Black' box on their casting requirements without actually having to include women who look too – how do I put this? – Black.

For many Black men, having a light-skinned partner is viewed as a sign of success, the ultimate status symbol. Hip-hop culture is rife with male artists making reference to bagging themselves a light-skinned babe, whether it's Jay-Z rapping *All the wavy light-skinned girls is loving me now* (from his 2003 single 'December 4th'), to Kanye West giving an interview to *Essence* magazine in which he expressed a preference for mixed-race women (or, as he referred to them, 'mutts').[12] In 2014, a casting call for the Dr Dre-produced N.W.A biopic *Straight Outta Compton* achieved viral status thanks to its explicit ranking of attractiveness according to skin tone. Put together by a casting company which, according to its website, had also worked on major films including *Argo*, *The Girl with the Dragon Tattoo*, *The Social Network* and *There Will Be Blood*, the casting call distinguished between A GIRLS – 'the hottest of the hottest' – who could be 'black, white, asian, hispanic, mid eastern, or mixed race too'; B GIRLS – 'fine girls . . . light-skinned, Beyoncé is a prototype here', all the way through to D GIRLS, who were to be 'African American girls. Poor, not in good shape. Medium to dark skin tone'. Their requirements ended up being widely circulated online, and a predictable sequence of events ensued. The Twitterverse raged, think pieces were published, the casting company issued a hasty apology and Universal Pictures (the studio behind the film) quickly released a statement[13] distancing itself from the content of the casting call. As

I watched the controversy unfold online though, I couldn't help but reflect on how pointless the outrage ultimately was. Those casting requirements weren't particularly unusual – the producers behind them had merely been careless enough to formally codify something that is usually left unsaid.

The idea of light-skinned women as status symbols was perhaps most perfectly epitomised by a photo that circulated in the days after the 2016 MTV Video Music Awards.[14] In it, five titans of the music industry: Swizz Beatz, Jay-Z, Steve Stoute (an influential businessman and former record exec), Kanye West and Diddy were captured mid-laughter, drinks in hand, the picture of wealth and success. Behind them, their wives and girlfriends stood dotingly, also laughing, their hands lovingly caressing their partners' shoulders. Of the five men, four are dark-skinned Black men (Swizz Beatz being the exception), but each of the five women behind them: Jay-Z's wife, Beyoncé; Diddy's then girlfriend, Cassie; Swizz Beatz' wife, Alicia Keys; Kanye West's then wife, Kim Kardashian, and Steve Stoute's wife, Lauren Branche, are light-skinned Black or racially ambiguous women. Women who would pass the paper bag test with flying colours.

The message is clear: when you can have any woman you want, why pick a dark-skinned one?

It's not all doom and gloom, though. There *are* circumstances under which my Blackness is not only acceptable, but actually highly sought after – that is, if I'm willing to commoditise my own oppression, or at least allow others to commoditise it for me. For people of colour working within creative industries – the media, the arts, the cultural sector – there is often a pressure so intense as to verge on obligation to trade off our identities and lived experiences as a way of gaining entry to industries that remain stubbornly and overwhelmingly white. Often we're asked to draw universal conclusions from singular experiences, and leveraging your own oppression can sometimes feel like the only way to make a name for yourself, particularly in the realm of digital media, which by algorithmic design rewards the extreme, the harrowing, the dramatic and the outré, as stories of racialised trauma often are. Journalist Tiffany Curtis observes that 'many women of colour writers and creative freelancers are hired (if hired at all) to boost a client's reputation by performing creative emotional labour and developing high-performing content around otherness – sharing their thoughts on the latest brand's cultural style snafu or commenting on the fact that racism, unsurprisingly, still exists. And then they are underpaid (if paid at all) for that work.'[15]

So ensues the economics of Black identity, and often Black rage. My experience as a Black writer working with mostly white commissioning editors is that I'm often expected to perform outrage, or gratitude, or displeasure over things that, quite frankly, I simply don't give a shit about. Often they already have a script in mind and just need a Black person to attach to it as a byline. The intent is rarely one of explicit malice – quite the opposite. These commissions often come from well-meaning white liberals eager to signal that they 'get it', and to absolve themselves of the sins of their forefathers. But it's rare for journalists of colour to be allowed the same range as their white counterparts. Instead, we're pushed to actively and continually demonstrate our ethnicity, becoming the go-to spokesperson for issues relating to race – which is fine, except we're often asked to comment *only* on issues relating to race, whereas white journalists can (and do) speak on everything, their identities seen as neutral, their experiences universal.

If, as Nora Ephron famously said, everything is copy, in catering to these demands are you being exploited, or simply milking your advantage? Are you selling yourself short or selling yourself out? Am I a fool for refusing to play the game, or a pragmatist if I do? And most important, where do you draw the line?

At the start of my foray into professional writing, not long before I left Vice, I found myself in a strange situation. A friend who worked at a leading newspaper and was aware that I was keen to break into journalism, had forwarded me an email that his boss had sent to him. The editor of the paper's online comment section, she was urgently looking to commission an article about some inflammatory comments the singer Tom Jones had made about race during a recent interview, and had asked my friend if he knew anyone who'd be up to the job. In media circles these sorts of articles are known as 'hot takes' – highly reactive and often divisive opinion pieces published in response to a recent event, usually with a quick turnaround. They are of questionable value to the media landscape – one description, by *Salon*'s Simon Maloy, defines them as 'deliberately provocative commentary that is based almost entirely on shallow moralising'.[16]

The editor's first choice to write the piece, another young Black journalist, had for some reason fallen through, so she was now frantically casting around for someone else who could perform the requisite combination of outrage, hurt and finger-clicking sass, to the tune of roughly 500 words, and preferably by noon.

'*Hi Otegha,*' the email began.

What do you make of the fact that Tom Jones is having a DNA test to determine whether he has any Black ancestry – just because he's got curly hair and a low voice. I'm keen to commission a piece responding to his decision, ideally saying that it's insulting nonsense. Would you be interested in writing it, today? If not, can you put me in touch with anyone who you know to be free to write, today?

The assignment was unpaid, but desperate to get my foot in the door at a respected media outlet, I accepted almost instantly. My first commission! *What an arse Tom Jones is*, I thought to myself, sharpening my metaphorical pencil as I settled in at my desk, ready to give him the drubbing he so rightly deserved.

Except.

Me: Fuck . . . Tommy I've just sat down to actually read that Tom Jones interview

Tommy: Yes?

Me: Yeah. And his comments were actually pretty reasonable

Not offensive at all

But I've committed to writing it now

Tommy: Well can you un-commit?

Me: No I can't 'un-commit'

Tommy: OK . . . well what exactly did he say?

Me: 'A lot of people still think I'm Black. When I first came to America, people who had heard me sing on the radio would be surprised that I was white when they saw me. Because of my hair, a lot of Black people still tell me I'm just passing as white. When I was born, my mother came out in big dark patches all over her body. They asked if she had any Black blood and she said she didn't know. I'm going to get my DNA tested. I want to find out.'[17]

Tommy: Mmmmmm

Me: ???

Tommy: Yeeeaah I feel like that brief is clutching at straws a little bit

Me: Me too!!
He basically wants to find out if it's possible he has Black ancestry which is . . . sort of legit?

Tommy: Yeah. 'Insulting nonsense' is pretty strong

I started to panic. The editor was obviously keen for me to contextualise Jones's comments within the discourse on racism that was then beginning to emerge online, clearly hoping to generate outrage – whether in support or critique of my article, I still don't know. Too late, I realised I had been selected as that day's sacrificial lamb, a placatory offering to the insatiable demands of web traffic targets and a click-based algorithm.

Me: What should I do??
I already said I'd write it, I can't back out now
It would literally just be clickbait – I don't even think he's done anything wrong
I'm gonna look like a complete twat if I write this
Fuck. Can I call you?

Tommy: Yeah sure, let me just find a meeting room

For the next half hour Tommy and I schemed, trying to come up with an angle that I wouldn't be entirely embarrassed to put my name to, the two of us swinging between utter incredulity and hysterical laughter at the sheer absurdity of my dilemma.

'I *cannot* believe your big journalism debut is going to be a poison pen letter about *Tom Jones* of all people,' Tommy gasped, barely managing to finish his sentence before once again dissolving into hysterics. Even in my panic, I could appreciate the bizarre comedy of the situation.

In the end, I decided I couldn't in good conscience write an article excoriating national treasure Tom Jones, an individual about whom I'd never once had a considered thought in my life. I emailed the editor a flimsy excuse about suddenly being rushed off my feet with work and backed out of writing the piece. She never responded, but less than an hour later, an article by another young Black journalist fulfilling the required brief appeared on the paper's website. It made for painful reading, a giant non sequitur of an article that cynically attempted to invoke the rhetoric of Black Lives Matter and other activist movements, and was (rightly) torn apart in the comments below. It also, as intended, generated plenty of clicks. A little counter in the corner of the web page displaying how many times the article had been shared made clear that by one metric at least, it had been a resounding success.

Of course, the pressure to monetise your identity or personal trauma online isn't limited solely to writers of colour. The rise in recent years of digital media platforms publishing personal essays of often staggeringly intimate proportions is a trend that at its peak in 2015 warranted a *Slate* essay by the journalist Laura Bennett scrutinising what she called the 'first-person industrial complex'.[18] Bennett, a veteran of digital media platforms including *Slate*, *Salon* and the *New Republic*, explores the pitfalls of what

131

she termed 'the new age of digital self-disclosure' – the practice of baring your soul online in exchange for a few thousand clicks and (if you're lucky) maybe a few dollars as well. 'For writers looking to break in [to journalism], offering up grim, personal dispatches may be the surest ways to get your pitches read,' Bennett wrote, before going on to explain why it is so often women who are at the mercy of 'the Internet's bottomless appetite for harrowing personal essays' – 'many of the outlets that are most hungry for quick freelancer copy, and have the lowest barriers to entry for publication, are still women's interest sites.'

Not all Black creatives are as uneasy with this dynamic as I have come to be. US-based writer Morgan Jerkins, author of the bestselling memoir *This Will Be My Undoing*, has spoken in the past about how a series of infamous police brutality cases paved the way for her early career gains. Of the period immediately after the Black teenager Michael Brown was shot dead in August 2014 by a police officer in Ferguson, Missouri, an incident of police brutality that triggered heated protests and fuelled the then emergent Black Lives Matter movement, Jerkins writes:

> I began receiving emails from white editors
> commissioning stories about Black suffering and trauma.
> They needed me. No longer could they depend on their
> white colleagues to talk about lived experiences that did
> not apply to them. Racial tensions had reached feverish
> heights, and I capitalised on this moment – one I
> believed to be ephemeral – as a career opportunity . . .
> I realised that my anger could be a form of currency:
> more bylines, money, contacts, influence.[19]

She later reiterated that sentiment during an interview[20] on the *Dear Sugars* podcast, where she described that period as 'very, very profitable'. The idea that the murder of a young Black man might be leveraged in service of one's personal ambition and bank balance is patently distasteful, even ghoulish, and yet Jerkins's turn of phrase – 'currency', 'capitalised', 'profitable' – draws a direct line between Black trauma and her own economic gain.

Still, Black creatives feeling squeamish about the idea of monetising their Blackness needn't worry, given the number of people more than willing to do so on our behalf. Mainstream white culture has a long history of co-opting Black culture and aesthetics for commercial gain, merrily colonising everything from beauty trends to music and even modes of speaking. Consider rock 'n' roll, a genre originally invented by African-American musicians in the 1950s before being repackaged and sold to white audiences by artists such as Elvis Presley; or the ubiquity of streetwear, for which we have hip-hop culture to thank. Consumer brands strive for cultural relevancy by sprinkling AAVE (African-American Vernacular English) across their social media accounts, words like *lit* and *bae* uprooted from their origins within Black America and shoehorned into bland corporatese. Black people, and in particular Black youth, have long been architects of cool, the creative directors behind contemporary culture.

A more generous reading than the one I'm about to offer might consider this sort of appropriation to be a form of homage, and note (correctly) that the development of culture necessarily requires that we absorb, borrow, trade, and yes, even steal influences from existing genres to create new forms of art. Certainly, cultural osmosis is not in itself a sinister phenomenon, and the 'mainstreaming' of Black culture – so long marginalised – is no bad thing. Where things sour is when cultural osmosis goes hand in hand with the erasure of Black originators, who are rarely credited or given their dues; when exploitative commercial practices mean that Black people don't get to share in the spoils their creativity generates; when double standards make it so that Black aesthetics are only socially acceptable when adopted by non-Black individuals.

Take, for example, the fashion industry's current love affair with Black culture, specifically hip-hop and its attendant aesthetic. As fashion critics Lou Stoppard and Antwaun Sargent write in the *Financial Times*, 'Black is in fashion – as ugly as that sentence sounds. Fashion fetishises Black cultural icons. Hip-hop style is tapped into like it's a utility. Brands are happy to acknowledge Black talent and hire Black faces to front their campaigns, relying on their huge reach for kudos and attention.'[21] This is a phenomenon that the political writer Naomi Klein refers to as 'cool hunting' in *No Logo*, the seminal anti-brand, anti-corporatisation polemic she published in 1999. Tracksuits, trainers, hyper-visible designer logos – these are the hallmarks of hip-hop style that first emerged in the 1980s and 1990s, disseminated to the masses by way of MTV and often dismissed as gauche, until all of a sudden, they weren't. At the time of writing, a pair of Gucci logo-emblazoned tracksuit bottoms will set you back a cool £890, the matching zip-up hoodie a further £1,100. Both items borrow heavily from the visual language of hip-hop culture. This is the same Gucci that in February 2019 was forced to remove a £690 jumper from stores after observers noted that it bore a striking resemblance to racist golliwog imagery.[22] Coming just months after the popularity of streetwear and logomania had helped boost the company's profits by 33 per cent to €8.29

billion,[23] the ensuing fallout forced Gucci – a fashion juggernaut with thousands of employees worldwide – to admit[24] that it did not in fact employ a *single* Black designer in-house. Indeed the popularity of Black culture within fashion is in stark contrast with the industry's track record on race and diversity, as evidenced by the events that unfolded during the summer of 2020, after the murder of George Floyd prompted a worldwide reckoning with institutional and workplace racism. Allegations of racist attitudes and discriminatory treatment emerged across the industry, including at stalwarts such as US *Vogue*, whose editor-in-chief Anna Wintour was eventually compelled to email the company's staff admitting that the magazine had 'not found enough ways to elevate and give space to Black editors, writers, photographers, designers and other creators.'[25]

Black women in particular have become prime targets for corporate culture vultures whose standard creative process involves sifting through global subcultures for new aesthetics to co-opt. We see it in the fashion brands and magazines that now style (often non-Black) models with elaborately gelled baby hairs and bamboo hoop earrings as standard. Both these trends originated within the Black and Hispanic community, along with nameplate necklaces, which, as journalist Collier Meyerson writes, are 'a cultural touchstone of Black and brown urban fashion', intended as 'a flashy and pointed rejection of the banality of white affluence'.[26] Same too with long acrylic nails, particularly those of the elaborate, square tip, heavily embellished variety long worn by Black women the world over, from 'around the way girls' to hip-hop superstars, and until recently dismissed as 'ghetto'.

Growing up, my parents warned me and my sisters against adopting those trends, though I can't remember whether they expressly forbade us from wearing our hair and nails in certain ways or just hinted (strongly, as Nigerian parents do so well) that those styles would not be welcome under their roof. Throughout my adolescence, a frequently repeated warning was the risk of looking like a 'Peckham girl', my parents' rather geo-specific way of signalling 'ghetto'. Their admonishments didn't stem from snobbery, but rather an awareness of how Black teenage girls who adopt those styles tend to be perceived, and a desire to help us avoid the negative preconceptions so many people already have about Black women. Their warnings stuck. Even as an adult, free to dress and style myself however I want, and as someone who enjoys experimenting with fashion and beauty, the so-called 'Peckham girl' aesthetic is still one I avoid, not because I don't like the way it looks – far from it – but because I know how I'd be interpreted by the outside world (read: white people) if I were to lean into it. A Black woman wearing a tracksuit and crystal-studded acrylics scans very differently from a white woman doing the same.

The double standard whereby certain culturally Black aesthetics are deemed acceptable only when sported by non-Black people was perfectly illustrated in September 2016, when the fashion designer Marc Jacobs styled the models walking for his New York Fashion Week show with pastel-coloured dreadlocks. Dreadlocks are a traditionally Black hairstyle rooted in the Rastafari movement, and for many who choose to wear them, they are weighted with considerable cultural and spiritual significance. So, of course, Marc Jacobs assembled a troupe of mostly white models (including the likes of Gigi and Bella Hadid, Kendall Jenner and Karlie Kloss) to wear the colourful dreadlocks his design team had purchased in bulk via Etsy, a move that prompted US *Vogue* to describe the hairstyles as 'jaw-dropping' in an article[27] that made no mention of their Rastafarian origins. At the same time as Jacobs's parade of white models were sashaying down the catwalk, dreadlocks in tow, the US Army was still enforcing a ban on serving officers wearing the same hairstyle, only lifting said ban[28] the following year. On rich white women dreadlocks are *haute couture*; on Black people they are 'unprofessional', even a fireable offence. Stories of Black men, women and children being denied employment or education because of their dreadlocks are a dime a dozen, as even a cursory analysis of recent news stories will demonstrate: in 2018, a 6-year-old boy in Florida was denied entry on his first day of school for wearing dreadlocks (*HuffPost*);[29] that same year, a 12-year-old boy in London was put into isolation and ordered to either cut off his dreadlocks or face suspension (*BBC*).[30] Expand your field of vision just a little, and it becomes clear that the problem extends far beyond dreadlocks to include Black hair in general: a Black woman applying for a job at Harrods in 2017 was reportedly told she had to chemically straighten her natural hair to be in with a chance of landing the role, her hair deemed not 'professional enough' by the recruitment agency in charge of hiring (*Independent*).[31]

Of course, no individual or conglomerate has been more ruthlessly efficient in bending the Black aesthetic to its own gain than the Kardashian-Jenner clan, whose adoption of Black cultural signifiers and aesthetics has been instrumental to their success. I was both deeply shocked and not at all surprised when a friend once revealed to me that for years she had always assumed Kim Kardashian to be of at least partial African-American heritage. Who could blame her? The Kardashian sisters do not look like white women. Through a series of body alterations rendering them fuller of both bottom and lip, by and large their bodies now conform to physical phenotypes typical of Black women, while their commitment to fake tan and body make-up has darkened their skin to the point of racial ambiguity. Simultaneously, and arguably as a result of their increasingly spectacular proportions, they have also become extremely wealthy, and extraordinarily famous. Of the five sisters, Kylie and Kim are the two most committed to emulating hip-hop culture, frequently wearing hairstyles and clothing that draw from the Black community. They are also the two richest – as of April 2021, Kim was officially certified a billionaire by *Forbes* magazine, with her younger sister Kylie likely not far behind.

But whither thou credit? Like many cool-hunters before them, the Kardashians rarely opt to cite their influences, often going so far as to obfuscate the origins of their fashion and beauty choices instead. When describing the braided hairstyles she occasionally wears, Kim uses the terms 'Bo Derek' and 'boxer' braids, though most Black people will immediately recognise them as the Fulani braids and cornrows that have been the domain of our communities for centuries. Meanwhile, when Guido Palau, the hairstylist behind the Marc Jacobs show previously mentioned, was asked whether Rasta culture had been an inspiration to him, he replied simply 'No, not at all', quickly distancing himself from Black culture[32] (while being only too happy to benefit from the faux-bohemian connotations his bulk-bought dreadlocks had lent the show).

Though the context might change, the pattern is always the same. From the transatlantic slave trade right through to the present day, Blackness has long been – quite literally – bought and sold. If not our actual bodies, then select elements of them, and if not those, then it is our identities and our ideas which become commodities: assets to be mined, monetised and merchandised for commercial gain. Black culture and Black ideas are often most in-demand, and most lucrative, when divorced from the people who created them. As a saying popular among Black Americans goes, 'they want our rhythm but not our blues'. The gatekeepers of commercial culture want 'Black cool', but not the 'Black'.

Blackness has always been profitable. Actually being Black – well, that's another matter entirely.

Chapter 6

THE BEAUTY TAX

Two summers ago I resolved, at last, to do something I'd been meaning to do for a while, but had always been too busy or too distracted to actually follow through on. I wanted to understand exactly how much of my life I devote to carrying out the seemingly never-ending list of beauty-related admin I've deemed necessary to face the outside world each day, and so I decided to document it. All of it. I began keeping a beauty timesheet, jotting down notes on my phone before I went to bed each night. I say 'summer' – the month was May, but England being England, temperatures were cool and it rained a lot. Still, those early summer showers brought with them an unexpected silver lining – I didn't have to spend anywhere near as much time on my beauty regime as I do at the height of summer, when pedicures and regular leg shaves get added to the mix. (Life's too short – and I'm too lazy – to shave year-round.)

The rules for the timesheet were as follows: over the course of one month, I would log everything I did that might be classed as 'beauty work', counting anything that went beyond maintaining basic standards of hygiene and presentability. That meant showering, brushing my teeth, applying deodorant and so on weren't included in this log. Neither was moisturising, because

I am Black, and for Black people being moisturised is a matter of basic human decency. In order to get as full a picture as possible of the amount of time I spend on personal grooming, I also included travel time whenever I had to leave the house for a beauty treatment, or made a detour I wouldn't otherwise have needed to make. I can only explain my instinct to account for my beauty outlay in terms of the hours and minutes incurred by noting that at that point in my life – flailing under the weight of various work deadlines that constantly made me feel as if there weren't enough hours in a day – time felt like my most prized commodity. At other less hectic periods, it has been the cost of these beauty habits that has weighed on me most heavily, though being self-employed, accounting for my time as money and vice versa is really second nature. I quote project fees in terms of day rates, and quantify time off in terms of income foregone; the two measures exist as a fluid conversion chart in my head. Still, I tracked the financial cost of these efforts as well, as best I could.

I wasn't sure what to expect, or whether my experiment would even prove to be a worthwhile exercise, but I reasoned that if I was going to write authoritatively about the cost of beauty, then surely it made sense for me to first examine my own outlay. So. Here's what I found.

Day 1 (going to a party tonight):
Morning: Shave legs (15 minutes). DIY pedicure
    (15 minutes). Deep condition and twist out hair
    (1hr 30 minutes).
Evening: Pluck eyebrows (5 minutes). Remove twist
    out and style hair (10 minutes). Apply make-up

(15 minutes). Realise I can't be bothered to go to the party (60 seconds). Remove make-up (5 minutes).

Day 2: Nothing. Working from home all day.

Day 3: Again, nothing. Buy a new body butter on my way to meet a friend (£15).

Day 4: Wash, deep condition, detangle and blow-dry hair (1hr 30 minutes).

Day 5: Visit a hair salon to get cornrows (4hrs 15 minutes including travel there and back; £30).

Day 6: Hair maintenance – oiling scalp, taming a few stray hairs (30 minutes).

Day 7: Gel my edges (5 minutes). Apply make-up (10 minutes). Remove make-up before bed (5 minutes).

And on it went, for the next three weeks. By the end of that first week alone, I'd spent a total of 9 hours and £45 on personal grooming. By the end of the month, that number had gone up to 21 hours and £150, an amount that didn't even factor in the cost of the various hair, make-up and skincare products I already owned.

As it turns out, keeping a beauty timesheet is a rather imperfect science. Early on I realised that even the most rigorous system couldn't account for the little fragments of time that, cumulatively, are likely my most significant outlay. The times where I spend an entire bus journey scrolling through Pinterest for a new hairstyle to trial (30 minutes), or those evenings where, having removed the day's make-up (5 minutes), I proceed to paw gloomily at my face in the bathroom mirror, cataloguing each new blemish or spot before climbing into bed to scour the Internet for some sort of cure (15 minutes). What started out as an experiment borne of mild curiosity had by the end of that month morphed into what felt, to me, like a catalogue of my own folly. Because beauty work is usually so spread out – an hour one week, an afternoon the next – I'd never fully grasped *quite* how much time I spend actively tending to my appearance, administering various ointments and gels, or sitting stationary while someone else fusses over my face, or hands, or feet. It was equivalent to three working days a month, a figure I still find depressingly high. Then there was the cost to consider: my expenditure of £150 over the course of one month works out at £1,800 a year.

I thought guiltily about all the things I could have used those hours to do instead – the exercise I could have done, the friends I could have seen, the pages of *this book* I could (and should) have written. I felt guiltier still when I realised that, besides trying to schedule my beauty appointments more efficiently, perhaps block booking them into one afternoon every few weeks instead of tending to things in dribs and drabs, I had absolutely no intention of cutting back on any of it.

For starters, I actually *enjoy* much of the beauty work I do. I love the ritual of getting a gel manicure, of picking out a colour worthy of committing to for the next two weeks, and then having an excuse to sit still for an hour while someone else does all the work. I love the anticipation of trying out a new hairstyle, and the near spiritual bliss of submitting my hair to someone else's hands for a few hours so that they can detangle and blow-dry it far more expertly than I ever could. These rituals serve a purpose far beyond the aesthetic for me, providing temporary respite from the daily onslaught of notifications and constant decision-making that otherwise consume my days. For many women, beauty work constitutes a form of emotional caretaking as well as physical maintenance. And of course, there is the communicative potential that beauty offers. Beauty choices can function as their own language, visual shorthand for our state of mind. They can be a potent form of self-expression and a medium by which we communicate to others, whether that is a new haircut that 'means business', or a slash of red lipstick intended to seduce.

Still, for all the enjoyment I derive from these habits, there's a not-insignificant part of me that feels compelled towards them by forces other than my own personal satisfaction. Like most women, I am constantly aware of my appearance and that the way I look is one of the main things I am judged on by strangers. Years ago, on my way to a speaking engagement, I opened my handbag only to discover – to my horror – that I'd left my make-up bag at home. Running late that morning I'd decided (as I often do) to save time by doing my make-up en route to my destination, but I'd been in such a hurry that, of course, I'd forgotten my make-up bag. As my train rattled into Victoria station I pulled a mirror out of my handbag, weighing up my options as I scrutinised my face. I could go ahead and deliver the talk as I was, barefaced but otherwise presentable. The event wasn't being filmed or photographed, so it wasn't as if my make up-less face would be documented for posterity, and I'm usually fairly unashamed about going make up-free otherwise – my vanity could certainly bear it. But I worried that turning up barefaced would signal a lack of effort that might undercut my credibility, and affect how well my talk was received. The irony wasn't lost on me that the speech I'd been invited to give was about how I'd navigated some of the common challenges women face at work, and here I was grappling with a predicament that almost too perfectly encapsulated one of our greatest challenges: the requirement that we look a certain way in order to be taken seriously. *Why does it matter if I'm not wearing any make-up?* I thought to myself, annoyed, but I knew that it did, and today wasn't the day I wanted to make a political statement. I made an emergency detour via Boots to pick up a new mascara and eyebrow pencil, applying them quickly on the last few stops to my destination.

The correlation between being physically attractive and having a higher income is well documented, and one that applies to both men and women. Indeed, the branch of economics dedicated to studying how physical attractiveness affects a person's economic opportunities even has its own name: pulchronomics. In a 2016 study that explored the impact of personal grooming on salary prospects and how that differs by gender, sociologists Jaclyn Wong and Andrew Penner found that for women, higher pay wasn't actually contingent on physical attractiveness, but rather on the amount of *effort* we put into our appearance.[1] Attractive but poorly groomed women earned nearly 40 per cent less than their well-groomed 'unattractive'[2] peers, leading Wong and Penner to conclude that 'while good grooming is beneficial for men, it is imperative for women . . . Women's grooming practices help to convey credibility and allow women to assert power in the workplace.' Wong and Penner also suggest that – certainly in the workplace, if not elsewhere – for women, grooming and beauty work is often less about actually *beautifying* ourselves, and more about demonstrating conformity to 'a prescribed set of social rules governing the presentation of bodies'. What matters for women is that we're seen to adhere to the social norms that demand we carry out beauty work.

In some workplaces, particularly within the hospitality industry with its abundance of customer-facing roles, that requirement is often more overt, and even codified into employee handbooks. It was only in 2019 that the famously image-conscious airline Virgin Atlantic dropped a previously mandatory requirement that its female cabin crew wear make-up while on the clock, issuing this statement to the media at the time:

> Female cabin crew are no longer required to wear any make-up, *if they so choose. They are however, still very welcome to wear any of our existing palette of make-up* (including lipstick and foundations) set out in Virgin Atlantic's guidelines.[3]

(Italics: mine. Begrudging language: Virgin Atlantic's, though perhaps I should give a little more credit – its rival airline British Airways still requires its female cabin crew to wear lipstick and blusher 'as a minimum', even going so far as to outline permissible shades of lipstick.[4])

And yet despite all this, women's beauty habits are often dismissed as mere frippery, the time and money we 'choose' to spend on beauty work simply the price we pay for our gender's innate predisposition to vanity – but my regular manicures have long felt akin to a professional requirement, an investment in my earning potential as pragmatic as a master's degree or an MBA. I didn't wear make-up to give that talk because I'm especially worried about covering up the acne on my jawline, or making my eyebrows look more defined, but because I wanted to signal competence and professionalism, and I knew that wearing make-up was an easy – dare I say necessary – way of doing that.

I mostly try not to think too hard about how my complying with these standards perpetuates them, and makes me complicit

146

in a values system that I generally abhor. I feel slightly ashamed of the occasional sliver of gratitude I feel for the social currency I'm awarded for being slim and passably attractive, knowing full well that those characteristics probably afford me opportunities denied to women who are not. As African American sociologist Dr Tressie McMillan Cottom writes in her essay collection *Thick*, 'Beauty is not good capital. It compounds the oppression of gender' – but in a culture where so many institutions and structures seem to penalise women for the mere fact of their gender, who can blame us for trying to crib whatever advantages we can? Per Professor Heather Widdows, whose book *Perfect Me* explores the changing nature of modern beauty ideals, 'striving for beauty is ultimately a rational choice in a world that values it so highly.'[5]

Sometimes I wonder whether the pleasure I derive from beauty work is a kind of Stockholm syndrome, my brain's way of trying to ease the sting of the indignity of it all. The term Stockholm syndrome was originally coined to explain the strange psychological phenomenon whereby hostage victims occasionally begin to identify, sympathise with, or even defect to join their captors, and supposedly manifests because in the midst of horrendous conditions even the smallest acts of kindness are received with extreme gratitude, prompting a patently irrational psychological response.[6] Perhaps I've only learned to find satisfaction in visiting the beauty salon where a woman routinely rips the hair from my bikini line because the scented candles and tasteful furnishings feel like a blessing amid the horror of a wax.

Though if enjoying beauty work is a form of Stockholm syndrome, then it seems logical to ask: who are my captors – and why are they holding me hostage?

In Naomi Wolf's feminist polemic *The Beauty Myth*, she argues that modern beauty standards are a mechanism designed to keep women distracted from advancement in both domestic and public spheres, by means of the Sisyphean cycle of tweezing and buffing that seems to be our lot. First published in 1990 – the year I was born – save for a few era-specific substitutions (Instagram instead of fashion magazines, influencers instead of movie stars), *The Beauty Myth* could have been written yesterday. Wolf's argument positions the demands of contemporary Western beauty standards, and the effort they require from women to achieve and maintain, as having evolved as 'a violent backlash against feminism'. In her view, the compulsion I feel to spend £60 on vials of scented water that promise to eliminate my pores, or to get my nails done every time I have an important meeting, is the patriarchy's counter-attack against feminist gains of recent decades, the death throes of a system desperate to maintain its dominance. So follows Wolf's theory of 'the beauty myth', by which she means the beauty standards and norms that dictate female appearance. 'The beauty myth was perfected to checkmate power at every level in individual women's lives,' she writes, 'undermining – slowly, imperceptibly, without our being aware of the real forces of erosion – the ground women have gained through long, hard, honourable struggle.'

Wolf joins a long line of feminist thinkers in suggesting that at every point in history where women have made significant strides towards emancipation – from the suffrage movement that originated in the late 1800s, through to the sexual revolution of the 1960s – our gains have been met by pushback and retrenchment by the (male) powers that be. As the twentieth-century feminist movement began to dismantle long-standing social norms pigeonholing women as the domesticated sex, so emerged ever-higher beauty standards for us to abide by. 'Inexhaustible but ephemeral beauty work took over from inexhaustible but ephemeral housework,' Wolf writes, as a way to 'take over the work of social coercion that myths about motherhood, domesticity, chastity and passivity no longer can manage.' The journalist Susan Faludi's 1991 text *Backlash: The Undeclared War Against American Women* more fully explores 'backlash politics' as a historical trend, documenting the wave of anti-feminist sentiment that followed the second-wave movement of the 1960s and 1970s. 'The anti-feminist backlash has been set off not by women's achievement of full equality,' Faludi writes, 'but by the increased possibility that they might win it. It is a pre-emptive strike that stops women long before they reach the finish line.'

Take the #MeToo movement, for example, the world's first mass movement against sexual harassment, and arguably one of the biggest shifts in gender norms that the twenty-first century has seen. Not more than a month after it exploded into the public consciousness in October 2017, so too came the assertion that the movement had turned into a 'witch hunt', as the first few offenders began to face redress for their actions. In December 2017, the *New York Times* – the same publication that just two months earlier had broken the allegations of sexual misconduct against Harvey Weinstein[7] that were the touchpaper for #MeToo – ran an op-ed under the headline 'When #MeToo Goes Too Far'. In it, (male) journalist Bret Stephens described another (male) journalist who had been fired after multiple allegations of workplace sexual harassment as 'a pillar and champion of his hometown'.[8] According to a survey commissioned by the Lean In organisation in January 2018, in the three months after the

#MeToo movement emerged, the number of male managers who felt uncomfortable mentoring female colleagues more than tripled.[9] Given that men occupy the vast majority of managerial positions within the workplace, this development presents a clear obstacle for women's career advancement. Somehow the system has found a way to ensure that we are the ones penalised for having the audacity to call out men's transgressions.

Meanwhile, as American women agitated for the right to live and work unencumbered by the spectre of sexual abuse, the response from Donald Trump's ultra-conservative government was to double down on its agenda of curtailing women's bodily autonomy. As I write this, abortion rights in the USA, first granted in 1973 as part of the landmark *Roe v. Wade* ruling, are on the verge of being rolled back. When Brett Kavanaugh's appointment to the United States Supreme Court in 2018 ensured the balance of the court remained tipped towards conservatism, dozens of other states proceeded to either introduce or pass so-called 'heartbeat bills' prohibiting abortion once a foetal heartbeat can be detected, which can happen as early as six weeks into a pregnancy (and before many women even realise they're pregnant).[10] In May 2019 the state of Alabama passed a law banning abortion in nearly all cases – even for rape victims – and during the global coronavirus pandemic that began in 2020, Republican legislators in several states sought to capitalise on their nation's strained healthcare system by halting access to abortions, arguing that such procedures were 'non-essential'.[11] These developments almost certainly foreshadow a more concerted effort by anti-abortion advocates to mount a Supreme Court challenge to *Roe v. Wade* in the near future. After Justice Ruth Bader Ginsburg died in September 2020 leaving a vacancy on the Supreme Court,

Republicans moved quickly to appoint the staunchly conservative and anti-abortion Judge Amy Coney Barrett to the Court as her successor.[12]

Two steps forward, one step back. When women gain agency and freedom in one area of our lives, we almost always encounter pushback in others. Contemporary beauty standards are simply one of the more sophisticated enforcement mechanisms the patriarchy has developed to keep us in check.

Given that much of contemporary feminism now insists that individual women's choices automatically constitute acts of feminism in and of themselves, regardless of the actual *nature* of those choices, it is now deeply unfashionable to position the beauty work so many women actively choose to perform as being performed under duress – to deny women their agency in making these choices can be construed as patronising, even paternalistic. Cultural critic Amanda Hess notes that 'part of the conditioning of the "patriarchal ideal" is to make women feel empowered by it on their "own terms". That way, every time you critique an unspoken requirement of women, you're also forced to frown upon something women have chosen for themselves. And who wants to criticise a woman's choice?'[13] In 2003, the satirical news website *The Onion* ran a headline that read 'Women Now Empowered by Everything a Woman Does', poking fun at 'a new strain of feminism . . . in which mundane activities are championed as proud, bold assertions of independence from oppressive patriarchal hegemony'.[14] As is the case with many *Onion* headlines, their words read less as satire and more as simple fact.

It would be easier to accept the idea that beauty work is a sign of female emancipation were it not for the fact that these predilections haven't evolved in a vacuum, as organic expressions of the (very natural) human urge to beautify. Women aren't born with an innate desire for hair-free labia or DD breasts. Those desires are a direct response to the constant barrage of images that suggest there is a 'correct' way to look, and a culture that rewards women who conform to that standard with the kind of status, wealth, social capital – even genuine agency – that is otherwise hard to come by. It's difficult to examine the considerable expense, effort and at times extreme physical discomfort required for the average woman to achieve current standards of female beauty, and deem it a wholly voluntary endeavour.

It's clear what we stand to potentially gain from engaging in beauty work, gains that economists refer to as the 'beauty premium'. But what does all of this cost? How do we quantify the price of being a woman in a society that makes our perceived value largely contingent on meeting a minimum threshold of attractiveness determined by a system that doesn't even have our best interests at heart? There is the time invested (in my case twenty-one hours or three working days per month, though your mileage may differ). There is the money spent, with women in the UK spending an average of £1,352[15] on beauty upkeep each year, or £70,000 over the course of a lifetime (though it's difficult to find an undisputed figure on this). There is the not insubstantial physical discomfort endured, from the sting of a chemical peel at one end of the spectrum to the pain that comes with having your jawbone chiselled away by a surgeon's scalpel at the other. The notion that beauty and pain are an unavoidable trade-off is deeply embedded in our cultural understanding not just of beauty, but of womanhood itself. What of the emotional and psychological toll that comes with constantly straining towards aesthetic perfection, the misery of dieting and low self-esteem; what of the body dysmorphia induced by the continual veneration of exceptional body types by almost every section of the media? The forced pursuit of ever-higher benchmarks of attractiveness is a tax on the female existence, one we have to pay in order to thrive in a system that has made physical appearance paramount. Not only are women subject to pay gaps, pension gaps and wealth gaps, but to add insult to injury we are then forced by social norms to reserve a chunk of our already diminished earnings for beauty work, in order to remain competitive in the labour market, a process Naomi Wolf referred to as 'do-it-yourself income discrimination'. The beauty tax is essentially a transfer of capital, one that uses psychological manipulation and the very real threat of negative consequences if you decline to pay it as its enforcement mechanism.

And, of course, it's even higher for Black women, who spend far more money on hair and beauty than their non-Black counterparts, much of that money going towards the relaxers and weaves required to achieve the 'good hair' that adheres to Eurocentric beauty standards. Even as a cash-strapped student, I would somehow find the £80 it cost to have my hair relaxed every eight weeks. I didn't know of any Black hair salons in Oxford, so when my touch-ups happened to fall during term time, I had to travel back to London (a journey that added another £15 to the cost). Often I'd conceal the real reason for those fleeting visits, mumbling something to my friends about having forgotten a crucial textbook or item of clothing at home in London, before slipping out of college early in the morning. In hindsight, I can see that on some level I felt vaguely embarrassed by how much time and money I devoted to maintaining a hairstyle that didn't even look particularly good, and would always be a poor approximation of the European hair that relaxed Afro hair is intended to emulate.

Still, like clockwork, every eight weeks I made the pilgrimage to a boutique salon in south London whose famously rude owner, and even ruder staff, saw no contradiction in charging me £80 for the privilege of shooting me dirty looks as they slathered tubs of pungent chemical solutions onto my head. Their surly demeanours only softened if and when they managed to upsell me one of their expensive but useless treatments, and sometimes I'd acquiesce just to pacify them. I hated those visits, but that salon was also one of the few places I knew of where I could count on being seen to by a properly trained hairdresser. Then – and to an extent even now – there were few options in the way of reputable Black hair salons, which speaks to another reason Black women are forced to spend so much money on hair and beauty. We are a demographic notoriously underserved by the cosmetics industry, and options for hair products or services that are both good quality *and* inexpensive are few and far between. Certainly a decade ago, it felt as though I could have one or the other but not both, and my brief exploration of the budget end of the market in my teens and early twenties – and the ensuing havoc wreaked on my hair – motivated me to find the cash to upgrade my hair regimen, cost be damned.

I was 24 when I finally found the courage to stop relaxing my hair, seven years after I'd first persuaded my reluctant mother to allow me to have it done in the first place, so I could wear a weave. ('You'll ruin your hair,' she'd warned, but I wasn't to be deterred. She was, as mothers often are, completely spot on). Then, in my early twenties, I was inspired by the burgeoning natural hair movement, which encouraged women of African descent to reclaim their natural hair texture, growing out the relaxers and shedding the weaves that until about a decade ago were pretty much de rigueur for Black women throughout the diaspora, and certainly those in public life. An Internet-led movement originating in the USA and disseminated globally by way of YouTube channels and chat forums, I became obsessed with the sudden wave of natural hair bloggers preaching the gospel of protective styling, often illustrating their own 'natural hair journeys' by way of dramatic before and after photosets.

Slowly, tentatively – hopefully – I began to decipher the language of curl patterns and 'big chops' in preparation for my own come-to-Jesus moment. By my early twenties, my thin, damaged hair had all but disintegrated thanks to years of constant chemical processing. The images I saw online – of Black women with thick, healthy-looking hair, cute curls and elaborate updos – were a world away from my own reality: harassed-looking strands that stubbornly refused to grow past my chin. Still, it took me years to finally take the plunge, at which point I had to relearn how to care for my own natural hair in what would be a time-consuming and often expensive process of trial and error.

And yet even within the natural hair community, a movement rooted in the celebration of Afro hair, colourism – or rather texturism – abounds. One need only scroll through the online forums and Pinterest boards dedicated to swapping hair care tips, or consider the bloggers selected to front campaigns for the growing number of natural hair brands to see that it is overwhelmingly the looser curls typical of biracial women that are positioned as the face of the movement. For most 'naturalistas', a twist out is likely to be one of the first hairstyles we'll attempt to master. The precise alchemy of heat, product and sheer force of will required to achieve a passable twist out is the subject of countless blog posts and YouTube videos (it took me at least half a dozen frustrating attempts to master a technique that worked for me). And yet, if done correctly, the final effect of a successful twist out simply emulates the looser curls and hair texture of mixed-race women. Even in its 'natural' state, Afro hair is most enthusiastically celebrated when it happens to be mixed with European heritage, or if you're prepared to spend the time, effort and money required to pretend it is. Tellingly, I still spend about the same amount of time and money on my hair now that I'm natural as I did when it was relaxed.

Over the past decade, social media campaigns and activism aimed at broadening our conception of beauty have become staple features of our media diets, but the majority of the images we're bombarded with on a daily basis still position the standard issue version of female beauty as being young, skinny and white. If you deviate from that norm in any way, chances are you'll find yourself paying an even higher beauty tax. In *Thick*, Cottom writes about discovering as a teenager that whiteness is the prevailing standard of beauty within wider society. She goes on to assert that by virtue of being Black she will always be 'unattractive', because those prevailing standards 'definitionally exclude' Blackness. It's a confronting assertion, which Cottom unpacks at length (and it's worth reading her argument in full), but it rests on this belief: that contemporary beauty standards have deliberately been constructed to elevate and protect whiteness, that that is their very function.

So what does the beauty myth that Naomi Wolf identified in 1990 look like today, now that we have smartphones and Facetune, and the creeping ubiquity of Internet pornography and social media; now that the democratisation of access to digital technology has made it easier than ever to create, disseminate and alter images? Our beauty role models now come in pin-sharp HD, bolstered by algorithms that affirm those who most faithfully conform to their increasingly stringent terms. Where once celebrities existed at a remove, seen only in the context of movies and glossy magazines, the advent of paparazzi culture and a growing thirst for increasingly candid celebrity photos – coupled with the proliferation of mediums through which they can broadcast and we can consume – has dissolved the barriers between celebrities and normal people. The beauty standards previously only expected of actresses, models and entertainers – in other words, the 'professionally pretty' – are now expected of regular women.

All you have to do is open Instagram and pick your poison: are you striving for the effortless natural beauty of a Glossier girl, the millennial make-up brand fronted by 'ordinary' women who apparently only need a few dabs of concealer to achieve model-worthy good looks? (Not for nothing has Glossier been jokingly christened a purveyor of make-up for people who are already beautiful.) Or perhaps you're partial to the immaculately contoured faces that seem to have taken over my Explore page, their Fenty highlighter winking seductively in between holiday #throwbacks and videos of puppies misbehaving. The beauty myth seems to have crystallised into two opposing camps: in the blue corner we have the hyper-augmented Kardashian paradigm, and in the red, the beauty minimalism supposedly practised by the likes of Gwyneth 'Rarely Wears Make-Up'[16] Paltrow and co. Both ideals are oppressive in their own ways, though the Kardashian standard is perhaps more overtly so, with its reliance on artificial fillers and plastic surgery, and the family's glassy-eyed endorsement of 'flat tummy teas' and 'waist trainers' (otherwise known as laxatives and corsets).

But even though the supposed effortlessness of the natural beauty camp comes with its own fair share of obligation, it's often viewed as being somehow more authentic, more readily embraced by those who might dismiss the Kardashian clan's aesthetic – and open commitment to beauty work – as déclassé. The allure of not looking like you've tried too hard is a social norm that long predates the Goops and Glossiers of modern times. In 1528, the Italian courtier Baldassare Castiglione wrote an etiquette guide, *The Book of the Courtier*, in which he outlined the ideal qualities that members of high society might aspire to. Among them was the quality of *sprezzatura*, which roughly translates as 'studied carelessness'. According to Castiglione, one's ability 'to practise in everything a certain nonchalance that shall conceal design and show that what is done and said is done without effort and almost without thought' was the height of sophistication.

Centuries later, there is still a strange shame associated with sharing that maintaining your appearance requires substantial effort, especially for women. The goal is to convince everyone that, to quote Beyoncé, you woke up like this. In a 2018 paper published in the *Journal of Consumer Research*, researchers examining how beauty work shapes perceptions of moral character found that 'effortful' beauty work tends to evoke negative judgements, and is viewed by both men and women as evidence of 'poorer moral character'.[17] Women thus face the double bind of having to conform to modern beauty standards, while also having to downplay our efforts to that end, for fear of being seen as too frivolous, too shallow, or too vain, knowing that history has rarely been kind to vain women. (Consider Jezebel, said to have 'painted her eyes and adorned her head', and later thrown to her death from a tower, her corpse devoured by wild dogs.) The same research paper found that the more time women spent getting ready each morning, the more reluctant they were to actually disclose the lengths to which they'd gone, the burden of concealment becoming part of the labour required of them.

Often the solution is to package these efforts as 'self-care', or that increasingly bastardised buzzword 'wellness', thereby medicalising and valorising the pursuit of beauty. Instead of applying a full face of make-up every day (vain), you schedule a monthly appointment with your dermatologist (virtuous), or buy a Goop-branded sachet of powder that promises to make you 'glow from within' (healthy). Never mind that this approach often requires just as much effort and money as the more obvious ministrations of the Kardashians and their ilk, as noted in a 2019 *Atlantic* article entitled 'The Best Skin-Care Trick Is Being Rich'. Describing the practice of celebrities and other influential women sharing their skincare routines in interviews, journalist Amanda Mull observes that 'when affluent people name just one trick that supposedly works like magic, usually when prompted by a women's publication, that elides hundreds of dollars' worth of creams, serums and peels'.[18] These accounts tend to obscure the reality that unless you happen to be appropriately genetically blessed, attaining this particular version of beauty is, more than anything else, a function of wealth.

Consider the example of soul singer Alicia Keys, who in 2016 adopted a highly publicised 'no make-up' stance as a rejection of the pressure women are under to embody physical perfection. 'I don't want to cover up any more,' Keys declared in an impassioned essay for *Lenny Letter*, framing her decision to give up make-up as both deeply personal and a civically minded stance against the tyranny of modern beauty expectations.[19] Even in an era where famous women sharing #nomakeup selfies as proof of their normalcy is so common as to verge on unremarkable, a world-famous singer forgoing make-up entirely – at awards ceremonies, during live performances, on her album cover – *was* remarkable, and the media responded accordingly.

Except you don't have to look that far to uncover the amount of effort that went into allowing Alicia Keys – a woman who, with or without make-up, is objectively very attractive – to adopt this position. In an interview with *W* magazine some months later, Keys's personal make-up artist revealed a regime of regular facials, acupuncture and something called 'ice work', alongside a cocktail of eye-wateringly expensive serums and face masks; before revealing that the singer *did* in fact wear make-up for high-profile appearances, applying individual false lashes to her eyebrows to make them look fuller, drawing on freckles, and wearing self-tanner on her cheeks.[20] Keys's no make-up stance wasn't quite the wholesale rejection of modern beauty standards that she had positioned it as, and likely imagined it to be. Instead she merely traded one version of the beauty tax for another, deploying her considerable resources in service of an outcome that the rest of us cash-poor Normals have to emulate with bog-standard concealer instead. 'Natural beauty', as practised by high-profile women and the brands they endorse, is as demanding of women's time and money as the frequently derided Kardashian standard, which at least is relatively transparent about the level of effort required (though the family's repeated denials of cosmetic surgery are a notable omission). If any woman is justified in going to such lengths over her appearance, it is a high-profile celebrity subject to a level of scrutiny far beyond that of the average woman, and for whom personal grooming (much like for female air stewardesses) is a de facto requirement for success in her field. But Alicia Keys's Goop-esque approach to beauty isn't a world away from that of the Kardashians. It's an exemplar of a different aesthetic preference – au naturel as opposed to high glamour – not a rejection of beauty work, as suggested.

And, as if the demands on our bodies weren't enough, the scope of things that must be considered beautiful now extends far beyond women's physical beings to encompass our entire existences. Now, on top of having beautiful bodies – perky breasts and flawless skin, gleaming white teeth and a perfect hip-to-waist ratio – we must have beautiful lives as well. We are to wake up in our beautiful, tastefully decorated homes, and select a beautiful outfit from a tastefully curated wardrobe full of more beautiful clothes, before consuming a suitably photogenic (and healthy!) breakfast at an imported marble countertop in our beautiful custom-built kitchens, and . . . you get the gist. Anyone who consumes digital media in any shape or form will be familiar with the plethora of lifestyle content dedicated to detailing the unfathomably aesthetic lives of a certain kind of woman, documenting everything from how she takes her coffee, to her wedding 'journey' and style 'philosophy'. Similarly to expectations of physical appearance, where once these lifestyles were expected only of the rich and famous, they are now held up as everywoman examples, a billionaire heiress's Belgravia apartment positioned as a realistic aspiration for a generation of twenty-something freelancers living in laughably precarious rentals.

It feels curiously anachronistic that women are still so frequently judged by their ability to keep a beautiful home. It isn't that long ago that the demands of the home were the yoke that kept women out of public life and away from the workplace, before the swinging sixties and free-loving seventies brought with them the emancipatory potential of second-wave feminism. In 1963, Betty Friedan's era-defining manifesto *The Feminine Mystique* sought to galvanise a generation of women trapped by domesticity to throw off the well-manicured shackles of their subjugation, and for a while, it seemed as though the ideal of the 'happy housewife heroine' equating womanhood with domesticity and motherhood had been vanquished. And yet a half-century later, it feels as though the pendulum has quietly begun to swing back in the other direction, that we are at a cultural inflection point, or worse, have unwittingly passed it and begun the downward swing back towards the veneration of female domesticity. There are now a glut of women building public personas – and often making a lot of money – by proudly celebrating the sort of retrograde pursuits long associated with housewifery: Instagram influencers meticulously documenting interior decoration projects, and socialites broadcasting their colour-coordinated table settings. The domestic obligations that our foremothers fought so hard to reduce the importance of – one's ability to maintain a beautiful home, or the pressure to play the gracious hostess – have once again become a bewilderingly important yardstick of success for women, the fruits of their labour proudly displayed on Instagram. Domesticity is back in vogue, and back in *Vogue*.

There have even been attempts to repackage *cleaning* as something aspirational, as demonstrated by Essex-based Instagram influencer Sophie Hinchliffe, or as she's known to her followers, Mrs Hinch (not Miss, or Ms, but the wifely Mrs). Part-time hairdresser and full-time 'cleanfluencer', Hinchcliffe's love of cleaning has earned her nearly four million Instagram followers and a hotly contested bidding war for her first book, *Hinch Yourself Happy: All the Best Cleaning Tips to Shine Your Sink and Soothe Your Soul*, which upon publication in 2019 became an instant bestseller. Her feed is a careful homage to domestic duty, bright yellow Marigold gloves and bottles of Fairy washing-up liquid photographed against the backdrop of her pristine if somewhat bland home. That a woman has been able to build a lucrative career out of something as pedestrian as cleaning her own home, successfully capitalising on the domestic drudgery that has for generations served as a barrier to women's emancipation, might potentially be celebrated as some form of empowerment were it not for the fact that for the vast majority of women, housework will never be a monetisable activity. (Quite the opposite in fact – the average woman will do about fourteen hours of unpaid housework *per week*.[21]) A select few women celebrating acts that are barriers to progress for the vast majority feels fundamentally incompatible with the project of feminism.

So where does all of this money – the £70,000 debt that each of us will pay down over the course of our lifetimes – where does it all *go*? Who stands to gain from our losses?

The most obvious beneficiaries are the brands, corporations and media outlets that, as Naomi Wolf writes, 'depend for their considerable livelihood on selling women a feeling of terminal ugliness'. From fashion to pharmaceuticals, it's no secret that Big Business depends on making people feel as though what they have, how they look – who they *are* – is not enough. Modern consumer culture is sustained by a mixture of aspiration and dissatisfaction with the status quo, and the belief that *this* product or *that* brand is capable of transforming our lives; capable of making us happier, sexier, richer; capable of allowing us to self-actualise. When it comes to women, the default strategy is to either exploit or manufacture insecurities, shifting the acceptable baseline standard for our appearances to one that requires external intervention. Culture writer Anne Helen Petersen describes this as the 'unsolvable lack' created by capitalism. 'If a lack isn't readily visible . . . make it so – and then provide the means to solve it.'[22]

There are the usual suspects, brands like the nightmarishly horny Victoria's Secret, whose annual display of G-string clad 'Angels' constituted little more than a paint-by-numbers tribute to the notion that sex sells. Throughout its twenty-four-year existence, the Victoria's Secret fashion show remained staunchly committed to quite literally the narrowest possible definition of female beauty. In 2018, its now-ousted chief marketing officer Ed Razek defended his decision not to include plus size or transgender models in the show's line-up by suggesting that such women wouldn't fit in the 'fantasy' of his vision.[23] But where once the Victoria's Secret show was a spectacle largely unquestioned by commentators, its final few years brought with them plummeting viewership figures and increasingly vocal critiques of the brand's out-of-touch positioning.[24] In 2019, the Victoria's Secret show was officially cancelled, a relic of a bygone era forced to capitulate to the public mood.

Concurrently, brands, media outlets and the corporations that own them have become savvier, aware of the need to be seen to be changing with the times, to be more inclusive, to not so obviously assail women with suggestions of their physical inferiority.

Enter wellness, a Trojan horse that allows brands to mask the unrealistic beauty standards underpinning their existence beneath the benign veneer of science, to imply that their concern is one of health and that their products are the solution to the bone-crushing grind of modern life that can make even the healthiest of women worry that they might be sick. The wellness industry, which encompasses everything from fitness and nutrition to spirituality and mental health, is now worth over $4.2 trillion, a figure that according to the Global Wellness Institute will hit $5.6 trillion by 2022.[25]

Alternatively, you could disguise your agenda under the label of body positivity. A radical movement first instigated by self-described 'fat' women whose bodies exist outside the boundaries of traditional beauty norms, body positivity has been slowly co-opted by the same entities that once excluded fat women – that still exclude fat women – and who have scrubbed it clean of its political origins in service of profit. It's this kind of obfuscation that in 2019 allowed women's razor brand Billie to be celebrated for creating an ad campaign that deviated from the norms of its category by actually *showing* body hair. The campaign hit all the key notes required for it to be celebrated as a feminist statement. Billie had commissioned a 'feminist photographer' to shoot the advert, which was soundtracked by the raucous beats of Princess Nokia's 'Tomboy', giving the film a punky riot grrrl edge that implied Billie was being in some way subversive. The supporting press releases and interview sound bites read like a tick list of contemporary feminist tropes.[26] 'Female gaze.' 'Normalise body hair.' In fact, the video was so well crafted that no one seemed to notice the hypocrisy inherent in it having been created by a company whose entire business model is reliant on women feeling sufficiently ashamed of their body hair to purchase its products. Instead, the campaign was met with rapturous applause both on social media and by the many women's media outlets that covered it. (The latter is perhaps not surprising, given that most of these outlets are engaged in a constant hard sell of fashion and beauty products, dependent as they are on advertiser money for their continued existence). Billie describes itself as 'body-hair positive'. Its brand messaging frequently describes shaving as a 'personal choice', using the same 'my body, my choice' rhetoric of pro-choice feminists, and thereby subtly absorbing some of their legitimacy – all while conspicuously avoiding the question of why a woman might want to rid herself of body hair in the first place. That brands like Billie (or Dove, with its relentless commitment to 'real beauty') are able to have their cake and eat it – paying lip service to body positivity while profiteering from the same oppressive standards that make body positivity necessary – is a progression that prompted Amanda Hess to coin the term 'beauty-standard denialism'. By that Hess means the contradiction that although beauty standards for women have never been higher, we are now also tasked with practising serene self-acceptance, often by the very same entities that make their living from steering us in the opposite direction.

There are individuals who profit too – men, of course, because even if they don't individually enforce or endorse these beauty standards, they do benefit from the patriarchal norms that have created them, and so profit by default. Part of the theory of beauty Tressie McMillan Cottom presents in *Thick* is that without men, 'the socio-cultural institution of Big Beauty could not be as powerful as it is'. Perhaps counter-intuitively there are also women who benefit from, and have a vested interest in, this status quo. In Jessa Crispin's *Why I Am Not a Feminist*, her 2017 manifesto decrying the corruption of feminism's once-radical agenda, she observes that 'women who profit from the patriarchy will help keep it in place'. After the actress and body-positivity activist Jameela Jamil labelled Kim Kardashian a 'double agent for the patriarchy' in 2018, I observed many people on social media rush to Kim's defence, suggesting she is in some way playing the patriarchy at its own game, as though her primary audience isn't, in fact, women.[27] It is women, not men, who are literally as well as figuratively paying the price as Kim lines her own pockets by flogging them appetite-suppressant lollipops,[28] and inviting them to believe that it's these lollipops – and not, say, her army of dieticians and personal chefs, punishing exercise regime or (alleged) cosmetic surgery – that are responsible for her insane physical proportions.

I return again to Heather Widdows' suggestion that beauty work is 'ultimately a rational choice in a world that values it so highly'.[29] It is a rational choice for women, and perhaps even a necessary one given what's at stake for us: social positioning, economic advancement, career progression. But the pursuit of beauty also presents a double-edged sword, one that serves to make us materially, physically and spiritually poorer, even as we strive for the very opposite. Despite how visible its physical manifestation can be, beauty work is merely another type of invisible labour, the hours we spend on it largely unquantified, and ultimately unpaid.

Chapter 7

INVISIBLE LABOUR

Today you are going to work for free. And if you don't do it today, you'll do it tomorrow. And if you don't do it tomorrow, you'll do it next week, or you'll have done it last week, or you'll do it next month.

Working for free is, unfortunately, an inescapable part of the female condition. Entire economic systems are predicated on women assuming the burden of responsibility for the constant trickle of low-level organisation and emotional caretaking that greases the wheels of life. We are the invisible worker bees holding together family units and friendship groups, global conglomerates and entire societies, and yet – in addition to being unpaid – this work, crucial as it is, is very often also unacknowledged.

This is what I call invisible labour, a term that sociologists, economists and feminists have all defined differently over time, but by which I mean to encompass the following:

Domestic labour – household chores and all the various bits of admin that go into the maintenance of a home. Paying council tax, stocking up the fridge, emailing your landlord about the broken boiler.

Caregiving – for young children, elderly relatives and other dependants.

Office housework – the low-level admin that's essential to office life but to which no designated employee is assigned. Ordering lunch for a team meeting (and clearing up afterwards), planning the office Christmas party, organising birthday celebrations and leaving cards.

Mental labour – which often adds another layer to all of the above. This is the 'worry work' of remembering to send thank you letters, of factoring everyone's dietary preferences into the weekly supermarket shop. It's the work of anticipating needs and making sure they're met, of weighing up and reminding, of creating the to-do list and keeping track of the items on it even if you don't actually have to do them all yourself.

Emotional labour – a term increasingly used as a catch-all to denote the presence of invisible labour in general, but which actually refers to the fairly specific requirement within certain jobs to keep one's emotions in check (more on that below).

All of the above overwhelmingly fall to women – in the instance of care work, over three quarters of the unpaid care work done globally is carried out by women, who do more than three times the amount men do.[1]

'Not only has housework been imposed on women, but it has been transformed into a natural attribute of our female physique and personality, an internal need, an aspiration, supposedly coming from the depth of our female character.' So wrote the activist and writer Silvia Federici in her radical 1975 manifesto *Wages Against Housework*. Federici is most well-known for arguing that women should be paid for their domestic labour, though as the writer Jennifer Schaffer observes this demand was 'more radical provocation than concrete policy proposal',[2] an attempt to highlight the extent to which our global economic system relies on women's unpaid labour. But *Wages Against Housework* also offers valuable insight into *why* the division of labour has evolved thus: the belief that there is some natural order that makes women somehow predisposed to it. 'They say it is love,' Federici writes. 'We say it is unwaged work.'

Perhaps the most zeitgeisty – and the most misunderstood – component of the invisible workload women have to shoulder is emotional labour, a term first coined by the sociologist Arlie Hochschild in her 1983 book *The Managed Heart*. Emotional labour, as Hochschild conceived of it, refers to the requirement in certain professions that workers manage their own emotions in order to make others feel comfortable, either forcing or hiding certain emotions as necessary. Hochschild illustrated her point by using flight attendants as an example (who by my count seem to suffer an extraordinary number of indignities at the hands of employers desperate to retain the glamour of flying while providing services that are anything but). The obligation flight attendants have to – at least in principle – welcome passengers on-board with a smile, and deal graciously with all manner of drunk, impatient, fussy and anxious flyers, while suppressing any fatigue or irritation they themselves might be feeling, is a prime example of emotional labour, which is often a facet of customer service roles. Anyone who has ever waitressed or worked in a retail job and smiled through gritted teeth while dealing with a rude customer will understand instinctively what emotional labour looks like, and how it feels to perform it. Research has shown that over time, constantly having to suppress your own emotions and project ones that you might not necessarily be feeling – enthusiasm, cheerfulness, warmth – can take a real psychological toll. This is when you'll find yourself getting home from work and snapping at your housemates or your kids because you've run out of 'nice' for the day. In the longterm, performing excessive amounts of emotional labour can lead to increased anxiety, stress and a greater risk of burnout.

And though it's often interpreted as being a uniquely female burden, in fact both men and women have to perform emotional labour at work – consider your (likely male) Uber driver, painfully accommodating of your every whim, aware that his livelihood depends on you finding your journey pleasant enough to leave a 5-star rating. The power dynamics built into the on-demand economy (Uber, Deliveroo, TaskRabbit, and so on) make it a rich setting for emotional labour, given how easy it is for customers to feed back on their experiences and the effect of that feedback on gig economy workers' future opportunities. Still, emotional labour occurs within most jobs, to a degree. There are few of us who can get away with being completely transparent about our more negative emotions at work. The lower down you are on the pay, power or seniority ladder though, the more emotional labour you'll find yourself doing, which is why it's so frequently characterised as a specifically female obligation. Women are more likely to find themselves tasked with emotional labour because we are more likely to be employed in the sort of customer-facing, low-wage service jobs that demand emotional labour as a key function of their execution.

We also have to contend with social conditioning and stereo-types about traditional gender traits. In media, culture, history, even some areas of science, it's almost impossible to escape the message that performing emotional labour comes 'naturally' to women, that we are inherently better at it, and that we *enjoy* doing it – that it is not actually labour at all. The archaic theories

171

of gender essentialism Silvia Federici railed against when exploring why household chores so frequently fall to women are as easily applied to the work of managing one's emotions. What woman has not at some point felt the burden of expectation that, as the memoirist Deborah Levy puts it in *The Cost of Living*, we are to be 'the architect of everyone else's well-being'?

Then there's the 'likeability' factor – an ability to effectively perform emotional labour is a social lubricant women generally need to rely on more than men, courtesy of societal expectations that we are agreeable and nice, and the social penalty levied if we are perceived to be otherwise. Mastering the performance of emotional labour is pretty much mandatory for any woman who wants to move through the world with a degree of ease.

As awareness of the concept has grown in recent years, other types of invisible labour also taken on by women have been increasingly corralled under the umbrella term of 'emotional labour'; its meaning expanding to encompass pretty much any type of unpaid and/or feminised labour, especially if that labour happens to be particularly unpleasant, and regardless of whether it might be reasonable to expect payment for it. Particularly on the Internet (i.e. the place where nuance goes to die) the understanding of what does and does not constitute emotional labour has become confused. Now everything is discussed in those terms, from reminding your flatmate to take out the bins to making small talk at a dinner party, regardless of whether it actually involves the intersection of formal employment and emotion management that sits at the core of the concept Arlie Hochschild had in mind. Even explaining the concept of emotional labour to another person, as I am doing now, has become reclassified as emotional labour.

In 2017, US *Harper's Bazaar* published an online article titled 'Women Aren't Nags – We're Just Fed Up', in which the journalist Gemma Hartley detailed her attempts to get her well-meaning but slightly oblivious husband to pull his weight around the house, and more broadly, analysed the amount of unacknowledged work women carry out on a daily basis.[3] Perhaps unsurprisingly, the article touched a nerve and quickly went viral, eventually spawning a book, *Fed Up*, in which Hartley offered up a new, broader definition of emotional labour as:

> the unpaid, invisible work we do to keep those around
> us comfortable and happy. It envelops many other terms
> associated with the type of care-based labour I described
> in my article: *emotion work, the mental load, mental
> burden, domestic management, clerical labour, invisible
> labour.*

Another Internet explainer published in 2018 by the business journal *Quartz*, somewhat overconfidently titled 'An extremely clear definition of emotional labour for anyone who still doesn't get it', included such examples as 'texting to help siblings through break-ups' and 'evaluating whether friends' hook-ups were fully consensual' as examples of emotional labour that one might (presumably) expect to be paid for in an ideal scenario.[4] This is, of course, a frighteningly bleak lens through which to view the maintenance of personal ties, but one that exemplifies many recent analyses of emotional labour. If it seems pedantic or pointlessly academic to fuss over the strict boundaries of the term, given that language is a constantly evolving thing and no concept or definition is immutable, it's worth considering the rather mercenary and hyper-capitalistic implication of the behaviour required to maintain a sense of community and inter-personal relationships falling into a bracket of activity – labour – that, by definition, one should be paid for. Still, the instinct to expand the meaning of the term points to a need to find a way to recognise all the unpaid and uncredited work women do, an understandable response to centuries of those efforts being over-looked.

One of the most jarring realisations I had when I first started working was of how clearly the burden of invisible labour in most offices is split along gendered lines. At 21, I had a fairly naïve out-look about what sexism within the workplace would look like, expecting it to be painted in broad brushstrokes and easy-to-spot clichés – a bottom-pinching boss or male colleagues entertain-ing clients at a strip club. The reality, as most women know, is usually far more subtle. Almost immediately, I picked up on the uneven distribution of what I now know to be invisible labour, and the unspoken expectation that women would be the ones to host and facilitate, troubleshoot and housekeep. It was a dynamic that felt both incredibly alien and glaringly obvious and once I'd become aware of it, I saw it everywhere. The way women in the office had to walk the fine line between assertiveness and humil-ity, couching requests in a flurry of would-you-possibly-minds and sorry-to-pesters, aware that failing to show the appropriate level of amiability would have them labelled 'bossy', or worse. To say I didn't particularly care for those gendered norms would be an understatement – in my first job, I took a perverse pleasure in stubbornly refusing to conform to them, an attitude that was responsible for the 'bolshy' comment I once got from my boss.

I had taken his words as a compliment, evidence that I'd managed to resist being subsumed by the patriarchy, but the truth is I didn't really care about that job, so it was easy for me to go against the grain. When I started working at AMV, a job I'd fought for and hoped to make a career out of, all of that changed.

It didn't help that ad agencies tend to thrive on a pretty rigid sense of hierarchy. Whether you're at the top of the food chain or the bottom of it, everyone in an ad agency knows their place, and acts accordingly. As I soon found, that kind of hierarchy rarely caters to the interests of female employees. Then there was the job I was doing – account management – a role a colleague once sardonically likened to being the agency equivalent of a septic tank, in that we had to 'take shit from all angles'. Account managers serve as an ad agency's connection to its clients, managing that relationship while trying to keep everyone involved in the process of making an ad happy. That means balancing various conflicting demands: the clients who want blockbuster campaigns (and results) on a shoestring budget; the creative teams jaded from years of flogging buy-one-get-one-free deals to Middle England; the producers trying in vain to keep shoots from going wildly over budget; and literally *everyone* pissed off at getting three weeks to work on a campaign they should have had three months for. Thus, account managers occupy an inherently tricky position and are the ones who bear the brunt when any of the million and one things that can go wrong, do. I found we were often regarded with a mixture of pity and contempt by other departments, and rarely given the credit we deserved for what I still think is one of the most challenging jobs in advertising.

Even though the job description of an account manager necessarily involves plenty of organising and planning and making sure that things run smoothly, I often felt as though that requirement was exploited to make young women in particular the office dogsbodies. About two thirds of ad agency 'account men' – as account managers are often colloquially referred to – are actually women,[5] and account management tends to be gendered as a female space, particularly at the junior level. (This is in stark contrast to the overwhelmingly male creative and strategy departments, which are also the more prestigious, better paid and high-status departments within an ad agency.) Collectively, we were expected to play the role of nurturer and facilitator to those mostly male creatives and strategists, endlessly mollifying, cheerleading and coddling often startlingly fragile egos.

Again, I found these gendered dynamics endlessly frustrating, given my preferred style of communication is rather more direct – inappropriately so for a woman in her early twenties doing a job that stipulates deference as one of its key functions.

About a year into my time at AMV, I had to deliver some tricky client feedback to an art director assigned to one of my accounts. We were at the end of a protracted creative development process that had dragged on for far longer than was necessary, and now – just when we thought it was finally over – the client had sent me an email asking for more changes. I swore under my breath before getting up to go and break the news, knowing it would go down like a bag of wet sand. Having recently been assigned a new intern to train up, I decided to take her with me, thinking I'd show her how to tackle these tricky situations like a pro.

The meeting lasted all of three minutes, and ended with the art director throwing a book across the room and literally screaming at me, before storming out of his office and striding up and down the hallway shouting, protesting about what was expected of him. Curious heads popped out of other offices along the corridor to see what the commotion was about. I was mortified, worried that his reaction would be perceived as a negative indictment of my ability to properly 'manage' the situation. When it became clear he wasn't coming back, I left his office, intern in tow.

'Is that sort of thing . . . normal?' she asked, as we took the lift back down to our floor in startled silence, both of us shaking.

I looked at her, weighing up my answer. What was I supposed to say? Answer honestly and say *'Yes, that's far more normal than I'd like to admit,'* and potentially put her off the industry for life? Or lie and say *'No,'* and risk misleading her about what she was getting herself into?

'Eh . . .' I laughed nervously, trying to reassure her. 'It's not usually *that* bad.' I felt guilty for having exposed her to such an unpleasant situation, but also immensely grateful that she'd been there with me, that I hadn't been in that office alone. I managed to make it to the bathroom before bursting into tears. Then I went back to my desk.

The emotional labour needed to squeeze myself into the role of a compliant account man day in, day out required an enormous effort, one that made me increasingly unhappy over time. In hindsight, I suspect I wasn't the only one who struggled with having to smile appeasingly while trying to persuade middle-aged men with frustrated creative ambitions to do the work they were being paid a salary many multiples of mine to do. I do know that my experiences weren't particularly atypical. Ad agencies throughout the industry are built along the same framework of intensely gendered power dynamics.

Another way that invisible labour frequently manifests itself within the workplace is as office housework – all those little bits of admin that help things run more smoothly, like finding a time when everyone can meet, or taking notes in a meeting. Not long before I decided to leave AMV, I found myself working under two account directors, Fergus and Jim, who seemed to interpret my relative juniority as licence to treat me like their own personal secretary. By this point I was a senior account manager, but under Fergus and Jim I began to spend more and more of my time on low-level admin, far more so than even at the very beginning of my career. Some days my job consisted of little more than booking meeting rooms and carting printouts to Fergus's desk, who loved nothing more than to send things to the printer and then email me to ask that I bring them over to him. Desperately worried that without more substantive work to do I'd never get the experience I needed to be promoted, I tried to voice my concerns to my head of department. This was the same person who only months earlier had told me she found my ambition 'hard to manage'. Unsurprisingly, nothing changed.

Late one night, Jim sent me an email about a client meeting scheduled for the next morning, asking me to come into the office early to print out the 100-page PowerPoint presentation he'd just finished and stick all the pages up on the walls of the meeting room. I emailed back reminding him that I had a long-scheduled training course early the next morning that I really didn't want to miss, and suggested some other, less time-consuming, options. Perhaps the clients could look at the presentation on a screen or – if they really needed physical copies to look at – perhaps I could just set the printer to run off a few copies while I attended my training session and have them ready for the start of the meeting?

'My bad – I'd foolishly assumed you'd be around tomorrow morning (!) Not ideal that you aren't,' Jim responded, his email dripping with passive-aggression. 'But we definitely need the presentation up on the walls.'

Why, I thought to myself, *in the age of laptops, and the Internet, and mobile fucking phones, do you need 100 pieces of FUCKING paper printed out and Blu-tacked to a FUCKING wall?*

'Sure, no problem!' I tapped out, too tired to argue. I'd only left the office about an hour before.

My BlackBerry buzzed again. *For fuck's sake.*

'Also, what's the situation with breakfast?' Jim had written.

'Hey. I've arranged with catering for there to be teas and coffees, hope that's all right.'

'Mmmmm . . . not ideal that we don't have a full breakfast sorted. Can you get everyone some yoghurts and smoothies on your way in?'

'Sure.'

The next morning, just as I was finishing setting up, the business lead on our account (who was several rungs senior to Jim), walked past.

'What are you doing?' he asked, confused.

'Oh, er, Jim asked me to print out the deck and stick it up on the walls. For the meeting.' I responded, immediately feeling foolish.

'No, stop doing that. We don't want you looking like a runner. Go downstairs and say hello, everyone's arriving.'

I was surprised and slightly grateful, though I now realise I was probably being billed out to clients at rates that suggested a level of seniority that would have been called into question if they'd walked in on me playing Art Attack on my hands and knees. Of course no one – not even Jim – so much as glanced at the pieces of paper stuck on the wall at any point in the meeting. As I'd suspected, it was the sort of pointless busywork that had absolutely nothing to do with practical necessity, and everything to do with Jim's ability to email me at ten o'clock at night (I should never have replied) and have me in the office doing bitchwork at seven the next morning. I'm sure a few people reading this will dismiss me as just another moaning millennial, too precious and entitled to roll up my sleeves and get stuck into the more unglamorous side of a nine-to-five – and yet I always recognised that low-level admin was part and parcel of being a junior employee, and readily accepted that obligation. The problem was that, even as I progressed, that requirement didn't seem to change. When I looked around and saw women far more senior than I was still bound by those same responsibilities, I knew something was rotten.

It doesn't take a genius to figure out what all those hours spent playing the role of office helpmate might mean for women's progress in the workplace. Office housework generally consists of 'non-promotable tasks', defined by the *Harvard Business Review* as tasks that 'benefit the organisation but likely don't contribute to someone's performance evaluation and career advancement'.[6] Spending time helping to coordinate an office move instead of, say, landing a new revenue-generating client might earn you a grateful mention in a company-wide email, but it's probably not going to get you a pay rise. Even merely being *seen* to be doing office housework subconsciously affects your colleagues' perceptions of you, perceptions that go on to influence your promotion prospects, wage levels and general career advancement. Optics matter. Just as my business lead was sensitive that our clients catching me setting up the meeting room would undercut my credibility, the same applies to the people you work with on a day-to-day basis, whose observations are likely to have an impact on your career progression. And then of course, as always, there is the issue of race – studies have shown that women of colour more frequently report being asked to do office housework than white women, and certainly more than white men.[7]

One of the strangest things about office housework is that women aren't just *assigned* more of it than men – they're also more likely to *volunteer* for it. Research published in the *American Economic Review* in 2017 concluded that this propensity to volunteer 'did not appear to result from gender differences in preferences, but rather from a shared understanding that women will volunteer more than men'.[8] In other words, women don't volunteer for office housework because of some innate feminine quality or because they're 'just better at that sort of thing' (as people often like to suggest); they do it because they know it's expected of them, and because they realise that they'll be penalised if they don't. Another study, published in the *Journal of Applied Psychology*, found that women who decline to take on office housework – in this example, helping prep for a meeting – are perceived more negatively than men who show the same reluctance.[9] On the flip side, men who *do* help out around the office enjoy a significant reputational boost in their colleagues' eyes. Women who do the same, however, get nothing. It's simply expected that we'll do it anyway.

The dynamic where women are assigned the role of office helpmate or 'den mother' was actually formally codified at an ad agency I freelanced at shortly before quitting agency life for good. Here, account directors and account managers were referred to respectively as 'Mothers' and 'Nannies', a supposedly quirky tradition whose oddly gendered connotations seemed invisible to everyone but me. Aside from playing into the already gendered dynamic of (usually but not always) female account managers playing den mother roles to (almost always) male creatives, it also felt deeply patronising. I wanted the work I did to be recognised as that – skilled professional work, not some untrained primal urge or servile instinct. Still, the domestic qualities those labels imply are strangely fitting, given that for many women the home tends to be the greatest source of invisible labour.

Though the gap varies according to age, income and socio-economic class, in pretty much every country in the world, heterosexual women do considerably more housework than their male partners. On average women in the UK do about 60 per cent more unpaid housework than men,[10] or ten additional hours a week – work that, if Silvia Federici's *Wages Against Housework* were actual policy, would earn them about £13,500 a year.[11] This gender chore gap starts depressingly early, with numerous studies finding that even in childhood, girls end up doing more chores than their male siblings.[12] When women become mothers the gap grows significantly, given women are more likely to assume the role of primary caregiver. But even when both parents work full-time, women still end up doing more domestic labour than their partners, taking on what Arlie Hochschild labelled 'the second shift' in her 1989 book of the same name. Women go to work and do their first 'shift' in the office, before coming home to another round of work, this time the business of household chores and childcare. And while the rise in domestic responsibilities women experience after marriage and children is matched by a permanent drop in earnings, for men the opposite is true. Getting married and having children tends to boost a man's income. As housewife-turned-activist Judy Brady posited in 1972 'who *wouldn't* want a wife?'[13] That this is only true for heterosexual couples also demonstrates how deeply rooted the division of labour is in gender stereotypes – numerous studies have shown that same-sex couples divide household chores much more evenly, perhaps because, as Jennifer Petriglieri writes in the *Atlantic*, they are 'already well accustomed to challenging gendered social norms'.[14]

It would be easy to focus only on quantifying the economic impact of women's unpaid labour, but there's a huge emotional cost to be reckoned with as well. The constant decision-making and deputising involved in the role of household project manager can be incredibly draining, and is a real source of overwhelm for many women. Researchers investigating the psychological and emotional ramifications of the gender chore gap have found that women who believe the split of household responsibilities in their relationships is unfair are more likely to suffer from depression, loneliness, anger and psychological distress.[15] That these emotions are often met by a lack of understanding from their male partners (who often think the domestic workload *is* being shared equally) can put a significant strain on relationships.

Given the lost hours and quietly sacrificed opportunities, the energy expended and the negative impact on one's earning power, that women have been taught to aspire to marriage seems to me one of the greatest scams the patriarchy has pulled off yet. How strange that tradition dictates brides wear white, and not black.

Chapter 8

DEATH OF THE GIRLBOSS

girl·boss /gɜːl bɑs/

noun

An ambitious, successful woman with an enviable career.
Often (but not always) an entrepreneur or self-employed
in some capacity. Highly driven and impossibly well
groomed. Probably younger than you.

Somewhere around the mid-2010s, as we collectively pieced
together our post-recession existences and began to succumb
to social media's poison embrace, entrepreneurship got itself a
makeover. In the space of a few short years, a career path I'd never
before contemplated suddenly exploded into my consciousness.
The word 'entrepreneur' stopped being synonymous solely with
grey-suited businessmen like Bill Gates and Warren Buffett,
people with personal fortunes that read more like the GDP of a
small country and who might as well have lived on the moon for
all the relevance they had to my life.

All of a sudden, it felt as if entrepreneurs were everywhere,
and they were actually kind of . . . cool. Running a start-up was

Cool. Closing a funding round was Cool. Selling your business to another bigger business and using the proceeds from that sale to start a new business? Very Cool. Start-up founders routinely began to ascend to a level of celebrity previously reserved for members of the glamour professions, their lifestyles commanding a similar cultural fascination to those of movie stars and models. The aspiration du jour for much of my generation was (and to an extent still is) to be the next baby-faced CEO on the cover of *Forbes* magazine, or at the very least to work for ourselves. And who could blame us? The media loves an ingénue, is saturated with stories of wunderkinder whose brilliant minds have catapulted them onto 'Under 30' lists and made them fat fortunes, stories that were at first concentrated in the esoteric recesses of Silicon Valley but can now be found pouring out of every major global city. The language of entrepreneurialism has burrowed its way into wider workplace culture, phrases like 'productising' and 'growth hacking' taking hold of middle managers in offices thousands of miles from the tech start-ups that birthed them, carried by emails and spreading impossibly fast, like cancer, or weeds. In London, the area surrounding Old Street's chaotic, traffic-clogged roundabout has rather hubristically been christened the 'Silicon Roundabout' by those keen to channel some of the cachet – and venture capital dollars – of the California original.

It's not hard to understand the appeal of entrepreneurship. Here, according to popular lore, is a career path that allows you to captain your own ship and to work in a profession where inexperience can be passed off as a form of currency; to actually reap the full financial rewards of your labour, instead of exchanging your time and ideas for wages that carry increasingly little value in the current economic landscape. Mine is, famously, the first generation set to be poorer than the one that came before, a generation emerging into adulthood against the backdrop of a financial crash, unaffordable housing and rising higher education costs; with more and more of us making a living on the shaky foundations of the gig economy. The traditional rewards for career success no longer apply, so little wonder we look to entrepreneurship in the hopes of striking gold. We are trying to game the system, hoping to eke out some semblance of financial and emotional reward from a set-up that seems only to present us with increasingly dismal options – and even the old guard have cottoned on. These days law firms and management consultancies fearful of losing younger employees to the siren call of start-up life routinely encourage recruits to scratch their entrepreneurial itch by becoming 'intrapreneurs' instead, promising that the rigid structures of corporate life can offer the same excitement as one might find at start-ups with mantras like 'MOVE FAST AND BREAK THINGS' emblazoned in neon tube lighting on their office walls.

The B-side to all this – the ballast to the boundless optimism and seemingly limitless possibility promised by start-up culture – was the acceptance of deep personal sacrifice as fundamental to professional success, and the normalisation of aggressive workaholism. This was the age of hustle culture, all relentless ambition and 'sleep when you're dead' working hours; self-appointed business gurus cranking out tweet-length aphorisms about the virtues of failure; an obsession with self-optimisation and productivity 'hacks' that suggest the human body's natural limits are merely something to be out-manoeuvred, obstacles to be overcome rather than warning signs to be heeded.

Out of this cultural moment came the Girlboss, the result of start-up culture being refracted through the prism of fourth-wave feminism that was at the time also gathering pace. The term 'girlboss' itself was first propelled into public consciousness by American entrepreneur Sophia Amoruso, founder and former CEO of fast fashion brand Nasty Gal, who in 2014 published a memoir-slash-business manual called *#Girlboss*. A somewhat self-mythologising account of Amoruso's rags-to-riches trajectory, *#Girlboss* told the story of a dumpster-diving community college dropout who'd turned an eye for vintage clothing and an entrepreneurial mindset into a fast fashion company that at its peak was valued at $330 million. The book was a masterclass in personal branding, cementing Amoruso's image as the spunky outsider of the otherwise stuffy business world. She was relatable, and more unusually she was also *cool*, sporting a blunt fringe and leather biker jackets, and giving unvarnished interviews about 'getting shit done'.[1] Her origin story presented a refreshingly counterculture alternative to the corporate narratives peddled by other female business icons, with their tasteful shift dresses and stiff blow-dries, and her message – 'if a sofa-surfing college dropout can do this, then so can you' – took. At present the #girlboss hashtag has been used over 22 million times on Instagram alone, with the book itself selling more than half a million copies to date.[2]

In its wake, a host of female-focused websites, clubs, media platforms and conferences sprang up, most of which tended to focus on younger, self-employed women and members of the creative class. Two years later, I'd set up a platform of my own (more on that later). *#Girlboss* was nothing short of a cultural phenomenon, its publication marking the beginning of a shift that saw entrepreneurship and self-employment treated increasingly as a lifestyle choice. And, despite what girlboss culture would later come to represent, there was a genuine sense of optimism in that brief era, a belief that if women gathered together, connected and told our stories, good things were bound to happen. Often they did.

The key pillars of girlbossery were, of course, millennial pink: that softly muted, peachy sort of dusky pink that experienced a resurgence as Amoruso's book was published, and that has now reached total ubiquity. At least initially its popularity represented an ironic sort of reclamation of a colour women had long been suspicious of, thanks to brands who tried to sell us overpriced razors by manufacturing them in baby-pink and adding a 25 per cent mark-up, not to mention the studied ditziness of Paris Hilton's pink Juicy Couture and chihuahua-toting noughties alter ego. My first book, published in 2017, had a millennial pink cover too.

Then there was the obsession with successful women's morning routines, a lifestyle magazine-friendly subset of the self-optimisation drive sweeping through our wider culture (example: *'rise at dawn, meditate, journal, yoga. At desk by 6 a.m.'*). There was the popularisation of the pantsuit, courtesy of Hillary Clinton's ill-fated 2016 presidential run, an item of clothing that for a certain breed of young, urbane, relatively affluent and self-identified 'nasty woman', came to symbolise another form of subversion, this time of an item traditionally associated with male power. Words like 'She-E-O' and 'mompreneur' entered the lexicon, competing with 'girlboss' to most effectively condescend to women who were running their own businesses. The sleep-when-you're-dead school of work–life balance was alive and well here too, helped along by Beyoncé lyrics exhorting us to 'grind 'til we owned it'. Everyone had a side hustle, and everyone posted about it on Instagram.

In a way, it makes perfect sense that women, particularly millennial women, would embrace this narrative, given the gendered barriers that so often characterise our experiences of the workplace, and especially considering that at that time we didn't yet have the outlet of the #MeToo movement. Combine the generational plight of millennials with the gender-specific concerns most women face at work, and the emergency parachute for those caught in the middle of that particular Venn diagram starts to look a lot like a blush-pink bullet journal with the word HUSTLE stamped across it in gold foil. Indeed, the UK's self-employment boom in the decade to 2018 was primarily fuelled by women,[3] many of whom were disillusioned by corporate environments and looked to girlbossery as a way out. Living my own post-graduation nightmare, I embraced it too, galvanised.

And even as the word's inventor fell out of fashion (quite literally – Nasty Gal was forced to file for bankruptcy in late 2016), a new crop of female business icons sprang up to assume the mantle. Where Amoruso had fulfilled the role of the fashion rebel, her successors slotted neatly into other category-appropriate archetypes: there was *Vogue* staffer-turned-beauty mogul Emily Weiss, founder of billion-dollar millennial beauty brand Glossier; nice girl Whitney Wolfe Herd, founder of the 'female-friendly' dating app Bumble where 'women make the first move'; all-American wholesomeness courtesy of Ty Haney, the Texas-dwelling, sports-loving founder of athleisure apparel company Outdoor Voices; and political wonk Audrey Gelman, a former Hillary Clinton campaign staffer and co-founder of women's co-working space The Wing. Amoruso herself staged a comeback of sorts, eventually parlaying the girlboss brand into a media company of the same name, her positioning softer and less swaggering than in her first incarnation, perhaps more mindful of the potential for sudden catastrophe at a fast-growing start-up. A glossy posse of relatively affluent twenty- and thirty-somethings, to many millennial women – myself included – these female founders embodied the height of career success. They were aspirational in the way women in the public eye have learned to be, that is, carefully balancing their obvious success and considerable wealth with studied relatability. An Instagram post announcing the purchase of a plush new apartment would be followed by one in which they picked up their dog's poop. They were all, of course, very attractive. In another life they might have been models – some, like Glossier's Emily Weiss, actually had been.

They were also all white. Few of the female founders who've become household names among millennial women are women of colour – and why would they be? The vast majority of venture capital funding, which is the rocket fuel that's allowed most of these start-ups to flourish, overwhelmingly goes to white women (when it goes to women at all). Female founders get around 2.7 per cent of the venture capital pie, with women of colour getting virtually none: 0.2 per cent.[4] Black and brown women who've raised VC money are, to borrow the Silicon Valley parlance, actual unicorns.

But we've been here before. These women are all heirs to the Sandberg throne, only lightly tweaking the model of female ambition that the Facebook exec promoted in her 2013 career manual-slash-feminist manifesto *Lean In*. For a time, the workplace philosophy outlined by Sheryl Sandberg was formative in shaping what female success should look like, how it should be harnessed, what goals were the 'right' goals for ambitious women to strive towards. And yet for all the millions of copies sold, for all of the hype surrounding its impeccably slick roll-out and the gushing endorsements from high-profile names (Gloria Steinem, Arianna Huffington, Oprah), criticism of *Lean In* from its intended audience – feminist women – was both immediate and sustained, even spawning book-length ripostes, as with political journalist Dawn Foster's *Lean Out*.

The problem? That Sandberg seemed less concerned with challenging the status quo than she did encouraging women to adapt to it. The feminism *Lean In* promotes is also focused – almost obsessively so – on the idea that having more women 'at the top' will necessarily benefit all women. 'If we can succeed in adding more female voices at the highest levels', Sandberg writes, 'we will expand opportunities and extend fairer treatment to all,' displaying what Jessa Crispin refers to in her own book *Why I Am Not A Feminist* as 'the tendency of contemporary feminism to see women in power as an inherent good', regardless of how said women actually wield their influence.

Other criticisms of *Lean In* pointed out the fundamental classism of Sandberg's advice, much of which only feasibly applies to professional women of a certain milieu, and assumes a degree of agency that many working women simply do not have. One wonders if a minimum wage service worker on a zero hours contract would be able to successfully negotiate a higher salary by 'leaning in' and pushing for a raise at work. A more likely outcome is that she'd be fired. Then there's the fact that success as Sheryl Sandberg conceived of it for working mothers is only really possible if they are able to rely on the services of other women occupying low-paid, precarious and often racialised service roles – nannies, cleaners, housekeepers et cetera. *Lean In* makes little mention of what success might look like for the coterie of household staff required to make a career like Sandberg's – or the ones she seems most interested in championing – logistically possible. As the labour market specialist Professor Alison Wolf argues (most notably in her 2013 book *The XX Factor*), 'there are large numbers of women who are doing very, very poorly paid jobs, which make the lives of better paid women possible'.[5] Though *Lean In* encouraged women to smash the glass ceiling, it made little provision for the women on the ground floor who would have to walk over the shards of glass left in their wake.

Perhaps the most heavily contested aspect of *Lean In*'s feminist philosophy, and the one that would earn Sandberg most criticism over time, was the theory that gave the book its title – the idea that more women could rise to the upper echelons of corporate structures if they simply 'leaned in' more, by being more assertive and setting more ambitious goals. At one point Sandberg suggests there might be a 'leadership ambition gap' between men and women, writing that 'since more men aim for leadership roles, it is not surprising that they obtain them'. It's a logic that leaves little room for the harsh reality that even when women *do* lean in, we are often knocked back, hard. (After all, remember that we are more likely to be denied pay rises than men are, and are often penalised for even daring to ask.) The notion that women can overcome gendered discrimination by modifying our own behaviour also neatly elides the structural forces underpinning these disparities. As Michelle Obama would later comment in an unguarded moment during a live interview, 'it's not always enough to lean in, because that shit doesn't work all the time'.[6]

Sandberg and those who followed in her wake became poster girls for a certain type of contemporary feminism, one that critics say is lacking in substance and scope, and focuses only on the needs of a narrow subset of already privileged women; a version of feminism that is toothless and apolitical and fails to challenge the injustice of existing power structures, aiming only to insert women at the top of them. This type of feminism, commonly referred to as neoliberal feminism, tends to overlook the aspects of feminist thought concerned with collective social justice that necessarily place it in direct opposition to capitalism. Exploring this tension, the academic Nancy Holmstrom explains it thus: 'feminists should be concerned with ending the oppression of women whatever the causes, be they sexism, racism or economic, or some combination difficult to disentangle. *A feminism concerned only with ending the oppression of women based on gender would be a very limited version, far from the emancipatory vision at its core*' (italics mine).[7] That feminism necessarily aims to eradicate *any* inequality arising from identity-based discrimination makes it fundamentally incompatible with capitalism, an economic system that not only creates inequality, but actually *requires* it in order to work properly. Inequality isn't just an unfortunate side-effect of capitalism but rather the very basis of it, as essential to capitalism's effective functioning as wheels are to a bike.

And yet in recent years feminism and capitalism have become increasingly comfortable bedfellows, shoehorned into alignment by the simple fact that these days, feminism is big business. After a stretch in the wilderness around the turn of the century, when the myth of 'post-feminism' saw some claim that parity had been reached and that feminism's work was done, the early 2010s saw the emergence of a new wave of feminist discourse. This was (and is) a primarily digitally driven movement, characterised by discussions around sexual violence against women and the pervasiveness of everyday sexism; body positivity and the challenging of traditional beauty standards; empowerment narratives such as Sheryl Sandberg's and Sophia Amoruso's; and greater intersectionality (that is, consideration of female experiences beyond those of the relatively privileged white women who have traditionally been at the centre of mainstream feminist discourse). Feminism was once again back on the cultural agenda and, thanks to endorsements from various high-profile celebrities (Beyoncé, Emma Watson, Chimamanda Ngozi Adichie, to name a select few), it was actually also *cool*.

Of course, where there is cultural relevancy to be mined, capitalism will be there, pickaxe at the ready. These days nearly every brand marketing to women has found a way to incorporate feminist rhetoric or visuals into its marketing, whether that's Dove's ongoing 'Real Beauty' campaign, a pioneer of the format, or Nike's 2019 'Dream Crazier' advert, a 90-second Serena Williams-narrated clip in which women are urged to rethink our stance on 'hysterical' necessarily being a pejorative. There are self-styled feminist brands, like the period underwear company Thinx, and advertorials published in women's magazines combine inspirational feminist narratives with a plug for whichever brand has underwritten the publication's bills for the month. Such is the potential for profit that so-called 'feminists' are emerging from the unlikeliest of corners, with public figures including Kim Kardashian and Ivanka Trump rushing to align themselves with feminism. That their respective CVs encompass flogging appetite-suppressant lollipops to teenage girls and playing handmaiden to a regime hell-bent on curtailing women's access to abortion, is an irony the duo seem to have overlooked.

This is what writer Andi Zeisler refers to as 'femvertising'[8] – a heavily sanitised, commerce-friendly strain of feminism-as-sales-tactic. Mainstream feminism has gone from radical anti-capitalist ideology to a product to be bought and sold and used to burnish personal brands, and as is often the case, the message adapts to fit the medium. While social media has been instrumental in allowing this wave of feminism to reach a wider audience, it also often reduces it to caption-length maxims that fail to convey any meaningful political intent. '*The future is female.*' '*Support your local girl gang.*'

Perhaps the most high-profile example of how effectively this cultural moment came to be commercialised appears in the form of The Wing. An exclusive women-only members' club and co-working space that opened in 2016, its stated mission was 'the professional, civic, social, and economic advancement of women through community' – and from the moment photos began to emerge of its inaugural space, an airy twelfth-floor penthouse in Manhattan's Flatiron district, The Wing became an instant phenomenon. Dozens of enthusiastic press features followed, and the waitlist for membership quickly ballooned into the thousands. The club's target audience appeared to be a certain class of urbane, social media-literate and politically liberal career women, who wore their feminism proudly on their sleeves and more importantly, could also afford the $185–$250 monthly membership fee. Women not unlike The Wing's two co-founders, Audrey Gelman and Lauren Kassan, who perfectly fit the prevailing model of female success by virtue of being two relatively young and highly mediagenic female entrepreneurs who spoke about their business in mission-driven terms. Gelman in particular was already something of a New York It-girl prior to the club's launch, a stalwart of the city's social circuit and a regular fixture on the pages of *Vogue* and *Vanity Fair*. Her role as the company's CEO accounted for a good proportion of the initial buzz. So too did the club's roster of founding members, which read like a who's who of New York's most aspirational career women, a carefully selected mix of female founders and creatives that signalled the company's intended values, and whose names were judiciously deployed in its PR efforts. There was Glossier CEO Emily Weiss and J Crew's then president Jenna Lyons; writer Lena Dunham (a close friend of Gelman's) and former *Vanity Fair* editor Tina Brown. A few slightly less obvious choices marked The Wing out as being cut from a more discerning cloth than most: Bronx-born rapper Remy Ma, and the actress Natasha Lyonne; while a selection of editors from various New York media prestige titles rounded out the list by providing a measure of bluestocking chic (not to mention favourable press).

From the start, it was clear that The Wing had taken the Sheryl Sandberg formula and improved on it, and that this was the brainchild of women who had noted the criticisms levied against Sandberg's myopic version of feminism and hoped to circumnavigate them. For starters, there was a clear political strand to The Wing's efforts that had been notably absent from Sandberg's *Lean In* project. Wing members were bussed to the 2017 Women's March on Washington DC to protest Donald Trump's inauguration, and the club's events calendar kept up a steady stream of boldface political names the rest of the time, from progressive youth-favourite Alexandria Ocasio-Cortez to elder stateswoman Hillary Clinton. Even Michelle Obama was rumoured[9] to have quietly slipped in and out of an event at the company's DC outpost. Its membership base seemed reasonably diverse too, as evidenced by social media posts where women with bantu knots and box braids were pictured side by side with trans women and sex workers – the sort of women whose existence had seemingly never even occurred to Sheryl Sandberg; the sort of women who might describe themselves not as women, but as womxn.

Then there were the highly Instagrammable interiors, full of cutesy touches designed to appeal to its female demographic – an instantly recognisable pastel colour palette that made generous use of millennial pink (by now the designated colour of female ambition); plush velvet sofas and tasteful mid-century furniture; a dedicated 'beauty room' complete with vanity mirrors and illustrated wallpaper; a lending library in which books were arranged neither alphabetically nor by genre (as one might expect) but by colour. Each of The Wing's eleven outposts was carefully designed to encourage sharing on social media, and members and guests happily obliged, regularly Instagramming photos of the provided set pieces – a sign in the café that said 'I'll have what she's having', a neon light that spelled out 'No Man's Land'. It would be years before I actually physically set foot in one of The Wing's spaces myself, but the first time I did I had the almost physically disorientating sensation of having stepped inside my phone. My brain had become so used to experiencing the spaces as a flat two-dimensional amalgam of pixels that in 3-D the whole thing felt slightly unreal, even hallucinatory.

Impressively for what was at its core a co-working space, The Wing's brand of woke feminist Manhattanite cool became strong enough for the company to do a brisk trade in feminist-themed merch. Key rings inscribed with the motto 'Girls Doing Whatever The Fuck They Want' retailed on its website for $17.50; for $32 aspiring girlbosses could avail themselves of a T-shirt that said 'Casual Business Woman' on its breast pocket. That these products were available for both members and non-members to buy meant that even women who didn't live in one of the cities where The Wing had set up camp – or those who simply couldn't afford its membership fees – could still be monetised. Unsurprisingly, given the clear scope for profit, the concept spawned several imitators, with trendy female-focused members' clubs springing up everywhere from London (the AllBright) to Seattle (the Riveter). However none of them were able to replicate the specific alchemy of social cachet and savvy branding that saw The Wing's Instagram grow to over half a million followers, and the company raise $117.5 million[10] in venture capital funding.

And it was against this backdrop of enthusiastic commercialism that a groundswell of criticism began to build, turning The Wing into an ideological battleground, a proxy for long-running arguments about how mainstream feminism addresses class and race and privilege, and how it intersects with the demands of capitalism. Because although The Wing's mission statement asserted that the company was 'intentional about creating an inclusive space where everyone belongs – regardless of race, ethnicity, religion, age, sexual orientation, ability, gender identity, or socio-economic background', a members' club requiring up to $3,000 a year in membership fees would never really be accessible to working-class or low-income women (who are statistically also more likely to be women of colour). The Wing's undeniable benefits – community, the opportunity to make valuable connections, its numerous amenities – were limited to the affluent middle- and upper-class women who could afford them, and had the requisite social capital to be accepted as a member. Consequently, it became a symbol of the worst sins of neoliberal feminism; though where Sheryl Sandberg had been somewhat more oblique in excluding certain women, The Wing more clearly delineated who it was 'for'. You were either a member, with all the attendant benefits, or a non-member, in which case you had to make do with a branded key ring. This was pay-to-play female empowerment, where already privileged women could buy the resources and connections that would allow them to become even more so. In that sense The Wing probably came closer to emulating the patriarchal dynamics it sought to counter than it did to disrupting them (and lest we forget, for a time its biggest investor was WeWork, the pinnacle of the fratty 'beers and ping-pong' co-working culture The Wing's co-founders had positioned themselves against at launch. At one point WeWork owned a 23 per cent stake[11] in the company).

Then there was the company's use of feminist rhetoric and visual language as a marketing tool, which ranged from the predictable – posting vintage black and white photos of feminist icons to its Instagram feed (and who among us) – to the crass. Days after Dr Christine Blasey Ford's 2018 testimony against soon-to-be Supreme Court Justice Brett Kavanaugh, in which she recounted the painful memory of having allegedly been sexually assaulted by Kavanaugh and friends as a teenager, I opened Instagram to find that The Wing had unveiled a conference room[12] named in her honour in its newly opened San Francisco space. Looking at the gold-stencilled sign on the room's glass doors, Ford's name set against a backdrop of cheerily patterned pink and red wallpaper, I cringed. It felt tacky and opportunistic, as though The Wing was capitalising on a private individual's public trauma to funnel attention towards its brand, specifically the 8,000 square feet of San Francisco real estate it had just leased. Translating the magnitude of that moment to a twee stencil decal felt like a strange flattening of Ford's suffering, an insistence on relentlessly aestheticising feminist discourse and finding a way to cram something as big and as raw and as fundamentally ugly as Ford's experience into the confines of The Wing's pastel pink ecosystem. It simply didn't fit.

The problem for The Wing's founders was having built their house on an ideological fault line. As Linda Kinstler wrote for the *Guardian*, it was a business 'founded upon a paradox: its brand is steeped in the feminist language of emancipation, empowerment and equality, while its business is based on one of society's most elitist institutions: the private members' club'.[13] It's tempting to explain away the intense scrutiny The Wing has been subject to as being rooted purely in sexism (as the company's founders, members and supporters have on occasion done), and it's certainly true that The Wing was criticised more frequently and with a vigour that other similarly exclusive members' clubs largely seem to avoid. Whether published by feminist website Jezebel, with its trademark anti-establishment snarkiness, or the more measured tones of the *New York Times*' culture section, there was and is an undeniable sense of schadenfreude underpinning the many, many takedowns of The Wing that have been published over the years. Its founders, Gelman especially, seemed to make headlines for transgressions that one suspects are par for the course among company executives but which largely go unreported on when the perpetrators are male. At times they were criticised for transgressions that were not really transgressions at all – one such takedown focused on Gelman's refusal to wash dishes at one of the club's spaces,[14] which seems to me not an unreasonable position for a company CEO to take.

But then again, none of The Wing's competitors – the Soho House Group for instance, or even competitor-turned-investor WeWork – claimed to be enacting some form of social good, nor had they benefited from the cultural equity of so vociferously aligning themselves with a political ideology built on equality. A feminist project that discriminates based on income, class or social capital cannot accurately describe itself as feminist, and it was this perceived hypocrisy that put a target on The Wing's back. The problem was not what The Wing was but what it claimed to be, and that it purported to be something that it demonstrably was not. We do not like it when individuals or companies claim to be something they are not, and go on to make money out of that deceit – that is the dictionary definition of a con. In Jia Tolentino's essay collection *Trick Mirror*, girlboss feminism and companies like The Wing are cited as being among the definitive scams of the millennial generation, an analysis that helps explain why the company's existence became so controversial. Commoditised feminism offends because it patronises its audience by assuming we aren't smart enough to realise that our beliefs are being distorted in order to sell us things; because the productisation of feminism and positioning of consumer purchases as somehow revolutionary lulls us into a false sense of achievement, diverting attention away from the sort of actions that might actually enact social change; and because it is cynical and disingenuous and ultimately, self-serving.

Now here's the kicker: I was, for a while, a member of The Wing.

A few months before the company opened its London outpost in 2019, I was offered a free membership and invited to become one of its founding members – a perk of my career as a writer having given me something of a public profile. (Of course there's no such thing as a free lunch, or a free co-working membership. I was always aware of the unspoken terms of the deal, that The Wing was aligning itself with me as a way of signalling its brand values, and that in exchange for my lending them some of what little social capital I've managed to acquire in recent years, I would be allowed to use the space for free.) I deliberated over the offer for a while, WhatsApping a few friends to ask whether saying yes would make me a 'bad feminist'. *Don't be such a bloody martyr*, came one response. *What's The Wing?*, read another. In the end, I accepted. In exchange for a free membership, access to The Wing's network of career-minded women, its roster of events, and the use of a co-working space in central London, all I had to do was . . . well, I didn't have to do anything. There was a photo shoot for a spread in *Vogue*, but that wasn't exactly a hardship. Still, as soon as the *Vogue* article was published, essentially pegging me as an unofficial brand ambassador, I began to field questions from friends and acquaintances, usually nomadic freelancers like me, anxious about whether or not to join. They all seemed to be weighing up the decision with a seriousness that far outstripped the level of thought I imagine they'd usually dedicate to deciding whether or not to join a members' club. I sensed that on some level many of them were looking for approval, worried about what joining The Wing might indicate about their own feminism – similarly to how I'd consulted with friends before accepting my own membership. 'I mean, when you break it down it's really just a co-working space,' I began to respond. 'So if you need somewhere to take meetings and you like the vibe of it, then yeah go ahead and join. Don't overthink it.'

And I meant it. Arguments surrounding The Wing's feminist credentials resulted in the act of membership itself being framed as, if not immoral, then certainly somehow anti-feminist, imbued with a moral weight that I just didn't feel it warranted. I struggled to accept that there was something unethical about women who wanted to and could afford to join The Wing doing so (although of course there's a broader, non-gender specific, conversation to be had about the inherent elitism of members' clubs as a concept). That logic would imply that it's not possible to be a 'good' feminist if you want, or have access to, things that other women do not, which to me feels like an impossibly high standard to set, or achieve. Joining The Wing certainly wasn't a feminist act, but neither did it strike me as actively anti-feminist.

It felt strange too, the assumption that The Wing's members had necessarily bought into the company's feminist-themed marketing, that they might not just be interested in a women-only co-working space with the kind of thoughtful amenities that few other competitors provided, such as on-site daycare or pump rooms for breastfeeding mothers. Similar expectations are rarely made of other brand–consumer relationships – many of us patronise brands whose marketing we neither agree with nor like, but whose products we enjoy or find useful. (I personally can't stomach the condescending tones of Dove's 'Real Beauty' marketing spiel, but my conscience remains untroubled by the fact that their bar soap is a staple in my bathroom cabinet; it smells uncommonly good.) That The Wing's member base happened to be made up entirely of women somehow didn't feel incidental to that heightened expectation of total ideological conformity.

Still, I ended up terminating my Wing membership after only five months, a decision driven by lots of little things – that my experience of the company had often felt hollow and trans-actional (and really, what should I have expected); that it was far from the buzzing feminist kibbutz I'd envisioned; that suggestions I'd made about forming a steering committee to work on making the company's membership more diverse had been met with polite disinterest – and one big thing. In March 2020, the *New York Times* (having previously lavished The Wing with glowing praise[15]) published an article that struck an altogether more negative tone, a 5,000-word exposé detailing a culture of employee mistreatment, where casual racism by members frequently went unpunished and unaddressed by the company's management.[16] One incident described a Wing member referring to the company's Black employees as 'coloured girls'. Another member had taken umbrage with a group of local teenage girls who'd been invited to The Wing for an event speaking Spanish in her presence.

Even though aspects of the article felt thinly reported, based on my own experiences of toxic workplaces, it seemed obvious to me that what was being reported was likely only the tip of the ice-berg, and it didn't take much imagination to colour in what had been left out. One complaint in particular struck a nerve, and felt true to my experiences of the company as a member; accus-ations from women of colour who'd worked for The Wing that the company had used their ethnicity as a marketing tactic, liber-ally posting them on social media to give the illusion of diversity, without actually following through in its day-to-day operations. The Wing's community was not – despite its many claims to the contrary – particularly diverse. After my membership was confirmed, I had logged on to its online members' directory, and scrolling through page after page of tiny avatars, one thing quickly became very clear.

'Wow,' I texted a friend, who was considering also becoming a member. 'It is really, *really* white.'

That disconnect, between the social media presentation of its membership base and the clear reality of it, niggled at me. The company's vocal commitment to intersectionality suddenly seemed to be more about the optics than anything else, an attempt to counter accusations that projects like The Wing primarily benefit affluent white women by wielding the faces of Black, Latina, queer and trans women as shields against possible accusations of elitism.

Then there were the damning testimonials written by former employees on the company's Glassdoor page, many of which alluded to a hierarchy of race among its staff. 'Most of the "help staff" are people of colour, while the majority management (and members) are wealthy white women. It's like a country club,' one former employee had written. Another suggested that the company needed to 'get real about the fact that the WOC are supporting your spaces and that this is a white-focused company, despite the fact they show it differently in social media'. Yet another, 'it's also quite obvious that much of the help is WOC, while members are upper-class white women, which made me uncomfortable'.

In the end it wasn't The Wing's heavily commoditised brand of feminism that motivated me to leave. That bothered me somewhat, but truthfully (clearly) had not bothered me enough to prevent me from joining. I hadn't been naïve enough to imagine that my joining The Wing constituted some sort of feminist statement, or indeed that my membership somehow benefited anyone other than myself – and I was fine with that. I wasn't fine with the possibility that, particularly as a reasonably high profile Black woman, my continued membership might somehow help The Wing to airbrush its reputation, or with the comforts my complimentary membership afforded me being predicated on the exploitation of other women, particularly other women of colour.

The Wing's fall from grace was symptomatic of a broader cultural shift – a scepticism towards girlboss culture that was at first just a whisper among the feminist media commentariat whose literal job it is to criticise these things (a category in which I include myself), but which slowly began to claim even women who had previously been its most ardent fans. If 2014–2016 were the glory days of girlboss culture, then 2017 onwards was when things began to unravel. The initial chink in the armour was arguably the brutal shock of Donald Trump's election in November 2016, evidence of how powerless the pantsuits-and-pearls cosplay of Hillary-affiliated girlboss feminism was in the face of real, unadulterated evil. It was a stark reminder that there were far greater dangers than a mansplaining colleague or a disappointing performance review (which for a while had been framed as the greatest threats a woman might face). Even for those of us not in the USA, Trump's election was a wake-up call emphasising the need for a deeper, more substantive, more *political* version of feminism to combat the real crises that were likely to follow. Relying on girlboss feminism, with its Nasty Woman T-shirts and 'power poses', suddenly felt like rushing into the Battle of Waterloo waving a plastic toy sword.

This collective awakening was reflected by a shift in tone among mainstream women's media titles, who if nothing else, understood that they would need to evolve in line with the changing mood in order to stay relevant. *Teen Vogue*, a magazine previously dedicated to covering the exploits of New York teen socialites and their bedroom makeovers, aggressively pivoted towards politics and activism, to great success. Website traffic skyrocketed correspondingly, and the virality of an anti-Trump op-ed by journalist Lauren Duca titled *Donald Trump Is Gaslighting America* published in December 2016 saw the magazine sell more print subscriptions that month[17] than it had during the whole of 2016. Trump's ascent to power also precipitated the embrace of a more radically progressive political framework among many on the left, including among the sort of youngish liberal women who were otherwise the prime targets for girlboss rhetoric. The popularity of political figures like Jeremy Corbyn in the UK, and Bernie Sanders and Alexandria Ocasio-Cortez in the USA, introduced democratic socialism to many who had never before conceived of it, which in turn saw many young women seek a feminism more concerned with securing the rights of the masses than celebrating the successes of a relatively privileged few; a feminism focused on employees, not bosses, perhaps in recognition of the fact that employees is what most of us are.

Then there was the fact that the shortcomings of so many of the companies and individuals that had been at the forefront of the girlboss movement were slowly coming to light, exposing the inconsistencies between their marketing and their day-to-day operations. Even before Sophia Amoruso's Nasty Gal filed for bankruptcy in 2016, a spate of stories documenting employee mistreatment had made their way into the press, alleging that the company had systematically and illegally fired pregnant employees,[18] that multiple rounds of employee redundancies had created a culture of fear, and that Amoruso herself had fostered a toxic and bullying workplace environment.[19] Period-proof underwear company Thinx, whose provocative fruit-as-genitalia-themed adverts earned the company an army of fans and reams of positive press coverage faced similar problems. In 2017, the company's self-described 'feminist SHE-E-O' Miki Agrawal faced multiple allegations of employee bullying and sexual harassment, with female employees also alleging that they had been systematically underpaid and received inadequate healthcare coverage.[20] Shortly afterwards, Agrawal stepped down as the company's CEO. In 2019, Steph Korey, co-founder and CEO of luggage brand AWAY, who along with her co-founder Jen Rubio had greatly benefited from the wave of positive press tied in with the girlboss narrative, was reported[21] to have bullied and overworked several employees. Slack messages leaked to journalists revealed a mercurial and at times outright cruel leadership style that was deeply at odds with the inclusive, community-focused brand image that the company had crafted. As more and more of these nightmare female founder stories began to emerge, they called into question the gender essentialism that was the bedrock of girlboss theory, the idea that women are inherently good and moral leaders. Evidently, being a female leader didn't magically preclude you from mistreating your employees. The 'feminism' underpinning the girlboss model of success began to look increasingly shaky.

The Wing itself finally imploded during the summer of 2020. On 11 June, co-founder and CEO Audrey Gelman announced her resignation from the company, referring to the need to 'bring The Wing along into a long overdue era of change'.[22] Hours later, many of her former employees announced via coordinated social media statements that they were staging a 'digital walkout', citing poor management, incidents of racism, exploitation of Black and brown employees, and the toxic work culture first reported by the *New York Times* a few months earlier. Gelman's resignation came as part of a global reckoning with institutional racism and workplace discrimination triggered by George Floyd's murder in May 2020. As a new wave of Black Lives Matter protests surged, several high-profile brands known for their progressive, feminist stances were publicly taken to task for not adhering to those values in private, and for perpetuating abuses against Black and minority staff. On the same day that Gelman publicly resigned from The Wing, Leandra Medine Cohen, founder of fashion website Man Repeller, also stepped down as her company's CEO, in light of criticism of the website's lack of diversity and of her decision to lay off several Black employees in the middle of a pandemic that had affected Black Americans more severely than any other demographic. The next day, another *mea culpa*: Yael Aflalo, founder and CEO of cult clothing brand Reformation, resigned as her company's CEO following accusations from former employees that she had presided over a racist company culture where Black employees routinely faced discriminatory treatment. So too with Christene Barberich, co-founder and editor-in-chief at Refinery29, who resigned as stories emerged that several former employees had endured a litany of racist microaggressions while working for the company, including from Barberich herself.

The fantasy had crumbled, unable to withstand a social uprising that challenged the allocation of power and privilege along race and class lines – the very threads that had always been loose in the fabric finally coming completely undone. Still as these breakdowns unfolded in the press and across social media, more than ever it became clear to me that the cultural appetite for female founder takedown stories far outstrips that for male ones. There was a certain mocking glee that accompanied the news of these women's demise, a certain 'told you so' energy on social media that differed from the tenor of the reactions I'd observed in relation to two similarly high-profile male CEO exits in recent years: Travis Kalanick of Uber in 2017, and Adam Neumann of WeWork in 2019. To pretend that the *only* motivation behind the intensity of the backlash towards these female founders is a desire to hold them accountable, or dismay at their ethical transgressions, would be wilfully obtuse. For all their genuine missteps, these women were also unquestionably held to higher standards than those imposed on their male counterparts, who have to fall on their swords far less frequently, and certainly not for the level of company dysfunction most of these women had presided over. It took a disastrously botched IPO to compel Adam Neumann to resign from WeWork, having survived numerous reports over the years of fostering a frat-boy culture rife with sexual misconduct; while Uber's Travis Kalanick had survived a string of controversies[23] as CEO of the company, including high-profile sexual harassment claims, frequent regulatory and consumer complaints, and being caught on camera berating an Uber driver who had voiced concerns to him about the company's falling fares. There is a clear disparity in the treatment of and consequences for female founders who mess up – which isn't to say that excuses should be made for them simply because they are women, but rather that male founders ought to be held to the same standards.

It's worth considering too, why the narrative of the 'fallen girlboss' has such staying power. While I can easily reel off a list of 'toxic female founders', aside from the aforementioned Neumann and Kalanick I struggle to come up with a similar list for male ones – which, given that globally male founders far outnumber female ones, is certainly odd. Perhaps these sorts of stories fail to emerge about men because they are simply kinder, more empathetic, morally upstanding leaders, though somehow, I doubt that's the case.

In August 1990, feminist activist and writer Gloria Steinem published an article in *Ms.* magazine titled 'Sex, Lies & Advertising', detailing the struggles she'd faced as its founding editor in 1972.[24] One of *Ms.*'s founding principles had been a commitment to producing the kind of substantive, intelligent journalism then largely absent from the women's media landscape, which at the time was dominated by publications that often amounted to little more than a vehicle for branded advertorials. Admirable as this approach was, refusing to publish the fluffy lifestyle articles expected of women's titles in the seventies meant that *Ms.*'s publishers faced a constant battle to attract enough ad revenue to keep the magazine going. Steinem writes that the title was regularly blacklisted by advertisers who deemed its values dangerously progressive. She also documents the numerous occasions on which she and her team valiantly held the line against corporations used to parlaying their ad spend into editorial control, but concludes the piece with a reflection on how they too occasionally fell short: 'I'm just beginning to realise how edges got smoothed down – in spite of all our resistance.' She recalls changing the word 'Porsche' to 'car' in an article by Andrea Dworkin about Nazi imagery in German pornography, 'feeling sure Andrea would understand that Volkswagen, the distributor of Porsche and one of our few supportive advertisers, asked only to be far away from Nazi subjects.'

A half-century on from *Ms.*'s inception, the difficulty of trying to reconcile feminism – the logical endpoint of which has to be anti-capitalism – with more prosaic economic concerns is as complicated as it ever was, perhaps even more so thanks to the increasingly unrelenting conditions of modern globalised capitalism. For me, and I imagine for many other women, that challenge is further complicated by my desire to thrive under the prevailing economic system even as I recognise its many flaws, and my understanding that doing so requires me to have a certain amount of capital. Though girlboss feminism is rightly criticised for its tendency to frame wealth acquisition as feminist praxis, as a Black, female, first-generation immigrant who has witnessed first-hand how acquiring the trappings of wealth (namely a private education) can mitigate an otherwise marginalised social position, part of me finds that critique a little tough to swallow.

In *Why I Am Not A Feminist* Jessa Crispin takes aim at the notion that the ability to personally buy oneself respite from the crosswinds of patriarchy constitutes real progress for women as a class, writing: 'There is a way a woman can deflect the worst effects of patriarchal control, and that is through money. Make enough of it and you can escape the patriarchy's most obvious trappings . . . Money is a quick and easy way to check out of many pernicious forms of oppression.'

Of course, Crispin intended that analysis to be an indictment of corporate feminism's shortcomings and evidence of its ethical flimsiness – but rotated a little and viewed from a slightly different angle, I can't help but feel that it sounds like salvation.

Chapter 9

RUMSPRINGA

After I left Vice, for the first time in my life I felt like I'd truly failed. There I was, back in my teenage bedroom, with no job, no income, and no idea of what I was going to do next. My early forays into the world of work had been a bitter disappointment, and I was convinced my career would never recover from the impending gap on my CV, a fear further stoked by the colleague who in my final weeks at the company had warned that I was 'making a mistake' by leaving. For months afterwards his words weighed on my mind, crowding out all other thoughts.

You've made a mistake.

To his credit, I *did* feel as though I'd made a mistake, an enormous one – not just with Vice, but at every stage leading up to it. I was furious with myself for not having made different choices, for not having pursued journalism more seriously after graduating and submitting myself to the merry-go-round of unpaid internships that I imagined would by now have borne fruit. I worried that I would be unemployed for years, and began to panic at the thought of 'falling behind' when – overachiever that I am – I was so used to being ahead, so used to ticking the right boxes at the right time and knowing what the future held. I tormented myself for having been unable to stick it out at Vice, for not being thicker-skinned, for not having mastered the real-politik required to survive there.

You've wasted the last five years of your life, and now you have to start from scratch. Well fucking done.

I spent whole days in bed, and whole weeks indoors, crying, unshowered and (I later realised) deeply depressed.

And of course, true to form, I worried constantly about money.

My only objective was to start earning money again, and within a few days of leaving Vice, I'd found a tutoring gig with a company that specialised in farming out well-spoken Oxbridge graduates to the wealthy families who could afford its exorbitant rates. The money was good, and the work was easy – £60 an hour to spellcheck writing assignments, correct quizzes, and occasionally play board games with a slightly anxious 10 year old. I hated every minute of it. I was part of a coterie of expensive tutors and nannies assigned to the family's two children, and I felt deeply confronted by their obvious wealth; I found the idea of further smoothing the path of someone who already had so many advantages galling. I felt uncomfortable too, at the dynamic between me and the parents who'd hired me, who at times made me feel like a commodity they had purchased, plucked off the shelf and ready to be cast aside at a moment's notice. After only a few sessions I cried off sick, making limp excuses as to why I wouldn't be returning, and crawled back into bed to lick my wounds. Rather than being gentle with myself and taking time to regroup after the genuinely traumatic experience I'd had at Vice, I had forced myself back into work before I was really ready, only to find that I was too depleted, and too mentally exhausted to cope. Looking back on it now, it was an unnecessarily self-flagellating choice, given I had the good fortune to be living rent-free, and had thousands of pounds stashed away in savings – yet it was as if that money didn't exist. I'd only managed to accumulate it in the first place by creating a strict mental barrier, staunchly refusing to dip into my savings for any sort of indulgence, and that rigid approach followed me into this new income-less phase of my life.

You might remember that in a previous chapter I discussed 'money vigilance', one of the four money scripts that most of us adhere to, and the script that I've identified as my own particular persuasion. What I didn't mention was that while money vigilants tend to prioritise saving and frugality – ostensibly sensible traits – our excessive financial caution often prevents us from enjoying the benefits and sense of security that money can provide, and can manifest as its own dysfunctional behaviour.[1] In some cases healthy vigilance can tip over into compulsive hoarding: a fear-based need to accumulate money (or objects), which can have adverse psychological consequences. If you derive mental comfort from saving up money, as I do, then being forced to spend it can be a source of real anxiety. It's only with the benefit of hindsight and a good deal of introspection that I now realise I spent my early twenties building up a savings pot with no intention of ever actually *spending* that money. I wasn't saving money – I was hoarding it. The prospect of no longer having that buffer terrified me, and I would lie awake at night worrying about my now dwindling savings, plagued by a constant, bone-deep sense of foreboding. Every bank transaction and phone bill, every TfL charge or meal out felt like the slow unravelling of a safety net I so desperately needed to feel secure, even as the more rational part of my brain recognised that *this* was the archetypal rainy-day scenario that one is supposed to save up for.

Years later I would realise that I'd developed what data journalist Mona Chalabi referred to as 'money dysmorphia' in a *Guardian* article in which she described how her fear of one day encountering some sort of financial crisis had led her to deprive herself of things she knew she could comfortably afford. 'I live in worst-case scenario mode to protect myself from the financial perils of naivety,' Chalabi wrote, describing how she'd scrimped on healthcare (Chalabi is based in the USA, where of course being sick comes with a price tag), visiting a cheap therapist with no qualifications and a dermatologist who left her with a rash. 'I worry that if I actually let myself accept that I have money now, it will be even more of a shock if poverty does come. I feel like I do not have money, even though I do.'[2]

Reading those words for the first time felt as though someone had traced the pattern of my brain and unlocked the secret of why I felt the way I did about money. Throughout my twenties I had deprived myself of things I wanted, things I could afford, things I could have reasonably justified spending money on, because I feared that one day those purchases would come back to haunt me, that I would look at a pair of expensive shoes bought during times of plenty, or tot up the cost of holidays past, and feel like a fool. I suspect Mona Chalabi is, like me, a money vigilant, someone who prioritises the accumulation of money over the pleasure they'd get from spending it, and in her case, as with mine, this dysmorphia stems from previous experiences of scarcity: for her, growing up in a home with 'peeling wallpaper and ancient maroon carpets' and later living in a 'cockroach infested, 100 sq ft bedsit'.

This probably seems like a relatively good money problem to have. I realise that, in the grand scheme of financial worries, simply *feeling* unable to spend money you have ranks far below not actually *having* enough money. Summon the world's tiniest violin et cetera. But so often, financial anxiety isn't necessarily a function of your economic reality, but rather the product of the experiences you've accumulated in years gone by. It is possible to *feel* as though you don't have enough money – and act accordingly – even when you do. In fact, perceived shortages of money can substantially hinder our ability to think and act rationally. In one study, conducted by a Harvard-based behavioural economist, researchers found that simply *thinking* about scarcity significantly diminished an individual's cognitive ability.[3] Even within the context of an artificially engineered scenario, where participants were aware they were taking part in a research project with no bearing on their real-world finances, the mere perception of scarcity caused their IQ scores to drop by an average of fourteen points – a greater drop than if they'd been forced to stay awake for twenty-four hours straight. These findings hold true regardless of socio-economic status – what is scarcity for one individual might well be considered abundance by another, though unsurprisingly, this mentality is more prevalent in those who grew up in financially precarious households. Even after periods of scarcity have ended, it's hard to shake the mindset.

The definition of insanity is doing the same thing over and over again and expecting different results, or so the saying goes.

A month or so after I walked out of Vice for the last time, a letter from a pension provider landed on my parents' doorstep, cheerily informing me that I still had another forty years to go until retirement, and as I read it, a thought slowly began to take shape in my mind, possibly even more of a premonition than a thought – that this just wouldn't work. I couldn't spend the next forty years doing the same thing I'd spent the last five doing – trying to mould myself to fit a system that simply wasn't designed for someone like me to thrive in, and somehow expect to find happiness or fulfilment. I knew too, that I couldn't return to the shitshow of agency life without sacrificing the thin sliver of sanity I had left, that I couldn't face a return to endless rounds of client feedback on things that, ultimately, no one truly gave a fuck about; to CEOs who described the work we did as though our agency were next in line for the Nobel Peace Prize or an Oscar, as though we were not simply a bunch of underpaid and over-worked salarymen trying to sell people things they didn't need to add to the pile of stuff they already had; to creative directors who secretly fantasised about jacking it all in to write a screenplay but couldn't bear to part with the six-figure salaries and Soho House memberships that validated their sense of self, and so instead resentfully churned out scripts for baby food adverts and threw tantrums when clients insisted on cutting 'the best joke'. I realised I had to find a way of working that didn't entirely crush me, something that made me feel bigger rather than smaller, full rather than empty. And there lay the problem – I had absolutely no idea what that might be.

Within the Amish community, teenagers on the cusp of adulthood are often permitted to embark on what is called a *rum-springa* (which loosely translates as 'running around') – a period of experimentation during which they're allowed to try out aspects of modern life traditionally prohibited by their faith, things like drinking alcohol and wearing non-traditional clothes, driving cars and using mobile phones. The broad aim, or the hope, of this tradition is that having experienced the outside world, Amish teenagers will then actively choose to commit to the Amish way of life, and happily so, rather than spending a lifetime wondering what they're missing out on and potentially defecting from the community in later life.

I resolved that I too would have a *rumspringa*, my own period of no-consequence experimentation and 'running around'. Rather than jumping straight into hunting for a new job, I decided instead to have a career gap year and explore my options, taking advantage of the relative financial freedom that being able to live at home with my parents afforded me. If at the end of that year I hadn't yet figured out my next move, then I would return to advertising, or perhaps try to find a marketing job at a charity or brand that had a social mission I could get behind, somewhere progressive where my year of experimental living might even be viewed as a selling point. In the meantime, I would take on whatever freelance work I needed to in order to earn my keep, and try my best to resist caving in to the pressure I'd always put on myself to be relentlessly moving up the career ladder. The year 2016, I decided, would be a career write-off, a black hole on my CV that I would find a way to creatively manoeuvre around once it came time to return to formal employment. Anything positive that came from the year ahead would be a bonus, but not the goal.

I decided too, to properly pursue an idea that had been bubbling away at the back of my mind ever since I'd started at Vice and it had dawned on me just how much of a boys' club I'd landed myself in. I'd wanted to set up some sort of blog or online network for women with creative interests, something that might give me a sense of community to counter the intense isolation I was feeling, and that might be an outlet for the growing confusion and angst I had about work, unable to figure out why *none* of these jobs seemed to be working out for me. Though the concept I had in mind was indisputably rooted in and influenced by girlboss culture, which was then in the ascendancy, I also saw it as a potential corrective to the aspects of that trend that I felt put off or excluded by. After initial optimism about their intentions, I'd become increasingly cynical about the sudden proliferation of female collectives and 'girl gangs' promising to empower young creative women, but seemingly concerned with feminism only inasmuch as it allowed them to line their pockets with brand money; and where the price of admission seemed to be being deemed sufficiently 'cool' or well-connected. In the earliest iteration of what I rather grandly referred to as the 'guiding principles' I wrote for what would end up becoming a platform called Women Who, I specified that I wanted it to be anti-'hashtag feminism', to foster practical (if boring) conversations about navigating creative careers, and to be open to all. I'd spent the first few months of my time at Vice quietly working on this idea at the weekends, sketching out logos and coming up with potential names, tinkering with a prototype website and asking friends for their opinions. But Vice had been so intense that I'd lacked the energy or time to really do anything outside of work, and towards the end of my time there I had let my plans for the blog gather dust, too exhausted to contemplate spending even more time at my laptop at the weekends. Now, with all the time in the world at my disposal, I decided to blow away the cobwebs and see what I could make of it, as much for myself as anyone else.

And, most importantly of all, I decided to seriously pursue the one thing I'd always wanted to do but had been continually turning away from: writing. I realised, finally, that simply ignoring that aspiration and throwing myself into advertising – as I'd been doing for the past few years – wouldn't make it just go away, that I would continue to feel unhappy and unfulfilled and wistfully envious of other writers, and that I needed, for my own peace of mind, to at least try.

Even in those early months, I think on some level I was already committing to self-employment for the long haul. I went as far as to open a second bank account for business expenses and find myself an accountant, contacting HMRC to inform them of my change in employment status and buying special software for tracking invoices. In hindsight it was an awful lot of trouble to go to for what was supposed to be a year-long stint of casual freelancing, even for a compulsive planner like me. By the spring of 2016, I was officially self-employed. Now I just needed to find some actual work – though I was being as frugal as I could, I was still burning through my savings at a terrifying rate. London has a way of emptying your pockets if you so much as dare to leave the house, let alone actually try to do anything. After a particularly depressing week, where I'd repeatedly traipsed into town for various vague meetings about potential freelance work that I knew deep down would never materialise, and had been stood up by not one but two of my meetings, I decided to swallow my pride. Sitting down at my laptop, I proceeded to send a personalised email to any and every contact I had who might be able to throw work my way, simultaneously updating my Facebook status with a chirpy 'is now freelancing!' addendum. I cringed as I did it – would people think I was begging for work? *No-one wants to hire a desperate person*, I thought. But then again, I *was* desperate.

Just as I was really beginning to panic, a blessing arrived in the form of an interview for a three-month contract at a top

London ad agency. Leaving their offices afterwards, I could tell it had gone well, and sure enough they emailed the next day offering me their standard day rate to come aboard. But sensing that a) they were desperate to fill the role as quickly as possible, and b) my interviewer had taken a shine to me, I emailed back asking for a slightly higher day rate, what would amount to an extra £500 a month – an amount I knew an ad agency could easily afford. Almost as soon as I sent the email I regretted it, convinced I'd just negotiated myself out of an already generous offer, that they would think I was greedy and go with the next candidate. But within hours they'd responded saying yes, and could I start the next day. The confidence boost from having my first attempt at negotiating as a freelancer go well was immeasurable, and I felt a little of my old self-assurance start to creep back, the 21-year-old me who'd asked her boss for a raise after only four months on the job finally returning to the fray after years in the wilderness.

Now I started to really accelerate my plans for Women Who. Somewhat impulsively I decided to mark its launch by writing a mini handbook full of career advice, thinking of all the things I wished I'd known when I was starting out, of all the mistakes I'd made that I could have avoided had someone just clued me in. It felt wildly exciting to have a project that I was genuinely passionate about, and to have an outlet for my ideas that I had complete control over – a far cry from my professional experiences up until then. Having never previously resembled anything close to a 'morning person', I suddenly found myself jumping out of bed at 5 a.m. to put in a few hours on the book as the sun came up before commuting into central London for work, cheerfully turning down invitations to hang out with friends at the weekends so I could write instead. I felt, at last, as though I was doing what I was supposed to be doing: coming up with ideas, writing, *making* stuff not just marketing it.

Still, at times all of that boundless enthusiasm was tempered by moments of sickeningly intense, almost physically debilitating self-doubt, which only seemed to intensify as the launch date for Women Who drew closer. Twice I nearly pulled the plug on it all, overcome by anxiety at what people would say. I pictured former colleagues mocking my efforts and constructed imagined conversations in which fictional observers commented on the precocity of dispensing 'workplace wisdom' at the tender age of 25. But I pressed on, armed with pep talks from sympathetic friends, and coaxed out of a very serious last-minute bout of cold feet by my mother, who sat on my bed as I buried my face into a pillow and patiently reminded me of all the favours I'd called in to get this thing off the ground. More than anything, it was that – the prospect of having wasted everyone's time and what that might do to my reputation, the sheer embarrassment of it – that finally got me out of bed.

And then to my surprise, the Women Who launch event ended up being a runaway success, far beyond what I had hoped for. The little boutique shop in Shoreditch I'd convinced to host it was packed with people, overflowing out onto the street in fact, and probably violating a dozen health and safety regulations in the process. All 250 copies of the book I'd written, with its too-tight margins (a printing error) and its cover that got horribly scratched if you so much as breathed on it (another printing error), sold out in three days, and Women Who ended up getting a handful of positive press write-ups. I began being invited to give talks about the project, where I'd meet other women who, like me, had become disillusioned by bruising experiences of the workplace and were turning to self-employment as a way of clawing back some semblance of control over their careers.

By the end of that summer I knew for sure that I didn't want to go back to a full-time job at the end of the year. I wanted to see what I could do with Women Who, and I knew that being in an office all day would deny me the flexibility I needed to really make a go of what had been by far the most satisfying moment of my career. So I kept freelancing, and by the end of that 'gap year' I'd signed a book deal after an editor at a major publisher was tipped off about the DIY version of my book, and got in touch with an offer to republish it via traditional channels. My gambles – quitting my job, taking a *rumspringa*, launching Women Who, *writing a book* – somehow, all of it had paid off.

Despite this admittedly fairly charmed entry into self-employed life, actually figuring out how to make a living as a freelancer took me far longer than just that first year. Those first few years were a process of constant trial and error, of figuring out what was worth my time and what wasn't, what paid lots for relatively little effort (anything corporate), and vice versa (writing), what sort of work I genuinely enjoyed doing, and which assignments I'd rather peel off my own skin than repeat.

I began to realise that I had staked both my livelihood and my sense of self on the rapidly disintegrating quicksands of several dying industries. I learned that while most people ostensibly *do* value creative work – music, the arts, writing, photography – surprisingly few had made the connection that in order for those things to exist within a capitalist economy, the artists creating them would need to be paid, and people therefore bristled at the suggestion that they could not have those things for free, that

that was not in fact their *right*, an expectation with increasingly disastrous consequences for creators. I learned that the Internet is both a blessing and a curse, having created, as Hua Hsu wrote in the *New Yorker*, 'a situation in which it's easier than ever to share your creativity with the world, and harder than ever to make a living doing so'.[4] That while I had been revelling in the ease of access to my school friends brokered by MSN Messenger and Hotmail, and the capacity for self-expression afforded by MySpace and its infinite number of design possibilities, the Internet's other corollaries had been slowly demonetising huge swathes of the media, so that when the magazines I had read and dreamed of writing for as a teenager began – at last! – getting in touch to commission me, they couldn't actually afford to pay me very much, if at all. That many of those magazines were now going out of business anyway, and that every year there would be a smaller and smaller pool of editors for me to pitch my ideas to; that it was unlikely I would ever be able to make a living from writing full-time, and that publishing too was on its knees, hollowed out by Amazon's rapacious profiteering; that for all the initial hope and potential promised by the innovation of digital media, most online publications had ended up dependent for their survival on the algorithmic whims of a few increasingly hegemonic tech overlords, and that those companies were not particularly benevolent leaders, did not value creativity or ideas insomuch as they valued profit.

I learned that because much of my work existed at the more intangible end of the already slightly intangible knowledge economy, many people did not assign value to my skills in the way they did other professions (which is perhaps understandable – I'd probably rather be stuck on a desert island with a plumber or an engineer than a fellow 'marketing professional-turned-writer'). Still, I did not appreciate the stranger who emailed me suggesting we meet for a 'friendly coffee', before sending me a bullet-pointed meeting agenda the day before our rendezvous, at which point I realised she actually just wanted me to consult for the large media company where she worked, for free. After that, I became more vigilant about policing my time, learning to root out the increasingly inventive ways people would try to get me to work for free *before* I'd wasted time on the back and forth of emails, or travelled across town for meetings that could have been phone calls instead. These methods ranged from the age old 'exposure' argument to more philosophical and admittedly rather impressive attempts to dress up what was actually 'work' as 'not work': an ad exec describing the proposed consultancy he'd got in touch about as 'a peer to peer chat' (that would therefore, surely, not necessitate payment?), or the editor who had asked me to prepare a workshop for her team responding to my enquiry about fees by stating she viewed my involvement as 'more of a collaborative, hopefully mutually beneficial meeting of minds'. I reflected on how much work the word 'hopefully' was doing in that context, before deciding that I did not in fact want our minds to meet.

Another thing I hadn't anticipated about self-employment was that constantly having to negotiate my pay – every time I got a new commission, in fact – would make me strangely dispassionate about the mechanics of pay, and far more comfortable talking about money in general. My barrier for what might be considered polite to discuss in company quickly disintegrated, and I would find myself probing people at parties about the ins and outs of how they'd negotiated their salary at the job they'd just landed, hoping to gather intel that might better inform my own efforts.

But despite the advances I was making with money in my professional life, my emotional relationship with it remained as complicated as ever. The inherent unpredictability of freelancing, and the fact I never *really* knew where or who my next pay cheque was coming from, or how much it would be for, meant I never really relaxed. I was always in disaster-planning mode, my money vigilance and hoarding tendencies operating at full force. As a way of retaining some sense of control, I'd allocated myself a punishing budget of a few hundred pounds a month – half of which was promptly sucked up by TfL fares and other mundanities. I'd inevitably spend the last week or so of each month trying to stretch out the last £30 of my 'allowance', regularly landing in my overdraft as a result. After a period during which I'd unwittingly racked up several overdraft penalty charges in the space of a few weeks, I realised how irrational I was being. My overly cautious budget was actually *costing* me money rather than helping me save it – and it was making me utterly miserable to be working as hard as I was and never really allowing myself to have fun. I decided to relax the purse strings a little, allowing myself a few hundred pounds extra each month, and immediately felt my life become more enjoyable and less fraught, the result of not having to keep a constantly running tally of how much was in my bank account whenever I left the house.

At the same time, I put nearly as much pressure on my work as I did my finances. A lifelong perfectionist, I developed unattainably high standards for Women Who, obsessing over anything that didn't go exactly to plan, every tiny hiccup and not-so-tiny disappointment (and there were many of those). After each event I organised, I would rush home and write down everything that had gone wrong in a running document bluntly titled

MISTAKES so that I could 'learn for next time', rarely focusing on what had gone well or lingering on positive feedback, even as I advised others to do the same. Occasionally I wondered whether it would not be easier, less anxiety-inducing, to return to the relative ease of a straightforward 9–5, before remembering how thoroughly said 9–5s had wrecked me.

And, for a long time – probably for most of Women Who's four-year duration – I believed the true mark of success would be to turn it into a juggernaut of a business, to more aggressively monetise it, to raise investment and 'scale', having thoroughly absorbed the prevailing cultural obsession with entrepreneurial-ism. But I also began to realise that the things I'd have to do to make it more lucrative – charge more for the resources I produced, and team up with brands to organise corny events where I'd have to espouse the 'empowering' nature of this-or-that deodorant in exchange for sponsorship money – were things that were at odds with my vision for it, even as others counselled them as the best course of action. To help Women Who grow I needed money, and to get that money, I needed to do things that I quite simply did not want to do. At times I wondered if perhaps I wasn't being overly high-minded, especially as I saw other similar platforms pursue those strategies to great success and slowly professionalise, while Women Who continued to be a scrappily run, one-woman organisation. Events happened whenever I had the time and could convince someone to give me a venue for free, and I would play the part of host-slash-doorgirl-slash-social media man-ager, checking off names as people arrived before rushing off to moderate a panel, surreptitiously uploading photos to Instagram as everyone chatted afterwards. I was trying to create perfection part-time and on a shoestring budget, while comparing myself to slick million-dollar businesses flush with venture capital money and hundred-person strong teams.

Reading *Rookie* editor Tavi Gevinson's farewell letter towards the end of 2018, in which she announced the magazine's closure and explained her decision 'to not do the things that might make [the magazine] financially sustainable'[5] as a way of avoiding having to close it (i.e. accepting investment, or entering into brand partnerships that contradicted her values), I felt a sickening sense of recognition at the parallels between her predicament with *Rookie* and mine with Women Who. If Tavi – with her enormous platform and considerable influence and connections – had not managed to find a way to make *Rookie* 'work' without compromising her principles (and to be clear, *Rookie* was far more influential, successful and robust a platform than Women Who ever managed to be), was it really realistic to imagine that I could do what she had not?

That dilemma was just one facet of the fundamental predicament I would encounter now that I was self-employed – that creative work often doesn't pay very much unless it's backed by a corporate entity, and that some form of commercial shadow work is necessary for all but the most successful creatives to survive: freelance culture writers who also write copy for e-commerce giants, film-makers whose bread and butter is making corporate diversity training videos. Early on I realised that I'd need to lean on my advertising experience to get the sort of well-paid work that could offset the masses of unpaid time I was spending on Women Who and on writing (which is as close to unpaid as creative work gets, especially when you're just starting out). After years of plotting my escape from adland, I was suddenly profoundly grateful for that experience, realising that consulting for brands was quite literally buying me the time I needed to pursue my other interests, and that outside of the absurd machinations of agency life I actually quite enjoyed that sort of work. Then and now, I bristled at the stigma around 'selling out' that proliferates in creative circles, often perpetuated by those who needn't worry about money and could therefore afford to retain a certain moral purity, free from the grubby machinations of commerce. And yet I recognised that there were certain lines I myself didn't want to cross, certain commercial opportunities from which I instinctively and unavoidably recoiled.

Even before going freelance, I'd always been someone who defined my identity with reference to my career, so self-employment – and literally *becoming* my own boss – only further encouraged that overlap, to the point that my work and my identity are now virtually indistinguishable, though I'm not alone in this. The fraying of various social safety nets, an increasingly atomised society, and the effects of globalised capitalism have all conspired to make some form of self-branding increasingly necessary for securing employment, particularly within the creative economy. In a 2019 interview given to mark the twenty-year anniversary of *No Logo*'s publication, writer Naomi Klein observed that the biggest change since its 1999 publication was that 'neoliberalism has created so much precarity that the commodification of the self is now seen as the only route to any kind of economic security'.[6]

This is the age of the personal brand, where people's online identities function as adverts for their work, the boundaries between the two blurring particularly seamlessly on social media. For a certain sector of the labour market, participating in this economy of the self is crucial to our continued employment (though you will be hard-pressed to find someone who openly confesses to actively cultivating their personal brand – the concept has become slightly déclassé). The pleasantly aspirational Instagram account, the Twitter feed that oscillates between observational witticisms and news of your latest professional achievements – the more appealing your digital presence, the more opportunities will present themselves to you, an occurrence that some have pushed to its logical extreme by turning their digital presence *into* the locus of their work, as influencers.

This economic pressure – or incentive – to self-commoditise, unsurprisingly, weighs more heavily on women, as seen in the media narratives around high profile women that insist on parsing every detail of their lives, from how they drink their coffee to the interiors of their homes, in a way that rarely happens to men. These days to be a successful woman in the public eye is to offer up your entire lifestyle for consumption, dissection and ultimately emulation, or to at least be expected to. Women more frequently have to inject selfhood as part of the equation for success.

Musing on the growing phenomenon of 'writer as influencer', freelance culture writer Allegra Hobbs suggests that 'to be a writer today is to make yourself a product for public consumption on the Internet, to project an appealing image that contextualises the actual writing'.[7] While it's a bit of an exaggeration to suggest (as Hobbs does) that an online presence is 'all but mandatory for a writer who reaches (or hopes to reach) a certain level of renown' – there are plenty of writers who emerge to great success even today and remain resolutely anti-social, Sally Rooney is one who comes to mind, Phoebe Waller-Bridge another – she is correct that it certainly helps, that a writer who can present a corresponding lifestyle on social media (artfully scattered book stacks, references to writing retreats, reflections on 'process') will likely be granted the stamp of legitimacy more readily than one who does not, or cannot.

The pressure for creative women to be advertisements for our work, and for that work to be inextricable from our selfhood, is also a specifically young woman's concern. Ageism being what it is, one of the things that sells best in the marketplace of the self is youth, as applied to physical appearances, cultural tastes, lifestyle and output. It is either less expected – or less desired – that older women will offer up those aspects of themselves.

I often find myself torn between wanting to resist the kind of self-branding that is now seemingly par for the course for female writers, while recognising that there are certain things about me that are easily marketable – that I am young, with a keen interest in fashion; that I am a heavy social media user and part of a generation that almost reflexively brands itself, even if only as a means of survival; and that much of that work feels enjoyable, or at the very least unburdensome to me. Resisting that self-branding actually requires me to *hide* aspects of myself to avoid the illusion of artifice, which feels strangely counter-intuitive.

Scrolling through Instagram recently, I came across a selfie uploaded by a young female film-maker, juxtaposed with an unexpected, self-referential caption: 'the trade for creative autonomy is crafting the perfect selfies'. Increasingly, part of forging a career as a young creative woman seems to involve weighing up whether, and to what extent, I am willing to make that trade.

Chapter 10

A ROOM
OF ONE'S OWN

I moved out of my parents' home as soon as I could afford to, not long after I'd turned 23. I'm sure to older generations 23 probably seems relatively late to be cutting the cord, but the economic reality of young adulthood these days means that the tales of hotfooting it to the big city with only £100 in your pocket that boomers, Gen Xers – even older millennials – seem so fond of, are few and far between. My generation is an altogether more cautious bunch, and 23 was the first time I felt secure enough in a job to contemplate renting, having just joined AMV.

My own belated exodus was largely prompted by the fact that in the two years since I'd graduated from university and returned home, my relationship with my parents had become increasingly fractious (which I imagine is not uncommon for members of the so-called 'boomerang generation' – the estimated 3.5 million millennials who are forced to live with their parents well into adulthood as a result of rising housing costs and dismal employment opportunities). Eventually, our arguments became frequent enough to outweigh the advantage of being able to live in London rent-free, so when a close friend, Poppy, floated the idea of moving in together, I decided to go for it.

The site of my first real foray into adulthood belonged to one of Poppy's friends who'd been temporarily relocated abroad for work, leaving vacant a newly purchased two-bedroom house. I pushed aside the burning anxiety I felt over what I knew many – not least my parents – would consider to be pouring money down the drain, and focused instead on what I'd be gaining: a less stressful living situation, and greater independence. Not to mention that moving out would cut my then eighty-minute commute in half and, I hoped, allow for a livelier, more spontaneous social life, no longer dependent on catching the last train (and then a bus) back to deepest suburbia. Within weeks, Poppy and I were excitedly lugging boxes of our belongings up the steps of an idyllic terraced house on a leafy Hackney street, cobbling together a semblance of adulthood from IKEA trips and borrowed furniture.

We moved in together in mid-September, just as the heat of summer was fading and the air was turning cool and crisp. It was that time of year when the mind naturally turns to new beginnings, and the house felt ripe with possibility, filled with the promise of the first blank page of a new notebook. Still, the thrill of independence I felt in those first few weeks was tempered by a lingering guilt that would well up whenever I thought too long about the amount of money I was 'wasting' on rent each month, and how much that would add up to over a year, five years, a decade. One evening, after reading yet another article about London's housing crisis (which at the time was often frontpage news), I burst into hot, desperate tears. I felt racked with guilt at the thought that by choosing to move out of my parent's home, I was actively pushing the prospect of home ownership further out of my own grasp and consigning myself to a lifetime of serfdom – and yet I couldn't face the thought of going back.

Because the house belonged to Poppy's friend Arabella, our rent only came to about £550 a month each – which for a house share in a prime part of Hackney was an absolute steal, even by 2013 standards. Plus, there was no need to pay letting agency fees, or part with a hefty deposit while wondering whether you'd ever again be reunited with your money. For that, I was more than happy to put up with the temperamental boiler and occasional gas leak, although our domestic bliss was short-lived.

Poppy and I were relatively new friends, having only been close for perhaps a year, if that. We'd been thrown together by a few mutual acquaintances and quickly formed one of those intense friendships that I imagine most women experience at some point, going from barely knowing each other to being partners-in-crime and confidantes within the space of a few months. Poppy was gregarious and smart, and came from an affluent and extremely well-connected family. To me, her life seemed impossibly glamorous, full of exotic holidays and trips to second homes, photos of her wearing designer gowns splashed across the pages of society magazines, and a dramatic on-off relationship with her quasi-aristocratic boyfriend (not to mention a long line of suitors the rest of the time). Only a little older than me, she seemed infinitely more worldly, and at first I was flattered that she wanted to be friends – close friends – with me. I could never reciprocate the glamour or opportunities she brought to our friendship: the social capital of being her friend and turning up to parties as a duo; the trip we took to her family's villa in the south of France; or the work experience a relative of hers had arranged for me not long after I'd graduated. Compliance felt like the only currency I could offer in return. I didn't know it at the time but I was one of a long line of lapdogs Poppy had accumulated along the way, friendships dependent on their ability to play supporting act to her starring role.

Cracks started to appear even before we'd moved in together, but I was so desperate to escape home that I ignored them. Mutual friends who knew Poppy better than I did warned me against getting too close to her, telling stories of other friends she'd burned in the past, but I ignored them too, convinced that I knew her better than they did and determined to judge our friendship on its own merits, not years-old gossip. Poppy did undeniably have an unconventional relationship with the truth, stretching and twisting it (and often outright discarding it) to fit whatever narrative she deemed most prudent at the time. I'd often hear her retell the same story with slightly differing key details each time, details that varied even more when I heard the same story told by other people we knew. She was used to getting her own way, and also fairly spoiled – the sort of person who once had her parents send their cleaner across London to do her share of the chores in our flat. Both these personality traits came to a head a few weeks before we even moved in together.

Poppy had raised the question of who would have which bedroom in the flat, texting me saying simply that she'd prefer to have the larger bedroom, as though the mere fact of her expressing that she wanted something would render the matter settled, an expectation I'd probably been complicit in fostering. Instead, I texted back suggesting that, given I too wanted the larger bedroom, we ought to flip a coin for it the next time we were together, which we did. When I won, she pouted, clearly irritated, and then mentioned that I'd need to pay a larger share of our rent as a result. I was confused – just a few weeks earlier we'd agreed to split the rent equally regardless of who ended up with the larger bedroom, but when I reminded her of that agreement she accused me of accusing *her* of being a cheat, of being distrustful, and pointed out that paying more for a larger bedroom in a flat share is generally the norm (which is true – it just wasn't what we had agreed between us). Of course, I capitulated, not wanting to make it into A Thing, but that exchange bothered me for weeks. It felt as though Poppy had only wanted to split the rent equally on the assumption she would have the bigger bedroom, and her sudden volte face as soon as she didn't get her way unsettled me. I'd later reread the texts where we'd agreed to split the rent equally to see if it was possible that I'd somehow misinterpreted them, but they were clear as day. In the end I chalked the incident up to her having misremembered our agreement as opposed to any real subterfuge – in part, I think, to preserve my opinion of her. It was only later in the context of the demise of our friendship that I would recognise that as the red flag it was, one of many examples of how entitled and casually manipulative she could be.

The fact that our friendship would eventually unravel was probably inevitable; living together merely sped up the process. Poppy was not someone used to having her behaviour challenged by her friends, and I was not someone used to biting my tongue or playing the beta to someone's alpha, at least not for an extended period of time. The power dynamic our friendship had been built on – Poppy the worldly savant and me her adoring acolyte – began to shift, the spell starting to weaken as the mundanities of house-sharing crept into our lives. I wanted a real friendship, built on honesty and mutual respect and an equal footing, and Poppy . . . Poppy wanted a fan.

Six months in, all of her little half-truths and manipulations, and all of my unvoiced frustrations and slowly building disillusionment snowballed into a heated argument over nothing and everything (conducted entirely via GChat, of course). The plan had always been that Poppy would move back to her parents' house when Arabella returned to England and that I would remain as Arabella's tenant. But a few days after my argument with Poppy, I woke up to an email from Arabella coolly informing me that the 'mate's rates' rent she and I had reconfirmed just weeks before was now null and void, and that, effective immediately, my rent would be going up by £215 a month. I was shocked and slightly panicked, but I emailed back agreeing to pay it. Arabella responded: actually, given that I'd fallen out with Poppy (who was of course a friend of hers) she wanted me to move out. I realised that the rent hike had really been an eviction notice spurred by my argument with Poppy, and that Arabella hadn't bargained on me being able or willing to bear the suggested increase. I moved out a few weeks later.

On to the next flat share, found via a loose acquaintance from uni who'd responded to my increasingly desperate Facebook statuses with news that one of her own housemates was moving out and did I want to come check out her room? I felt a surge of gratitude – she and I had several friends in common, which to me felt infinitely preferable to the gamble of moving in with a group of strangers found via SpareRoom. At a viewing later that week, I overlooked the flat's obvious dinginess, and my would-be flatmates' vague shiftiness about the landlord, Renata.

'She's a bit shit, and quite hard to get hold of sometimes but . . . it's mostly fine.' 'Mostly fine' would have to do. The important thing was that the room was affordable – £600 a month – and available immediately.

Here, I had the pleasure of arriving home from work one evening to find that the ceiling in my bedroom had caved in. Weeks of heavy rainfall and a prolonged leak that our landlord seemed unable or unwilling to address had finally metastasised into a football-sized hole above my bed, and chunks of wet plaster were now strewn around my room. On the phone to Renata the following morning, she seemed infuriatingly relaxed about when she might get round to having it fixed. When I raised the question of where I was supposed to sleep in the meantime, wary of the rest of the ceiling caving in on me while I slept, she insisted that the only logical solution was for me to temporarily move in with her, neatly sidestepping the rather more obvious solution of her sending someone over to *fix the sodding roof*. By the time the pigeons moved in, I knew better than to broach the subject with her. I never did mention the infestation in the roof, choosing instead to tolerate my avian companions, who were at least thoughtful enough to wake me up at four o'clock each morning with a chorus of insistent cooing that I tried hard to convince myself was pleasant. *Being woken up by birdsong – it's sort of romantic if you think about it,* I told myself, as metres above my head an unseen horde of scabby grey pigeons fucked loudly in the darkness.

And yet I would have stayed there indefinitely were it not for the fact that I found my two new housemates to be completely unbearable. Things had got off to a bad start when, a few days after I'd moved in, they'd breezily informed me that as they were both off on holiday shortly, they'd rented out their bedrooms on Airbnb, and for the next few weeks I'd be sharing the flat with a revolving cast of strangers.

'Er, I'm actually not that comfortable with that,' I said hesitantly. 'Sorry. I just don't love the idea of sharing the flat with a bunch of strangers. It just feels a bit . . . hostel-y.'

An awkward silence ensued.

'Why didn't you mention that before I moved in?' I added. 'I'm guessing you've known this for a while . . . ?'

My housemates shifted uncomfortably. 'We didn't think you'd mind. Everyone does it.'

'Right. OK. Well. I'd really rather you didn't if that's alright. Especially as I'll be here on my own. I think I'll feel sort of responsible for them.'

I corrected myself. 'I *will* be responsible for them.'

If I'd hoped that that would be the end of it, I could not have been more wrong. An argument ensued that dragged on for days, as we went back and forth over our respective standpoints. At one point I received an email from the more bullish of the pair announcing that it was important for her to 'monetise the unused space' while she was away, breezily batting aside my concerns about my safety, the imposition, the fact I had told her repeatedly how deeply uncomfortable I felt about the arrangement. I held firm and eventually they cancelled the bookings, but from then on things between us were decidedly frosty. When a break clause in the lease came up after six months, I hightailed it out of there into a tiny Homerton flat share with two close friends I'd known for years. This, at last, proved to be a relatively uneventful tenancy, until, eleven months in, I faced the classic renters' conundrum of a departing housemate and a room to fill, or in my case two. One of my housemates was relocating to the Middle East for work, while the other had decided to move back home, finding the rent was taking up too much of her salary. That left me looking for two new housemates to fill their places – at least until Rat-gate, at which point I packed up my things and fled back to my parents' house (though not before our landlord tried to extract an extra two months' rent from us as a parting gift).

And yet I know that I am relatively lucky – as renting stories go, things could have been far, far worse. I've heard stories from friends who endured a winter's worth of ice-cold showers and a bedroom so damp that actual mushrooms began to sprout from the walls. A friend whose landlord insisted on using their flat as a crash pad whenever they visited London, installing themselves in the living room for days at a time. Another friend who discovered by accident that the monthly rent payments she'd been transferring to her housemate had not, as she'd thought, been going directly to their landlord, but had instead been spent on trips to New York and tickets to Barbra Streisand concerts, leaving them both months in arrears. Then there are the landlords who seem to think they're being magnanimous by letting you spend as much as half of your income paying off their mortgages while utterly neglecting their end of the bargain. Who turn up unannounced, or worse, ghost you altogether, deposit in tow. Who make jokes about your flat being their 'children's inheritance' in the same breath as informing you of a rent increase and expect you to laugh along, which you do, because the power balance is unequivocally in their favour and you've learned to be as acquiescent as possible where landlords are concerned.

It's difficult to convey to someone who hasn't recently undergone the vagaries of renting in a big, expensive city like London how profoundly dispiriting that experience can be, and how it wears away at you, bit by bit. How aside from the exorbitant financial cost, there are other, less obvious costs that can't be quantified as easily, measured out in the constant worrying and weighing up, and in the emotional toll that that takes over time. It's the countless hours you'll spend poring over Zoopla listings, wondering if perhaps a bedroom without a clearly discernible window might not actually be *that* bad, and the days you'll spend repeatedly packing and unpacking your possessions, packing and unpacking your possessions, packing and unpacking your possessions, until eventually you discard anything that can't be easily carted up stairs or loaded into the back of a car. It's the humiliation of turning up to a flat viewing alongside no less than fifty other young hopefuls and being invited to 'bid' on said flat by closed auction, knowing that there's not a hope in hell of you getting it but bidding anyway (we didn't get it). It's being repeatedly catfished by property listings that bait you with photos of a nice-looking flat that somehow happens to fall within your price range, and clicking through the photos trying to figure out why it's so affordable before realising that – oh, of course – it doesn't have a living room. It's all the times you'll apologetically duck out of work to make phone calls to bewilderingly chipper letting agents or infuriatingly relaxed landlords, begging them just for once to be reasonable and act like decent human beings (they won't). It's the frustration you'll feel at the pointless contractual prohibitions, at needing permission for something as basic as hanging a picture, and having to live in a perpetual limbo of undecorated walls and flimsy IKEA furniture. It's the uncertainty, fucking *hell*, the uncertainty. The specific taste of the panic induced by an unexpected rent increase, or worse, eviction notice. Never really knowing if you'll be living in the same place in three months' time. Never really feeling settled.

Bit by bit, it wears you down, all of it, until you are grateful for the smallest of mercies – a landlord who allows you to repaint a wall, or takes weeks rather than months to fix the hot water. And all this while knowing that at the end of it all, you'll have nothing to show for your efforts but an empty bank account. No equity, no savings. Nothing. Little wonder that renters suffer from higher rates of loneliness and mental illness than their older, home-owning counterparts.[1] More than anything else, it was the lack of security I felt during those years, the creeping sense that at any moment everything could go to shit that triggered my money-hoarding tendencies. The thought of not having a comfortable buffer each month to fall back on in case of an emergency – or a rent increase – terrified me so much that I deliberately rented rooms a few hundred pounds cheaper than what I knew I could stretch to, putting the extra cash into an emergency pot instead. That is not in itself bad financial practice. It is eminently sensible in fact – except that London's sky-high rents meant that, on my budget, I never lived anywhere particularly nice. Instead, I endured a series of miserable rentals, when in hindsight it would have been a good investment – in comfort, and in my happiness – to have paid a little extra each month to live somewhere nicer (even though this would have meant spending about half of my post-tax salary on rent, a proportion that most housing charities and policy organisations deem to be 'highly unaffordable'. The rule of thumb recommendation is that individuals spend no more than 35 per cent of their post-tax income[2] on housing).

The blessedly short period I spent renting in London – two years in total – was one of the most stressful periods of my adult life. My lingering memory of that time is of the tight coil of anxiety that was permanently lodged in my chest, occasionally anaesthetised by a heavy workload or raucous night out, until an innocuous incident – a flatmate meeting a boyfriend's parents for the first time, say, or a missed call from my landlord – would send me mentally cycling through the sequence of events that might conspire to, quite literally, pull the rug out from under my feet. That renting in London is an experience defined by its precarity is particularly true when you're renting at the cheaper end of the market, as I was. It makes a mockery of the basic human instinct to nest, and the idea that one's home should be a sanctuary, somewhere you go at the end of the day to shut the door on the chaos of the outside world. For Generation Rent (as we are often called) more often than not the call is coming from inside the house.

It didn't help that, as a consequence of having been first to a private school and then to Oxford, I was surrounded by friends who frequently weren't in the same position as I was, who had parents who could afford to give them huge sums for a deposit (and in a few cases buy them a property outright). Not that that's particularly exceptional these days – more than a third of first-time buyers in England have to turn to their parents for financial help to get on the property ladder,[3] a figure that jumps to over half when considering only the under-35s.[4] The so-called 'bank of mum and dad' is now the tenth-biggest mortgage lender in the UK,[5] and certainly in London I didn't know anyone who'd managed to get on the housing ladder without a significant financial contribution from their parents.

Particularly in my early twenties, I harboured a mixture of envy and resentment towards people who fell into that category, less because of the fact of their good fortune (though I'd be lying if I didn't admit to that being a part of it) and more because of how *oblivious* so many of them seemed to the extent of their privilege and how it would change the financial landscape of their entire lives, far beyond their twenties. I had friends who'd nod sympathetically when I recounted tales of workplace drama and office politics, before saying things like, 'God, I could never work in an office', meaning to compliment me by suggesting that I was made of sterner stuff than they were, while also slyly implying that such an environment would stifle their fragile bohemian dispositions. In reality, the only difference between us was that they didn't *have* to work in an office, and I did. Instead they had the luxury of experimenting with nebulous creative interests, free from the pressure to make money either in the short or long term, because there would always be a pot of gold waiting for them at the end of the rainbow. Working in an industry I'd entered largely thanks to my fear of financial insecurity, and at the expense of what I knew I wanted to do for a living, I envied them that freedom.

So I quietly seethed when one friend moaned about how 'stressful' the admin involved in buying her flat had become, which as far as I could tell amounted to little more than attending viewings and signing a few contracts, given that her parents had paid for the flat outright. Another time, I was so consumed with envy when a friend's parents bought her a flat that for months I couldn't bear to visit, making excuses whenever she invited me over. I even skipped her twenty-fifth birthday party because the prospect of having to conjure up the requisite enthusiasm over her plush new flat was more than I could bear, especially given that I was at the time residing in the leaky, pigeon-infested hellhole. Then there was the friend who complained to me over drinks about 'how hard' it was to find somewhere to buy on what would turn out to be a £600,000 budget (provided in part, of course, by her parents), which earned a furiously catty text to Tommy as soon as we'd parted ways. Worse was the strange sense of betrayal I felt towards friends who, in our early twenties, had joined me in complaining about the state of the housing market, who'd moaned about being 'skint' and allowed me to buy them dinner only to miraculously buy themselves flats a few years later, helped along by parental contributions. Why had they bothered, I thought, when they must have known that that was going to happen for them sooner or later, that they secretly had a financial parachute strapped to their backs? I felt deceived, and embittered by what I perceived to be a weird sort of class tourism, their middle-class experimentation with slumming it in London rentals 'for the story' before escaping to the safety of home ownership and Farrow & Ball.

There is a strange coyness, too, about homes bought with help from the bank of mum and dad (and why do we even call it that – why not just call it what it is: family money?). Few people are particularly forthcoming in noting the often-massive inheritances underwriting these purchases. Instead, we see the Instagram photos of beaming twenty-somethings standing proudly on the steps of their new home, or engage in polite dinner party chit-chat about paint swatches and mid-century Ercol furniture, even as we are silently wondering '*How?*' Or at least I did. I spent most of my twenties wondering how, crunching the numbers and trying to figure out how it was that people my age had managed to buy properties in London, and how much harder I needed to work, how much more I needed to earn, how many more rungs I needed to climb up the career ladder before it would be my turn; until at last the penny dropped and it dawned on me that none of these homes had been bought on an account manager's salary.

Perhaps the most extreme example of this coyness unfolded not long after I turned 28. I decided that, rather than simply giving up and resigning myself to never being able to buy a flat in London, it might be worth educating myself about the ins and outs of buying a house so that I could make a plan of attack. If I could set some targets and make a plan, or even fully understand how big the gulf was between me and home ownership, perhaps I'd feel more in control. In short – and true to my intensely Type-A personality – I decided to organise my way out of despair. I spent the next few weeks calling up different mortgage brokers and financial advisers, peppering them with questions and hypotheticals, sending them bank statements and asking them to make vague predictions about how much I'd be able to borrow 'if *this*, or *that*'. I texted a friend who worked as a financial journalist to interrogate her about interest rates, and devoured articles about credit ratings and LTV ratios. By this point I was self-employed, so I knew that getting a mortgage would be considerably trickier than it is for salaried employees. As a freelancer, you have to provide mortgage lenders with a record of income over a couple of years (as opposed to just three months of payslips) and given how irregular my earnings can be, it made sense to start planning my finances a few years out.

But no matter which way I cut it, no matter how firmly I massaged the figures or how optimistically I forecast my future earnings, it became clear that to buy even the tiniest, most run-down hovel in all of London, I'd need an insanely high salary – several times the UK average, and certainly far beyond anything I could realistically see myself earning in the years to come. Saving up for a deposit suddenly felt like the least of my troubles – I simply didn't make enough money. (As of November 2020, the average house price in London stood at £514,000,[6] nearly fourteen times the median London salary of £37,000. Most mortgage providers will only lend a maximum of 4.5 times an individual's salary, five times at a stretch.)

It just didn't make sense – my friend Amy had got a mortgage when we were both 24, and both on the same salary of £28,000. She'd mentioned at the time that her parents had helped her out with a deposit, but I still didn't understand how she'd got a big enough mortgage to afford what was a spacious two-bedroom flat in a highly sought-after postcode. Was there a specialist mortgage provider for average earners no one was telling me about? More importantly, would they lend to me? Lounging on Amy's sofa a few weeks later, I decided to broach the topic with her.

'I hope you don't mind me asking,' I began, couching my request in that tentative, almost conciliatory tone we're accustomed to adopting when it comes to talking to people – even our closest friends – about their finances.

'But, like, how did you go about getting a mortgage? What was the process?'

I continued, 'Sorry, I'm not just being nosy – I'm just trying to plan for the future and figure out whether I'll actually ever be able to buy my own place, and all this mortgage stuff just doesn't make *any* sense to me.'

Amy looked immediately uncomfortable.

'I mean, you don't have to talk about it if you don't want to . . .' I added quickly.

She took a deep breath. 'OK – it's not that I *mind* talking to you about this, and I'm obviously happy to help with anything I *do* know the answers to but . . . I have a bit of a confession to make.'

I waited.

'I don't actually have a mortgage.'

'What?' I responded, suddenly confused.

'I don't have a mortgage. I bought my flat outright.'

'But you've *mentioned* having a mortgage before,' I said, still confused.

'I know,' Amy replied, turning red.

Sheepishly, she explained the truth – that aged 24, her parents had given her enough money to buy herself a flat outright. Worried that being perceived as 'rich' might affect how people treated her and create an expectation of largesse among her friends, she'd pretended instead that she still had a mortgage, as a way of downplaying the extent of her financial freedom.

In a society where the accumulation of wealth is viewed as verging on moral good, where the poor are routinely excluded from key social and institutional structures and maligned by nearly all aspects of our culture, it is not particularly surprising when people who don't have a lot of money express shame about that fact. Shame as it relates to wealth is somewhat more unexpected because – despite occasional pockets of resistance and the growing anti-capitalist sentiment that has entered mainstream cultural conversations – on the whole, we tend to venerate the rich, assigning enormous social currency to traditional markers of wealth: nice cars, massive houses, designer clothes. But that's the thing about shame – it's an emotion that arises from our most base human instincts: the fear of being judged negatively by others; our desire to 'fit in'; the discomfort of feeling exposed; and those emotional responses transcend income levels. For wealthy people who also happen to be politically liberal – and so value the notion of social equity – being rich, and the advantages that wealth presents, can be a source of moral discomfort, particularly when said wealth is inherited. It is entirely possible (and common) to feel shame about having 'too much' money, though this remains a position that perhaps understandably is rather difficult for the majority of us to conjure up considerable sympathy for. In Amy's case, she had kept her inheritance a secret not just because she'd been worried about friends treating her differently, but because – by her own admission – she felt embarrassed about having had it so easy on that front.

Her fears that she might be judged weren't completely unfounded. In a paper focusing on the psychology of inheritance, Columbia Business School professor Eric Schoenberg observes that, 'the belief that reward should be commensurate with effort makes society wary of the wealth that inheritors receive without any effort on their own part'.[7] We subconsciously value sources of money differently, assigning individuals status depending on the origins of their wealth, meaning a self-made millionaire is perceived differently to an heiress with the exact same net worth. Most people see inherited money as ultimately legitimate, but also slightly unfair.

We carried on talking for a while, Amy explaining the details of her situation, while I rapidly tried to recalibrate my expectations of a conversation that had now gone wildly off-piste, to say the least. I would spend the next few days mentally combing over years' worth of our conversations, re-examining offhand comments Amy had made about money, or about her flat, against what I now knew to be true. In truth, I was reeling – not at the shock of Amy owning her flat outright, but at how far she'd gone in obfuscating the reality of her situation. She hadn't just misled me by way of omission or declined to correct an incorrect assumption. She had lied.

'Look it's fine,' I said eventually. 'I'm not angry or anything – it's not like I have a right to know the ins and outs of your finances. I'm just a bit . . . taken aback,' I added, trying to be as non-judgemental as possible, given that fear of judgement had been the main reason she'd lied to me in the first place.

I paused, weighing up my words carefully before continuing.

'The one thing I will say is – you not being honest about this sort of thing is, like, *actively* unhelpful. I mean, I've literally been using you as an example of it being possible for me to get a decent mortgage on my current earnings, and that just . . . isn't the case. I get why you wouldn't shout about this from the rooftops, but actively misleading people . . .' I sighed. 'It's just a bit unhelpful.'

And there lies the rub. When people conceal these enormous advantages – whether it is the inheritance underwriting a house purchase, or the career advancements facilitated by the privilege of financial support – it invites self-flagellation among those who aren't as fortunate, making them feel inadequate when they're unable to achieve those same milestones, not realising that there is a secret cheat code they simply don't have access to.

Your late twenties are generally the time when the individual fortunes and lifestyles of your friendship group begin to diverge, as careers accelerate and stall, salaries track accordingly and the choices people made in their early twenties start coming home to roost. Suddenly you'll find that the friends who've long served as your comrades-in-arms, elbow to elbow in brightly lit libraries and dimly lit clubs, aren't necessarily your peers. While some might think nothing of dropping £40 on a casual Tuesday night dinner, others will fret about that bill all the way home, because that £40 was supposed to cover their food shop for the week, but they didn't want to seem cheap (even though they didn't have any of that overpriced bottle of wine that *someone* insisted on ordering 'for the table'). In fact, some of your friends stop ordering the second-cheapest wine on the menu, and just go for the one they actually like. They start buying proper furniture, and going to destination weddings, and staying in (really) nice hotels when they travel, and *you* start to wonder how on earth they can afford it all, before realising that somewhere along the way they either started making a lot more money than you, or quietly saving up (dickheads), or, yes, had a helping hand from their parents. And, of course, some people start buying houses.

In the same way that housing serves as an effective proxy for class divisions and wealth inequality in Britain as a whole, dividing us into homeowners and renters, landlords and tenants, haves and have-nots, it also serves as a neat proxy for the financial – and at times social – divisions that begin to emerge within some friendships in their late twenties. Housing (or more specifically home ownership) is *the* line in the sand, the chalkboard upon which the culmination of those differences in lifestyle and class status are writ large. I was forced to reckon with that fact a little earlier than most, as within my fairly privileged social circle the exodus from renting to home ownership began almost as soon as I graduated. By my mid-twenties those who owned property outnumbered those who rented.

The divergence in our relative fortunes was brought home to me most memorably soon after I turned 27, around six months after my first book was published. I hadn't had a holiday, or even really taken any time off since I'd become self-employed two years earlier, having been too preoccupied with work and trying to adapt to freelancing. Unsurprisingly, my brain and body finally rebelled, grinding petulantly to a halt in protest. Bone-tired, I found myself unable to work and cancelling meetings at the last minute – important meetings, meetings about opportunities I'd ordinarily have jumped at – while checking my emails filled me with a level of anxiety disproportionate to the task at hand. It became clear that I desperately needed a break, and so I booked myself a trip to Mexico, escaping the depths of an especially grim British winter to recuperate first in a boutique hotel on the Yucatán Peninsula, where I lay immobile on one of the hotel's beachfront cabanas for five days straight, before moving on to Mexico City, a place I'd wanted to visit for years. There I toured the city's architectural landmarks, meandering through the gardens of Frida Kahlo's Casa Azul, and soaking up Luis Barragán's dramatic colourscapes. I ate out at the city's most talked-about restaurants, feasting on ceviche and churros and ice-cold horchata at local markets. I relaxed. I took siestas. I had fun. And, most remarkably for me, I didn't worry (too much) about how much money I was spending. Even the most fiscally cautious part of me knew that I'd well and truly *earned* this splurge, and so for once I didn't feel guilty about 'wasting' money (although a part of me also rationalised the trip as a necessary investment in my ability to resume productive work when I returned to London, which says a lot about how modern capitalism has colonised even the concept of leisure as being in service of revenue generation – but I digress).

Arriving back in London ten days later, I thought about my trip as I sat on a Piccadilly line train gliding out of Heathrow, contentedly scrolling through the hundreds of photos I'd taken on my phone. I'd had a nice holiday, that I'd paid for myself with the fruits of my hard work, *and* I'd managed not to beat myself up about how much money I was spending while I was there. It felt like an achievement on multiple fronts, and I felt proud. *See,* I said to myself, *work hard and you can have nice things.*

My phone buzzed.

A message flashed on screen, my friend Lea posting a link to a small WhatsApp group chat we were both part of.

Lea: Anyone want to buy a flat?

I swiped right, already smiling, expecting to be confronted with one of those property listings that occasionally go viral on account of their owners' vast collection of something creepy and unexpected – life-sized Victorian children's dolls, or botched attempts at amateur taxidermy. But to my surprise, the link accompanying the text led to a Zoopla listing for Lea's own flat, bought for her many years before by her parents – and now up for sale for a clean £950,000. It transpired that she and her boyfriend had decided to take the plunge of swapping their central London flat for a family home in the suburbs, and this was her announcing that to the rest of us.

I felt like I'd been punched. The warm glow of optimism I'd been basking in evaporated instantly. In the space of a few seconds I went from reflecting on how far I could go in life if I just *applied* myself, to being reminded that no matter how hard I worked, no matter how many late nights and articles filed, workshops hosted and books sold, I'd never in a million years have *this*, or anything close to this.

And then I got angry.

How could she be so fucking *insensitive.* Granted, Lea and I had never spoken directly about our respective circumstances, but it seemed obvious to me that perhaps I wouldn't want to have such a naked reminder of how starkly our situations contrasted thrust in my face – her moving effortlessly on to her second million-pound property, while I remained confined to my teenage bedroom, the idea of getting even a toehold on the housing ladder laughably out of reach. My fingers hovered over my phone, poised to reply. *Yeah, I'd love to, let me just ask my parents for a few hundred thousand pounds.* But I knew that she'd be mortified, and that everyone else in our group chat would be mortified too, and that that was an incredibly churlish way to respond to a friend's good news. *Maybe I should message her privately*, I thought, but I was too tired to come up with the right words. Instead, I muted the chat and carried on home, my post-holiday bubble burst before I'd even turned the key in my front door.

Perhaps it's thin-skinned or naïve of me to have been so confronted by the reality of other people having more than I do. I tried to remind myself that I largely exist in a class bubble, one that's distorted my expectations of what financial trajectory my life should rightfully take, and that it isn't actually the norm to become a homeowner in your twenties (in fact, the average age of first-time buyers in the UK is 32, rising to 37 in London).[8] And yet it still stung, to find that the friends I was once level pegging with were suddenly light years ahead of me. Through school and university, it had never really bothered me that many of my friends' families were wealthier than mine, I suppose because it felt irrelevant. I'd just sort of assumed our lives would all turn out roughly the same given we all got the same grades and degree results, all had similar levels of ambition. *Education, education, education.* That's supposed to be the big leveller, right? And yet seeing friends get an advantage that put us on completely different lanes so early on in adulthood exposed the fallacy of meritocracy, how the multiplier effect of class and privilege only increases rather than decreases over a lifetime, as wealth is passed down – or not – from generation to generation. As reported by the *Guardian* in 2020, 'In many large cities, it is now virtually impossible to break into the property market if you earn an average, or even above-average, salary . . . Inheritance, not work, has become the main route to middle-class home ownership.'[9]

I found it difficult, too, not to lament the gaping chasm between the twenties I'd dreamed of as a teenager (admittedly high on the fumes of shows like *Friends*) and the reality of it. The UK's housing crisis has dramatically transformed the experience of early adulthood for anyone born in the mid-1980s or beyond. Rising housing costs mean that 41 per cent of adults between the ages of 22 and 29 are still living at home with their parents,[10] often in the hope of saving up the average £42,000[11] needed to put down a deposit on a property. Grateful as I was even to have that as an option, the plan had not been to live with my parents throughout my twenties. It felt as if I'd had to trade in the independence of early adulthood I'd so longed for just to give myself a fighting chance of one day owning my own home, a trade-off that many twenty- and thirty-somethings are now having to make. Mine is a generation that will be denied many of the basic pleasures and rites of passage we had reasonably expected would be part of adult life, and that previous generations enjoyed: the joy of independence, of furnishing a space to your own tastes, even the freedom to start a family. I know couples who've decided against having children simply because they can't afford to buy, and the thought of raising a family in a series of precarious and increasingly unaffordable rentals doesn't hold much appeal. The idea that one's wealth or class background might determine your ability to start a family feels dystopian, at best.

And while in 2002 single women like me were cited in a BBC News report as 'a major force in the UK property market',[12] accounting for one in seven properties sold and 17 per cent of all new mortgage lending, one of the (many) knock-on effects of the gender pay gap is a subsequent gap in housing affordability. Women on average need more than twelve times[13] their annual salary to be able to buy a property in England, while men need just over eight times theirs. In London and the South East those figures jump to eighteen and fourteen times respectively (not to mention that it takes us longer to save up for a deposit in the first place). These days even well-earning professional couples struggle to get on the housing ladder. What hope then for a single, self-employed woman with no inheritance to bolster her deposit? It is a near impossible feat.

At times I felt slightly embarrassed that my preoccupation with getting onto the housing ladder read as the most predictable of middle-class obsessions, a desire to achieve what is becoming an increasingly rarefied status symbol so that I, too, could compete in the arms race of Instagram humblebrags and cornice comparisons. But much of my anxiety around home ownership actually arose from craving the long-term security it provides; a couple of years of being buffeted around by London rentals and the financial anxiety wrought by that constant uncertainty only intensifying the desire to buy. I was also painfully aware of how much home ownership affects your living standards in later life. It's really over the next few decades, as my generation reaches middle and then old age, that the difference between the renters and the homeowners will start to become clear, the fortunes of those who were able to spend their earnings paying off mortgages and thus accumulating wealth diverging wildly from those who were stuck renting. In 2018 the Resolution Foundation, a think tank geared towards exploring living standards among low- and middle-income households in the UK, predicted that one in three adults currently aged between 20 and 35 will never own their own home,[14] and are set to still be renting by the time they come to claim their pensions (or 'renting from cradle to grave' as the Foundation's report so succinctly put it). That's if they're even lucky enough to be able to afford to rent. In 2019, a government inquiry concluded[15] that members of Generation Rent unable to get onto the housing ladder face an 'inevitable catastrophe' of homelessness when they retire and are no longer able to afford rising rents. In my mid-twenties, tentatively beginning to explore a completely different and financially uncertain career path, and having entirely given up on the prospect of ever owning a home, it was the prospect of what would happen later on in life that truly haunted me. I realised that the divides I was already observing in my twenties would only become more entrenched over time, the difference between the haves and have-nots becoming increasingly stark. And of course – as always – once you throw race into the mix, the situation becomes even more bleak. While 68 per cent of white households in the UK own their own homes,[16] that number plummets to just 20 per cent among Black Africans (though Black Caribbeans fare somewhat better with a home ownership rate of 40 per cent). Wealth begets wealth, and property is a major source of intergenerational wealth transference as homes, or the funds derived from selling them, are passed down from generation to generation. Analysis of the increasingly important role that family wealth plays in the UK housing market tends to focus mainly on class, eliding the fact that people from ethnic or immigrant backgrounds very often don't have access to those sorts of funds, further compounding racial wealth disparities.

Virginia Woolf famously wrote of a woman needing only 'money and a room of her own', but the defining feature of my twenties was reckoning with the possibility of never having enough of the former to enable the latter. By far the greatest economic anxiety I experienced during that period revolved around the coveted but highly elusive status of 'homeowner', and my frustration – and often outright sadness – at the complete lack of control I felt over the situation. The insane contradiction of economic conditions underpinning the London housing market meant that it wasn't a matter of simply *working* my way towards home ownership the way I was used to doing with most other things, like good grades or a new job. At times it felt as though it would be easier for a camel to pass through the eye of several successive and increasingly tiny needles than for someone like me – a single, Black, self-employed millennial woman – to get on the property ladder.

And yet, somehow, late in 2019, that started to become a possibility.

The royalties from my first book (which had become a best-seller), and the advance for my second meant that – to my surprise – I suddenly found myself in a financial position where I might actually qualify for a decent mortgage. A few weeks before Christmas my accountant had crunched the numbers and informed me of the good news, and I'd celebrated with a friend over a boozy Soho lunch, which had turned into dinner, which had turned into us being politely turfed out at closing. The following

January, I began my search, approaching the process with a scientist's precision: registering with dozens of estate agents and setting up email alerts, checking Zoopla at least five times a day and combing the Internet for tips.

Funnily enough, looking for a flat turned me into one of the things I'd always hated most: a middle-class property speculator. Suddenly I – a staunchly left-leaning lifelong Labour voter – found myself reading the *Telegraph*'s property pages as I tried to get a feel for what was happening with house prices and whether now was a good time to buy, whether Brexit might prompt a crash, and which banks were offering the best interest rates. I began talking about things like areas having 'good housing stock', began *caring* about things like areas having good housing stock, and I came face to face with my own snobberies about what type of flat I'd be proud to call home, assessing listings on whether I'd be proud to invite people over, whether I could picture myself breezily welcoming guests into my flat while quietly noting the look of envy or admiration on their faces.

I didn't even care that I felt the need to put on a slightly posher accent when I spoke to estate agents on the phone, my way of counteracting the fact that my name is what it is. Copious research has found that estate agents routinely discriminate against Black and minority prospective buyers and tenants, so I turned up to viewings wearing a blazer and an expensive handbag, talking airily about increments of £50,000 as though that amount was a mere trifle to me, just so the estate agents *knew* I could actually afford this and didn't subconsciously favour the white people I sometimes passed on my way out of viewings. I didn't care, because at least I was in the ring. The idea of buying a property felt like an act of defiance, a middle finger to the economic and political forces that have conspired to slowly push people like me out of the boroughs and cities we grew up in. I thought constantly of the irony of so few Black women being able to afford spaces of their own given the kind of existential stress we have to contend with, and that it is us who need sheltering from the world more than anyone.

I had just got to the stage of being serious enough about my search to start making offers, though the first two flats I bid on slipped out of my grasp for various reasons.

And then the pandemic struck. And things fell apart.

Chapter 11

HOMECOMING

We went into lockdown at the end of March.

Like pretty much everyone else, I'd managed to completely misjudge the severity of the situation during the early days of the COVID-19 pandemic. As reports of this strange virus emerging from China began to spread in January, I'd filed it away as just another news story in a sea of noise, barely glancing at the headlines that had begun to appear with increasing frequency on my browser home page. In early February, a friend had sent a text as he boarded a flight to the USA, joking 'I hope I don't catch coronavirus!', though he'd spelled it *coronovirus*, and I'd rolled my eyes at the improbability of his suggestion, as though he'd substituted leprosy or the bubonic plague, or something equally outlandish. *Don't be absurd*, I wrote back. A few weeks later, I'd booked flights to Italy for a friend's July wedding, confident that even though parts of the country had now been put into lockdown, things were bound to have cleared up by the summer, surely? A few weeks after *that*, the UK was entering lockdown too – which meant that the housing market, like most things, was now effectively closed for business. Viewings were banned, and most of the banks stopped lending to first-time buyers. Anyone hoping to buy a property, or even just to move house, would have to sit tight and wait for the lockdown to end.

And that is when I began to panic – I couldn't afford to wait. Because I'm self-employed and my income varies considerably from year to year, I'd been advised by a mortgage broker who'd looked at my accounts that I absolutely needed to secure a mortgage by the summer – and that if I didn't manage it by then, I'd probably have to wait another few years before I could present the two years of consistent income most lenders want to see when assessing freelance mortgage applicants. The clock was ticking. Every day the lockdown continued made it less likely that I'd be able to buy a flat that year as I'd planned, a prospect that after all those years of saving and strategising felt utterly devastating.

I took to checking the news constantly, toggling from the BBC to Twitter and back again, ten, fifteen, twenty times a day, fervently searching for clues as to when the *fuck* all of this was going to be over. The outlook wasn't great. Scientists, journalists and politicians alike were forecasting months, if not years, of disruption, and I started to realise that even once the lockdown had been lifted and I could resume my flat-hunt, as a self-employed person looking to buy on my own, banks spooked about a looming recession would not look kindly on me when it came to mortgages – that is if they'd even look at me at all.

As the precariousness of my situation began to sink in, so too did an overwhelming feeling of despair unlike any I have ever known before or since. After all the penny-pinching and counting and planning and worrying, I'd thought that the *one thing* I wanted more than anything else in the world was finally within reach, had even allowed myself to relax into it ever so slightly, only to have that dream snatched away just as I'd come to cash in my chips. Had I jinxed it, I wondered, by allowing myself to get excited about the process, by letting slip to a few friends here and there that I was looking at flats, by starting a Pinterest board before the keys were in hand and the contract signed?

Even though I knew I was far from being the pandemic's worst victim – that I was lucky to still have my health and a roof over my head, to have savings and to be able to work from home, to not have lost anyone I loved to the virus, to still be *alive* – that awareness only took me so far. Truth be told, I didn't feel particularly grateful. I felt angry and upset and intensely hard done by.

'Well, at least if you end up having to wait a few more years, you'll be able to save up a bigger deposit! So that could be good?' one friend reasoned, trying to console me as I explained my predicament to her down the phone.

'Mmmm.' All I could think was that I didn't *want* more time to save, that I had *been* saving, and that this year was supposed to be the pay-off. As far as I was concerned, there was no silver lining to be found in any of this, only bitter and all-consuming disappointment.

'It just feels so fucking *unfair*,' I ranted. 'I feel like I've done *everything* right – worked really hard, sacrificed stuff and spent most of my twenties living at home . . . And it just hasn't made a difference. I *still* can't buy my own place.'

One of the most reliable causes of human unhappiness is the feeling of lacking autonomy over one's life, and perhaps most difficult to bear in all of this was how powerless I felt. Whenever I'd found myself in a difficult situation in the past, I'd always somehow found a way to take control of things, whether that meant quitting a toxic job or moving into a new flat or extricating myself from an unhealthy friendship. But this was so much bigger than me – this time I had no options, could not scheme or plan or manoeuvre my way out of a global pandemic, could not in fact do anything but sit at home and wait it out. It didn't help that my physical state so closely mirrored my emotional one – physically constrained by the pandemic restrictions, and deprived of the usual outlets that might allow me to escape myself or my thoughts for even a few hours. I was trapped at home with my own corrosive anxieties, turning the disappointment over and over in my mind and cycling through the same few thoughts: that I'd been supposed to celebrate my thirtieth birthday in my own flat, ready to enter the next decade as the independent, self-actualised adult woman I so badly wanted to be, and with the prolonged adolescence of my twenties finally behind me. Instead, what I'd hoped – planned – would be the best year of my adult life, a year that had started out brimming with dreams and options and forward momentum, had somehow turned into one of the most exhausting, challenging and depressing years I'd ever known.

In response I became, I am sure, completely unbearable to live with. Snappy, belligerent, deeply morose. Attempts by my mother to coax me out of my gloom were almost inevitably met with a tantrum and a slammed door (see: prolonged adolescence). The optimism she counselled felt pointless, even dangerous – I didn't want to risk getting my hopes up, only to end up being disappointed if things didn't work out.

More than anything, I felt cheated. As lockdown dragged on and the true extent of the pandemic continued to unfold, I began to realise that this wouldn't be a months-long or even year-long disruption, but something more akin to a generational upheaval – that the aftershock of this pandemic would affect my life for years to come, and that this might be a turning point in my economic trajectory, a line that divided my story into 'before' and 'after'. Friends I spoke to seemed equally disillusioned, feeling as I did like they'd just started getting their shit together – becoming established in their careers and earning real money, perhaps paying off the credit card debt they'd accumulated in their early twenties and starting to save, possibly even considering buying a home, as I was.

We'd done what we were supposed to – gone to university and gotten the grades, found 'good' jobs and worked ourselves to the bone trying to prove ourselves at them. And then, just when we'd thought things were starting to work out, a global pandemic had come along and lain waste to our carefully laid plans. Now we were all just clinging on grimly to the bucking bronco of 2020, trying desperately not to let go of the meagre gains we'd managed against the circumstantial odds. Our twenties looked set to be bookended by recessions that had irreversibly damaged our professional and financial prospects (data has consistently shown that graduating into a recession has a long-term negative impact on your earning potential[1]), and now, just as we were emerging into our peak earning years – another recession. All this compounded by a decade-long austerity programme and the gathering clouds of Brexit, the shock of which even four years later still hadn't subsided.

In almost all of my WhatsApp chats a grim gallows humour emerged, as we traded increasingly nihilistic memes about our impending financial doom, the saying 'laugh or you'll cry' suddenly a generational slogan. One friend reminded me of a pre-pandemic conversation we'd had where we'd vowed that '2020 would be our year', and we cackled despite ourselves, hysterical at the hubris of our past selves. In more serious, vulnerable moments, others confessed to the toll the pandemic was taking on them, and how depressed and anxious they were, that they were either beginning or resuming therapy to cope, that they were considering antidepressants.

And we were the lucky ones! Middle class, university educated, mostly working in jobs that had allowed us to pivot to working from home with relative ease. Even those who, like me, occupied the more precarious world of self-employment, were mainly knowledge workers insulated by a modicum of professional capital, as opposed to operating at the knife-edge of the gig economy as waiters or shop assistants – the sorts of jobs that had evaporated as soon as the lockdown kicked in. I felt a guilty relief too that I was at the tail end of my twenties and not the beginning, shuddering at the thought of what it must be like to be looking for an entry level job as businesses left and right yanked grad schemes and internships, pulling up the ladder while they waited out the storm.

Still as lay-offs swept through the media and publication after publication folded, I quietly wondered – and not for the first time – why on earth I'd been so insistent on hitching my wagon to this crumbling industry, where only a lucky few manage to carve out a meaningful livelihood or make a lifelong career for themselves. As soon as the UK lockdown had been announced, I'd lost most of my freelance jobs for the months ahead, and with them a good chunk of my income. For the first time since going freelance, I was forced to truly reckon with how uncertain my career was, and the fact that I'd decided to make a living by peddling something nebulous and entirely inessential, and which, when push came to shove, people could easily live without.

Unsurprisingly, women were one of the demographics worst affected by the economic fallout from COVID-19, more likely than men to lose their jobs[2] due to their overrepresentation[3] in the sectors hardest hit by the pandemic, and more likely to be employed in the sorts of temporary jobs that had disappeared as soon as the lockdown was introduced. Women were also more likely than men to be furloughed,[4] and more likely to *ask* to be furloughed so that they could look after children, finding that their employers either couldn't or wouldn't accommodate their (often drastically increased) childcare responsibilities.

The motherhood penalty women face at work only intensified under pandemic conditions, which exacerbated the already uneven division of household labour, though this is not new. In times of crisis, the gender chore gap tends to increase exponentially, with women and their time acting as the shock absorbers of economic hardship. During the recession that followed the 2008 financial crisis, it was women who overwhelmingly shouldered the increased burden of domestic duties that resulted from job losses and strained family finances, and so too with the COVID-19 pandemic. Stories I heard from friends with children and others I saw circulated via social media made it abundantly clear that it was women who were bearing the brunt of domestic duties. In April, only one month into the first UK lockdown, economists from the universities of Cambridge, Oxford and Zurich found that mothers were typically providing at least 50 per cent more childcare than they had pre-lockdown, and spending between 10 per cent and 30 per cent more time on home-schooling their children than fathers did, increases that added up to an extra hour and a half of unpaid labour each day.[5] In the USA, there were similar outcomes:[6] home-schooling (suddenly a necessity for many parents) was disproportionately handled by women, even where *both* parents worked full-time. Worse, because men so often out-earn their female partners, the closure of schools during the pandemic often meant that, realistically, only one parent could work full-time. In many cases it made financial sense for that parent to be the man, and for women to assume childcare duties, essentially taking a step back from their careers. One way or another, many women found themselves forced out of the labour market by the pandemic, and the professional and economic ramifications of the COVID-19 pandemic will almost certainly continue to manifest in the years to come, even if these career disruptions are relatively short term. In ten or twenty years' time, economists may well refer to a swathe of women as 'the corona-virus generation', referencing those whose incomes, careers and pensions were irreversibly depleted by the events of 2020.

The pandemic was equally, if not more disastrous for ethnic minorities, who contracted and died from the virus at dispropor-tionally high rates.[7] In the UK, Black Africans were more than three times as likely to die from the virus than white Brits,[8] not because of any inherent genetic weakness or racial differences (per the sort of uninformed armchair scientist theories that tend to attach themselves to these sorts of findings), but for the simple reason that Black (and Asian) people are more likely to occupy frontline key worker roles: doctors, nurses, bus drivers, delivery-men – the sorts of jobs where you couldn't just sequester yourself at home with a laptop and Wi-Fi connection, and where you were continually exposed to strangers, and to the virus.

Even for those who didn't contract the virus, or who did and were lucky enough to survive it, the impact on employment rates and finances was often dire. Again, minorities in the UK were more likely to work in the sort of low-paid and insecure service jobs that dried up as a result of the pandemic, and were also more likely to outright lose their jobs than to be furloughed.[9] As ethnic minorities generally have far lower levels of savings and assets, they were also less able to withstand the economic shock of suddenly having a reduced or non-existent income. The pandemic only served to worsen existing economic inequalities and racial wealth gaps in the UK, though again it could be years, perhaps even decades, before the true extent of its economic impact on Black and brown communities is laid bare.

And yet somehow, in the middle of all this chaos, I managed to find a flat. As soon as the restrictions on house viewings were lifted, I swung into action, adopting a daily routine of harassing estate agents with near-constant emails and phone calls, ever-conscious of the clock counting down to my summer deadline. My persistence paid off – within weeks, I'd found a flat that I loved and had had an offer accepted, though, as ever, I soon found that things were not to be as straightforward as that. Just as I'd feared, most lenders had responded to the pandemic by tightening their lending criteria, making it harder than ever for self-employed people and first-time buyers to qualify for a mortgage. A few weeks after submitting my application, my broker called – bad news. The lender I'd applied to – who pre-pandemic had provisionally accepted my application – had changed its mind. Application denied. It's something of a descriptive cliché to say that one's blood ran cold, but I am sure that in that moment mine truly did.

Frantic now, I applied to a different lender, and so followed nearly two months of emails back and forth between me, my broker, my accountant and the lender, as together we navigated the obstacle course of restrictions and endless bureaucracy. For weeks on end there'd be radio silence, and then we'd be asked for more information, more tax returns, more projections, my bank statements, proof of future income, a reference letter from my accountant, a reference letter from my accountant with a *letter-head*. I'd send whatever they'd asked for, and then . . . more silence. It felt as though I was gathering evidence for a court case, as though they were looking for reasons to deny me (which, I suppose, they were). On some days I would find I couldn't work, couldn't focus, couldn't *eat* due to the sheer frustration of it all. I knew that I was about to have my application rejected a second time.

But then finally, miraculously, two and a half months after I'd had my offer accepted – an approval. This was the moment I'd been fantasising about for so long, and yet my relief felt strangely muted somehow, far from the cascade of pent-up emotion that I had anticipated. I could only muster a detached acceptance of that fact coupled with a narrow-eyed distrust, by now wary of getting too attached to good news in the middle of a year that had shown me how unexpectedly one's fortunes could sour.

I had been badly bruised by the process too, and it took a while for my anger over it to subside – anger at how *difficult* it had all been, and how time-consuming. Anger at how many hoops I'd had to jump through, and how keenly I'd felt that those in charge were looking for reasons to count me out rather than in. And, despite their reputation for being famously untrustworthy characters, I'd *still* been shocked by the general mendacity of estate agents and how pointlessly complex they often made the process, how opaque it all was, and the almost arbitrary nature of house prices; how much emphasis is placed on homeownership in the UK and then how insurmountable that process often is, the cruelty of that dichotomy. How grotesquely flawed it is to have a system where the reward for having enough money to afford a home is making *more* money as your property appreciates in value, while those who can't muster up a deposit are stuck on a hamster wheel of rent payments, penalised for having the audacity to not be rich.

The irony hasn't escaped me that while my fortunes have improved over the past few decades, that trajectory exists in stark contrast to the broader status quo, and that things around me have largely gotten worse. In the twenty-five years since my family moved to the UK, increasingly austere economic measures and restrictive immigration policies have seen many of the pathways that enabled us to find our footing dry up, with governments on both sides of the political spectrum seemingly hell-bent on pulling up the drawbridge for families like mine – immigrant and non-immigrant alike – who dream of ending their stories in a different place from where they began. The UK has one of the lowest rates of social mobility in Europe, and economists have predicted that the long-term effects of the coronavirus pandemic are likely to exacerbate existing social inequalities.[10] I am often struck by the fact that what my family was able to do back in the mid-nineties – emigrating to the UK, finding decent accommodation and schools, having access to well-funded community programmes and spaces – wouldn't be possible today, and by the dishonesty of the politicians desperate to convince us that that is a good and necessary thing.

The past has a way of clinging to you, of informing your present – your desires, your needs, your aspirations, your values. Your ability to realise those things. In choosing my flat I had deliberately sought out my own past, ending up only a few minutes' walk from where my family had first lived when we arrived to the UK, back in the neighbourhood where I'd spent most of my childhood. I had felt drawn back to where I had started out, and that to put down permanent roots there would be a triumph, a symbolic closing of the loop. I tread old paths almost daily now, buying vegetables from the same market where my mother used to buy hers, and on sunny afternoons I sometimes sit in the quiet churchyard I used to skip through on my way home from school. The library I used to sequester myself in while my mother ran her Saturday errands is right on my doorstep, though it has long since closed, as I discovered after wandering in one morning, only to be told by a slightly bemused receptionist that the building hadn't been used as a library in years. That paradise where I'd sat and read and read, thumbing through *Nancy Drew* stories and Dorling Kindersley books, begging for just five more minutes when my mum arrived to pick me up. I mourned that closure for months.

The word nostalgia is derived from the Greek *nostos*, meaning homecoming, and *algos*, meaning pain. At times I am almost overwhelmed by these memories, by the bittersweetness of nostalgia, of 'homecoming pain'. Driving through the surrounding streets in the back of a taxi not long ago, I rounded a corner and unexpectedly found myself face to face with the tower block we'd lived in for those first few months, in that borrowed flat with its rose-pink carpets. I hadn't seen it since we'd left.

'Oh, that's where I grew up!' I blurted out to the driver, wanting to share the significance of that moment with someone.

'Yeah?' he replied, polite, uninterested.

I twisted round in my seat to get a longer look at the building through the rear window as we drove past, only turning back once it was fully out of sight.

Your past informs your present, and with every year that passes I realise more and more that mine is my greatest advantage. Once or twice, noticing me get unduly panicked about money, perhaps spiralling over an unexpected expense that on balance I could easily afford, my parents have, I think, recognised themselves in me, and expressed guilt that perhaps their earlier money worries have left an indelible imprint. And truthfully, they're probably right – but the cautiousness they instilled in me has also been a precious, unexpected gift.

Everyone has different coping methods when it comes to dealing with their money worries. Some people choose to bury their heads in the sand, others to spend with wild abandon. I have mostly dealt with my fears by choosing to confront them head-on, peeling back the covers and looking under every rock. Paying forensic attention to my finances has become my way of conquering my money demons, of retaining control over something that scares me, something I think might always scare me just a little.

I learned that – that forewarned is forearmed – from my parents, who I guess have taught me most of the important things I know about money. It's from them that I learned never to spend more than I earn, and to never depend on anyone else for money. To be as generous with others as I possibly can. To never ever be a cheat. It was my mother who took me to open a bank account when I was 8 years old, where we deposited the birthday money I'd been given by a generous aunt (the year before I had splurged on an ABBA compilation CD and suffered buyer's regret, so this was to be my introduction to delayed gratification). I learned to understand the concept of interest from the few pennies of it I accumulated each year, which I'd see on the annual statement the bank sent, thrilled at the idea that I was being given 'free money'. It was my parents who impressed on me that I was as smart as anyone else – smarter than (if they were to be believed), from them that I learned my value. My father waging war against any teacher who tried to diminish me taught me to do the same as an adult. To fight for myself, and stand my ground. To not accept the pickle juice. This flat – *my* flat – feels like the manifestation of all they have given me, of all those lessons made concrete.

I had just turned 30 when I bought it, and it felt so neatly symbolic to punctuate the end of my twenties that way. As I packed my books into boxes and stuffed clothes into suitcases, I thought about how much my relationship with money had evolved over the course of that uncertain decade, and the irony of it being my writing – the thing that I had been too scared to pursue – that has brought me here. I am not who I was a decade ago. I have begun to do things that for years I was too afraid to do: travelling more, and spending too much money on nights out, taking an Uber instead of waiting patiently for the bus, and even dipping into my savings for no other reason than because I fancy a bit of a splurge. It seems counter-intuitive that the way in which I've got 'better' with money has been by becoming objectively 'worse' with it, but these acts are about being less fastidiously responsible, and giving myself permission to loosen a grip made tight through fear. Bit by bit, I am shaking off the pessimism that defined my twenties.

I have begun to relax into the thrill of having a place of my own, to accept that this is finally my reality; that I am master of my own tiny fiefdom, to decorate and furnish and rule over as

I see fit. I often marvel at the miraculousness of it all, still unable to believe the enormity of my good fortune. At times a strange electric, almost chemical, feeling will bubble up inside of me as I turn the key in my front door and step over the threshold into my home, a surge of pride that *I have done this*. I feel as fiercely proud as though I had poured the foundations and laid the bricks myself.

The journey to get here has been as challenging as it has been uplifting, as painful as it has been eye-opening, and with every challenge has come a valuable lesson, lessons that are about far more than just money. They are about freedom and bias, judgement and control, shame, pride, compulsion, fear. Lessons about human nature and human vulnerability, about the world and my place within it.

It is a journey that has allowed me to see myself more clearly, and so I am as grateful for the bad times as I am the good, because even the bad times have made me who I am.

I wouldn't trade them for all the money in the world.

ACKNOWLEDGEMENTS

To my editor Michelle Kane. There aren't words to fully express how much I appreciate and adore you, but I am a writer so I guess I have to try! Meeting you has changed my life, and it is a pleasure and honour to get to work with you every day, and to know that I have you in my corner. A brilliant editor, but much more than that, a treasured friend. Thank you for all that you do for me.

To Naomi Mantin, the best publicist in the book game. I am so appreciative of how hard you work (and how effortless you make it look!) and for the intelligence you bring to the book promotion process.

To all at 4th Estate, for the ambition, care and originality with which you publish my work, and for the respect you show me as an author. I am truly grateful.

To Kathryn Holliday, a fact-checker extraordinaire and an intimidatingly knowledgeable brain, whose eagle-eyed mind I felt lucky to have gracing the pages of this book.

To Nick Rowland, for keeping me sane(ish) and always making me laugh, and for your support during That Time. I don't think I'd be here without you.

To Vicky Spratt, for your endless support during the writing of this book, and for the occasional tough love (remember when

I wanted to 'take a break' from writing it, and you point blank told me no? That was important).

To Dolly Alderton, for your friendship and humour, but most of all for your wisdom in guiding me through how to tackle some of the trickier aspects of writing a memoir.

And most importantly, thank you to my parents, for so graciously allowing me to tell part of your story in this book, and for the many sacrifices you have made for me over the years; for the lessons you have taught me, and the integrity with which you have always conducted yourselves, and for the unconditional love you show me. I owe everything that I have, and everything that I am, to you.

ENDNOTES

Scholarship Kid

1 'Pupil Exclusions: Ethnicity facts and figures', GOV.UK <https://www.ethnicity-facts-figures.service.gov.uk/education-skills-and-training/absence-and-exclusions/pupil-exclusions/latest>. See also Sally Weale and David Batty, 'Fears that cancelling exams will hit BAME and poor pupils worst', *Guardian*, 19 March 2020 <https://www.theguardian.com/world/2020/mar/19/fears-that-cancelling-exams-will-hit-black-and-poor-pupils-worst>.

2 Eula Biss, *Having And Being Had*, 2020.

Dreaming Spires

1 'Elitism in Britain, 2019', GOV.UK <https://www.gov.uk/government/news/elitism-in-britain-2019>. See also University of Oxford Annual Admissions Statistical Report, May 2020 <https://www.ox.ac.uk/sites/files/oxford/Annual%20Admissions%20Statistical%20Report%202020.pdf>. Nick Collins, 'Pupils from elite schools secure one in ten Oxford Places', *Telegraph*, 28 October 2010 <https://www.telegraph.co.uk/education/universityeducation/8090117/Pupils-from-elite-schools-secure-one-in-ten-Oxford-places.html>.

2 According to ACORN, a demographic tool used to categorise the UK's population in line with socio-economic status, this is a widely recognised measure used by marketing teams and public policy departments alike <https://acorn.caci.co.uk/downloads/Acorn-User-guide.pdf>.

3 University of Oxford website, 7 January 2020 <https://www.ox.ac.uk/news/2020-01-07-more-black-british-students-ever-choosing-oxford>.

4 Lucy Sheriff, 'UniLad Magazine Forced To Pull "Surprise" Rape Article After Twitter Backlash', *Huffington Post*, 31 January 2012 <https://www.huffingtonpost.co.uk/2012/01/31/unilad-magazine-forced-to-pull-surprise-rape-article-after-twitter-backlash_n_1244173.html?guccounter=1>.

5 Greta Keenan, 'Refreshers', *Cherwell*, 24 September 2012 <https://cherwell.org/2012/09/24/refreshers/>.

6 Charlotte Proudman, 'Port and prejudice – drinking societies are the dark side of Oxbridge', *Guardian*, 26 October 2015 <https://www.theguardian.com/commentisfree/2015/oct/26/drinking-societies-oxbridge-clubs-oxford-piers-gaveston-cambridge-wyverns>.

7 Richard Alleyne, 'Oxford University drinking group condemned for drawing up "fit list" of attractive freshers', *Telegraph*, 7 December 2011 <https://www.telegraph.co.uk/education/educationnews/8940800/Oxford-University-drinking-group-condemned-for-drawing-up-fit-list-of-attractive-freshers.html>.

8 Natalie Robehmed, 'How 20-Year-Old Kylie Jenner Built A $900 Million Fortune In Less Than 3 Years', *Forbes*, 11 July 2018 <https://www.forbes.com/sites/forbesdigitalcovers/2018/07/11/how-20-year-old-kylie-jenner-built-a-900-million-fortune-in-less-than-3-years/?sh=8ce25dfaa62c#6470ad33aa62>.

9 Vanessa Friedman and Jessica Testa, 'The Metaphysics of Kylie Cosmetics Being Sold to Coty', *New York Times*, 19 November 2019 <https://www.nytimes.com/2019/11/19/style/kylie-jenner-coty-cosmetics.html>.

10 Chase Peterson-Withorn and Madeline Berg, 'Inside Kylie Jenner's Web of Lies – And Why She's No Longer a Billionaire', *Forbes*, 1 June 2020 <https://www.forbes.com/sites/chasewithorn/2020/05/29/inside-kylie-jennerss-web-of-lies-and-why-shes-no-longer-a-billionaire/?sh=58a5daec25f7>.

11 Kerry A. Dolan, Here's What Forbes Means By Self-Made: From Bootstrappers To Silver Spooners, *Forbes*, 5 March 2019 <https://www.forbes.com/sites/kerryadolan/2018/07/13/heres-what-forbes-means-by-self-made-from-bootstrappers-to-silver-spooners/?sh=5ef51301ca3e>.

12 Lynn Steger Strong, 'A dirty secret: you can only be a writer if you can afford it', *Guardian*, 27 February 2020 <https://www.theguardian.com/us-news/2020/feb/27/a-dirty-secret-you-can-only-be-a-writer-if-you-can-afford-it>.

'Please Sir, Can I Have Some More?'

1 Orit Gadiesh and Julie Coffman, 'Companies Drain Women's Ambition After Only 2 Years', *Harvard Business Review*, 18 May 2015 <https://hbr.org/2015/05/companies-drain-womens-ambition-after-only-2-years>.

2 Hannah Riley Bowles, Linda Babcock and Lei Lai, 'Social incentives for gender differences in the propensity to initiate negotiations: Sometimes it does hurt to ask', *Organizational Behavior and Human Decision Processes* (103), 2007 <https://www.cfa.harvard.edu/cfawis/bowles.pdf>.

3 McKinsey & Company and LeanIn.Org, Women in the Workplace, 2016 report <https://womenintheworkplace.com/2016#!>.

4 Olle Folke and Johanna Rickne, 'All the Single Ladies: Job Promotions and the Durability of Marriage', *Research Institute of Industrial Economics*, 2016 <http://www.ifn.se/wfiles/wp/wp1146.pdf>.

5 Christin L. Munsch, 'Her Support, His Support: Money, Masculinity, and Marital Infidelity', *American Sociological Review* (80:3), 2015 <https://www.asanet.org/sites/default/files/savvy/journals/CS/Jun15 ASRFeature.pdf>.

6 Ashley C. Ford, 'Millennial Women Are Conflicted About Being Breadwinners', *Refinery29*, 14 April 2017 <https://www.refinery29.com/en-gb/2017/04/151684/millennial-women-are-conflicted-about-being-breadwinners>.

7 Erica Buist, 'Media stereotype women in financial coverage, study finds', 10 March 2018 <https://www.theguardian.com/money/2018/mar/10/media-stereotype-women-in-financial-coverage-study-finds>.

8 Jia Tolentino, 'Refinery29, Kylie Jenner, and the Denial Underlying Millennial Financial Resentment', *New Yorker*, 24 July 2018 <https://www.newyorker.com/culture/cultural-comment/refinery29-kylie-jenner-and-the-denial-underlying-millennial-financial-resentment>.

9 Richard Wheatstone, '"The Heart Bleeds", Millennial who earns £70k mocked on Twitter for moaning she is "struggling" and having to cancel her £150 gym membership so she can save for a flat', *The Sun*, 18 July 2018 <https://www.thesun.co.uk/news/6808745/millenial-moans-cancel-gym-membership-70000-salary-twitter-buy-flat/>.

10 Jessica Knoll, 'I Want to Be Rich and I'm Not Sorry', *New York Times*, 28 April 2018 <https://www.nytimes.com/2018/04/28/opinion/sunday/women-want-to-be-rich.html>.

11 Lacey Rose, 'Ellen Pompeo, TV's $20 Million Woman, Reveals Her Behind-the-Scenes Fight for "What I Deserve"', *The Hollywood Reporter*, 17 January 2018 <https://www.hollywoodreporter.com/features/ellen-pompeo-tvs-20-million-woman-reveals-her-behind-scenes-fight-what-i-deserve-1074978>.

12 Benjamin Artz, Amanda H. Goodall and Andrew J. Oswald, 'Do Women Ask', *Industrial Relations*, (57:4) <https://onlinelibrary.wiley.com/doi/abs/10.1111/irel.12214>.

13 Linda Babcock, Sara Laschever, Michele Gelfand and Deborah Small, 'Nice Girls Don't Ask', *Harvard Business Review*, October 2003 <https://hbr.org/2003/10/nice-girls-dont-ask>.

14 Sara Laschever, 'Younger women may be asking for pay rises. But let's not celebrate just yet', *Guardian*, 9 September 2016 <https://www.theguardian.com/commentisfree/2016/sep/09/women-equal-pay-negotiate>.

15 'In corporate America, women fall behind early and continue to lose ground with every step', Women in the Workplace, 2016 report <https://womenintheworkplace.com/2016#!>.

16 Women in the Workplace, 2018 report <https://womenintheworkplace.com>.

17 Itself based on the 1938 play *Gas Light* by the English playwright Patrick Hamilton.

Boys' Club

1 Hamilton Nolan, 'Working at Vice Media Is Not as Cool as It Seems', *Gawker*, 30 May 2014 <https://gawker.com/working-at-vice-media-is-not-as-cool-as-it-seems-1579711577>.

2 Hamilton Nolan, 'Vice UK Is Not as Cool as It Seems, Either', *Gawker*, 15 July 2014 <https://gawker.com/vice-uk-is-not-as-cool-as-it-seems-either-1604842641>.

3 Matthew Garrahan, 'Vice eyes 2015 "deal spree" and possible IPO', *Financial Times*, December 15 2014 <https://www.ft.com/content/06a24e18-8477-11e4-bae9-00144feabdc0>.

4 'VICE to Gawker: Fuck You and Fuck Your Garbage Click-Bait "Journalism"' <https://www.vice.com/en/page/response>.

5 Daniel Miller, 'Vice Media sued by former employee alleging systemic pay discrimination against women', 13 February 2018 <https://www.latimes.com/business/hollywood/la-fi-ct-vice-media-lawsuit-20180213-story.html>.

6 Todd Spangler, 'Vice Media to Pay $1.875 Million to Settle Lawsuit Alleging the Company Paid Women Less Than Men', *Variety*, 27 March 2019 <https://variety.com/2019/biz/news/vice-media-to-pay-1-875-million-to-settle-lawsuit-alleging-the-company-paid-women-less-than-men-1203173870/>.

7 Taken from a mixed-gender sample size of 5,814 employees. See 'Gender bias in workplace culture curbs careers' <https://www.murrayedwards.cam.ac.uk/sites/default/files/files/CWM%20Gender%20Bias%20REPORT%20FINAL%2020190211.pdf>.

8 See Emily Steel's Twitter thread <https://twitter.com/emilysteel/status/944622418345250824>, and her article, 'At Vice, Cutting-Edge Media and Allegations of Old-School Sexual Harassment', *New York Times*, 23 December 2017 <https://www.nytimes.com/2017/12/23/business/media/vice-sexual-harassment.html>.

The Right Type of Black

1 Contemporary intersectional feminist thought has since expanded Crenshaw's initial definition beyond solely Black women to include any category of womanhood that falls outside the boundaries of the middle-class white cis-gender female experience – so *all* women of colour, LGBTQ women, working-class women, and so on. See Kimberlé Crenshaw, 'Demarginalizing the Intersection of Race and Sex: A Black Feminist Critique of Antidiscrimination Doctrine, Feminist Theory and Antiracist Politics', *University of Chicago Legal Forum* (1.8), 1989 <http://chicagounbound.uchicago.edu/uclf/vol1989/iss1/8>.

2 Bim Adewunmi, 'Maria Sharapova's Rivalry With Serena Williams Is In Her Head', *Buzzfeed*, 9 September 2017 <https://www.buzzfeednews.com/article/bimadewunmi/maria-sharapovas-rivalry-with-serena-williams-is-in-her-head>.

3 Gene Demby, 'How Code-Switching Explains the World', *NPR*, 8 April 2013 <https://www.npr.org/sections/codeswitch/2013/04/08/176064688/how-code-switching-explains-the-world?t=1610582253549>.

4 Quoted from *Slay In Your Lane* (2018).

5 Kathleen Henehan and Helena Rose, 'Opportunities Knocked? Exploring pay penalties among the UK's ethnic minorities', July 2018 <https://www.resolutionfoundation.org/app/uploads/2018/07/Opportunities-Knocked.pdf>.

6 Marianne Bertrand and Sendhil Mullainathan, 'Are Emily and Greg More Employable than Lakisha and Jamal? A Field Experiment on Labor Market Discrimination', National Bureau of Economic Research, July 2003 <https://www.nber.org/papers/w9873>.

7 Alison Hewitt, 'A "black"-sounding name makes people imagine a larger, more dangerous person, UCLA study shows', UCLA Newsroom, 7 October 2015 <https://newsroom.ucla.edu/releases/a-black-sounding-name-makes-people-imagine-a-larger-more-dangerous-person-ucla-study-shows>.

8 Arthur H. Goldsmith, Darrick Hamilton and William Darity, Jr, 'From Dark to Light: Skin Color and Wages Among African-Americans', *The Journal of Human Resources* (42:4), 2007 <https://www. researchgate.net/publication/23780671_From_Dark_to_Light_Skin_Color_and_Wages_Among_African-Americans>.

9 Jenée Desmond-Harris, 'Study: lighter-skinned black and Hispanic people look smarter to white people', *Vox*, 28 February 2015 <https://www.vox.com/2015/2/28/8116799/white-colorism-racism-study>.

10 Lance Hannon, Robert DeFina and Sarah Bruch, 'The Relationship Between Skin Tone and School Suspension for African Americans', Springer Race Soc Probl, 5 September 2013 <https://link.springer.com/epdf/10.1007/s12552-013-9104-z?>.

11 Arthur H. Goldsmith, Darrick Hamilton and William Darity, Jr, 'Shedding "light" on marriage: The influence of skin shade on marriage for Black females', *Journal of Economic Behavior & Organization* (72:1) <https://www.researchgate.net/publication/222543696_Shedding_light_on_marriage_The_influence_of_skin_shade_on_marriage_for_Black_females>.

12 'Kanye West calls mixed girls "mutts"', *HipHopDX*, 1 December 2006 <https://hiphopdx.com/news/id.4685/title.kanye-west-calls-mixed-girls-mutts>.

13 'Universal Distances Itself From "Straight Outta Compton" Casting Call', *Billboard*, 18 July 2014 <https://www.billboard.com/articles/columns/the-juice/6165177/universal-straight-outta-compton-casting-racist-offensive-nwa>.

14 Brooke Bobb, 'The Ultimate Post-VMA Power Couple Dinner: Pizza and Wine With Bey and Jay, Kimye, and More', *Vogue*, 19 August 2016 <https://www.vogue.com/article/vma-2016-kanye-kim-beyonce-jay-z-dinner>.

15 Tiffany Curtis, 'We need to talk about women of color in creative industries when we discuss the wage gap', *HelloGiggles*, 5 April 2018

<https://hellogiggles.com/lifestyle/money-career/women-of-color-creative-industries-wage-gap/>.

16 Quoted from Elspeth Reeve, 'A History of the Hot Take', *The New Republic*, 12 April 2015 <https://newrepublic.com/article/121501/history-hot-take>.

17 Ben Machell, 'What I've learnt: Tom Jones', *The Times*, 31 October 2015 <https://www.thetimes.co.uk/article/what-ive-learnt-tom-jones-j0fpf9fj3rr>.

18 Laura Bennett, 'The First-Person Industrial Complex', *Slate*, 14 September 2015 <http://www.slate.com/articles/life/technology/2015/09/the_first_person_industrial_complex_how_the_harrowing_personal_essay_took.html?via=gdpr-consent>.

19 Morgan Jerkins, 'How I Overcame My Anger as a Black Writer Online', *Lenny*, 1 August 2017 <https://www.lennyletter.com/story/how-i-overcame-anger-as-a-black-writer-online>.

20 Amory Sivertson, 'Rage Is A Red Lesson', *Dear Sugars* on wbur, 12 May 2018 <https://www.wbur.org/dearsugar/2018/05/12/rage-is-a-red-lesson>.

21 Lou Stoppard and Antwaun Sargent, 'How fashion tripped over the hip-hop economy', *Financial Times*, 28 February 2019 <https://www.ft.com/content/8ecf1b40-3760-11e9-9988-28303f70fcff>.

22 Nick Squires, 'Gucci withdraws "golliwog" black polo neck amid accusations of racism', 7 February 2019 <https://www.telegraph.co.uk/news/2019/02/07/gucci-withdraws-jumper-blackface-backlash/>.

23 'Kering to improve profit and double in 2018', *mds*, 12 February 2019 <https://www.themds.com/companies/gucci-keeps-boosting-kering-profits-double-in-2018.html>.

24 Lou Stoppard and Antwaun Sargent, 'How fashion tripped over the hip-hop economy', *Financial Times*, 28 February 2019 <https://www.ft.com/content/8ecf1b40-3760-11e9-9988-28303f70fcff>.

25 'The White Issue: Has Anna Wintour's Diversity Push Come Too Late?', *New York Times*, 15 December 2020 <https://www.nytimes.com/2020/10/24/business/media/anna-wintour-vogue-race.html>.

26 Collier Meyerson, 'Nameplate necklaces: This shit is for us', 1 November 2016 <https://splinternews.com/nameplate-necklaces-this-shit-is-for-us-1793863356>.

27 Celia Ellenberg, 'How a Florida Mom and Etsy Star Handcrafted 12,500 of Those Jaw-Dropping Dreadlocks at Marc Jacobs', *Vogue*, 15 September 2016 <https://www.vogue.com/article/marc-jacobs-spring-2017-wool-dredlocks-pink-purple-hair-guido-palau-jena-counts>.

28 Christopher Mele, 'Army Lifts Ban on Dreadlocks, and Black Servicewomen Rejoice', *New York Times*, 10 February 2017 <https://www.nytimes.com/2017/02/10/us/army-ban-on-dreadlocks-black-servicewomen.html>.

29 Rebecca Klein, 'New Complaint Targets School That Banned Child With Dreadlocks', *HuffPost US*, 14 February 2020 <https://www.huffingtonpost.co.uk/entry/florida-school-banned-dreadlocks_n_5c000d0be4b08506231a95e5>.

30 'Fulham schoolboy dreadlock ban overturned', *BBC News*, 12 September 2018 <https://www.bbc.co.uk/news/uk-england-london-45499584>.

31 Zlata Rodionova, 'Black woman applying for Harrods job told she had to "chemically straighten her hair to get job"', *Independent*, 25 January 2017 <https://www.independent.co.uk/news/business/news/sexist-workplace-dresscodes-high-heels-row-women-dye-hair-blonde-revealing-outfits-female-employees-offices-a7544736.html>.

32 Kathleen Hou, 'Marc Jacobs Models Wore Dreadlocks From Etsy', *The Cut*, 15 September 2016 <https://www.thecut.com/2016/09/marc-jacobs-spring-2017-models-wore-etsy-dreadlocks.html>.

The Beauty Tax

1 Bria Balliet, 'Beauty is as beauty does', 24 June 2016 <https://news.uci.edu/2016/06/24/beauty-is-as-beauty-does/>.

2 A note on methodology, given the subjectivity of attractiveness as a concept – Wong and Penner didn't assess the study participants' attractiveness themselves. Here follows a (lightly paraphrased) extract from their research explaining how the 15,000 participants were rated: 'Attractiveness is rated by interviewers, who [after having met study participants] were asked to answer the question "How physically attractive is the respondent?" using a five-point scale ranging from "very unattractive", to "about average", to "very attractive". Interviewers are not given specific instructions about how to assess the attractiveness of respondents.' A similar methodology was used to assess grooming levels.

3 'Virgin Atlantic drops mandatory make-up rule for cabin crew', *Reuters*, 5 March 2019 <https://www.reuters.com/article/us-britain-virgin-atlantic-uniforms/virgin-atlantic-drops-mandatory-make-up-rule-for-cabin-crew-idUKKCN1QM1OG?edition-redirect=uk>.

4 Harriet Mallinson, 'Flight secrets: Female attendants still have to abide by this rule from the 1960s', *Express*, 18 August 2018

<https://www.express.co.uk/travel/articles/1001292/flight-secrets-british-airways-female-cabin-crew-beauty>.

5 Amanda Hess, '"I Feel Pretty" and the Rise of Beauty-Standard Denialism', *New York Times*, 23 April 2018 <https://www.nytimes.com/2018/04/23/movies/i-feel-pretty-amy-schumer-beauty.html>.

6 In recent years there has been some debate as to whether Stockholm syndrome is actually a valid psychiatric diagnosis, as explored in depth by the investigative journalist Jess Hill in her book *See What You Made Me Do: Power, Control and Domestic Violence* (2019). Hill suggests that Stockholm syndrome is merely a myth invented to discredit female victims of violence, one that ignores the psychosocial complexities of abuse and female victimhood.

7 Jodi Kantor and Megan Twohey, 'Harvey Weinstein Paid Off Sexual Harassment Accusers for Decades', *New York Times*, 5 October 2017 <https://www.nytimes.com/2017/10/05/us/harvey-weinstein-harassment-allegations.html>.

8 Bret Stephens, 'When #MeToo Goes Too Far', *New York Times*, 20 December 2017 <https://www.nytimes.com/2017/12/20/opinion/metoo-damon-too-far.html>.

9 'Working Relationships in the #MeToo Era', *Lean In*, <https://leanin.org/sexual-harassment-backlash-survey-results>.

10 Abigail Abrams, 'Here's How Conservatives Are Using Civil Rights Law to Restrict Abortion', *Time*, 1 January 2020 <https://time.com/5753300/heartbeat-bill-civil-rights-law/>.

11 Eric Levenson, 'Abortion laws in the US: Here are the states pushing to restrict access', *CNN*, 30 May 2019 <https://edition.cnn.com/2019/05/16/politics/states-abortion-laws/index.html>. See also Hannah Gold and Claire Lampen, 'Every State That's Tried to Ban Abortion Over the Coronavirus', *The Cut*, 14 April 2020 <https://www.thecut.com/2020/04/every-state-thats-tried-to-ban-abortion-over-coronavirus.html>.

12 Elizabeth Dias, Rebecca R. Ruiz and Sharon LaFraniere, 'Rooted in Faith, Amy Coney Barrett Represents a New Conservatism', *New York Times*, 11 October 2020 <https://www.nytimes.com/2020/10/11/us/politics/amy-coney-barrett-life-career-family.html>.

13 Referenced earlier. Hess, '"I Feel Pretty" and the Rise of Beauty-Standard Denialism', *New York Times*, 23 April 2018 <https://www.nytimes.com/2018/04/23/movies/i-feel-pretty-amy-schumer-beauty.html>.

14 'Women Now Empowered By Everything A Woman Does', *The Onion*, 19 February 2003 <https://www.theonion.com/women-now-empowered-by-everything-a-woman-does-1819566746>.

15 Sarah Young, 'Average British Woman Spends £70,000 on Her Appearance in a Lifetime, Research Finds', *Independent*, 10 March 2017 <https://www.independent.co.uk/life-style/fashion/average-british-woman-spend-ps70000-appearance-lifetime-cosmetics-beauty-products-groupon-uk-a7623201.html>.

16 'My Morning Routine by Gwyneth Paltrow', *Goop* <https://goop.com/beauty/skin/gwyneth-paltrow-morning-routine/>.

17 Adriana Samper, Linyun W. Yang and Michelle Daniels, 'How Beauty Work Affects Judgments of Moral Character and Consumer Preferences', 2018 <http://www.adrianasamper.com/uploads/1/0/8/2/108263827/beauty_work_full_document_-_cond_accepted_jcr.pdf>.

18 Amanda Mull, 'The Best Skin-Care Trick Is Being Rich', 3 January 2019 <https://www.theatlantic.com/health/archive/2019/01/skin-care-secret-wealth/579337/>.

19 'Alicia Keys: Time to Uncover', *Lenny*, 31 May 2016 <https://www.lennyletter.com/story/alicia-keys-time-to-uncover>.

20 Jane Larkworthy, 'Meet the Woman Behind Alicia Keys' No Makeup Look and Glowing Complexion', *W Magazine*, 5 October 2016 <https://www.wmagazine.com/story/alicia-keys-no-makeup-glowing-complexion-secrets/>.

21 Office for National Statistics, 'Women shoulder the responsibility of "unpaid work"', 10 November 2016 <https://www.ons.gov.uk/employmentandlabourmarket/peopleinwork/earningsandworkinghours/articles/womenshouldertheresponsibilityofunpaidwork/2016-11-10>.

22 Anne Helen Petersen, 'that unsolvable lack', 30 July 2018 <https://tinyletter.com/annehelenpetersen/letters/that-unsolvable-lack-1>.

23 Nicole Phelps, '"We're Nobody's Third Love, We're Their First Love" – The Architects of the Victoria's Secret Fashion Show Are Still Banking on Bombshells', *Vogue*, 8 November 2018 <https://www.vogue.com/article/victorias-secret-ed-razek-monica-mitro-interview>.

24 Mary Hanbury, 'The Victoria's Secret Fashion Show saw a big drop in viewership in the wake of exec's controversial comments about transgender models', *Business Insider*, 3 December 2018 <https://www.businessinsider.com/victorias-secret-fashion-show-2018-viewership-drops-2018-12?r=US&IR=T>.

25 Samantha Reed, 'Wellness Industry Reaches $4.2 Trillion Economy',

American spa, 8 October 2018 <https://www.americanspa.com/news/wellness-industry-reaches-42-trillion-economy>.

26 Rachel Lubitz, 'This New Campaign Features Models With Pubic Hair – & It's About Time', Refinery29, 26 June 2019 <https://www.refinery29.com/en-gb/2019/06/236377/billie-razors-pubic-hair-campaign>.

27 Thom Waite, 'Jameela Jamil says Kim Kardashian is a "double agent for the patriarchy"', *Dazed Digital*, 2 September 2018 <https://www.dazeddigital.com/life-culture/article/41183/1/jameela-jamil-kim-kardashian-double-agent-patriarchy-diet-appetite-suppressants>.

28 'Kim Kardashian called "toxic" for advertising diet lollipop', *BBC News*, 16 May 2018 <https://www.bbc.co.uk/news/newsbeat-4413 7700>.

29 Amanda Hess, '"I Feel Pretty" and the Rise of Beauty-Standard Denialism', New York Times, 23 April 2018 <https://www.nytimes.com/2018/04/23/movies/i-feel-pretty-amy-schumer-beauty.html>.

Invisible Labour

1 'Care Work and Care Jobs for the Future of Decent Work', *International Labour Organisation* <https://www.ilo.org/wcmsp5/groups/public/---dgreports/---dcomm/---publ/documents/publication/wcms_633135.pdf>.

2 Jennifer Schaffer, 'The Wife Glitch', *The Baffler*, April 2020 <https://thebaffler.com/outbursts/the-wife-glitch-schaffer>.

3 Gemma Hartley, 'Women Aren't Nags – We're Just Fed Up', *Harper's Bazaar*, 27 September 2017 <https://www.harpersbazaar.com/culture/features/a12063822/emotional-labor-gender-equality/>.

4 Leah Fessler, 'An extremely clear definition of emotional labor for anyone who still doesn't get it', *Quartz*, 24 May 2018 <https://qz.com/work/1286996/an-extremely-clear-definition-of-emotional-labor-from-adam-grants-podcast/>.

5 Institute for Practitioners in Advertising (IPA) Agency Census 2018.

6 Linda Babcock, Maria P. Recalde, and Lise Vesterlund, 'Why Women Volunteer for Tasks That Don't Lead to Promotions', *Harvard Business Review*, 16 July 2018 <https://hbr.org/2018/07/why-women-volunteer-for-tasks-that-dont-lead-to-promotions>.

7 Joan C. Williams, Su Li, Roberta Rincon, Peter Finn, 'Climate control: gender and racial bias in engineering?', Centre for Work Life Law and Society of Women Engineers, 2016 <https://worklifelaw.org/publications/Climate-Control-Gender-And-Racial-Bias-In-Engineering.pdf>.

8 Linda Babcock, Maria P. Recalde, Lise Vesterlund and Laurie Weingart, 'Gender Differences in Accepting and Receiving Requests for Tasks with Low Promotability', *American Economic Review* (107:3), 2017 <http://www.pitt.edu/~vester/aer_promotability.pdf>.

9 M. E. Heilman, and J. J Chen, 'Same Behavior, Different Consequences: Reactions to Men's and Women's Altruistic Citizenship Behavior', *Journal of Applied Psychology*, (90:3), 431–441, 2005 <https://psycnet.apa.org/record/2005-05102-002>.

10 'Women shoulder the responsibility of "unpaid work", Office for National Statistics, 10 November 2016 <https://www.ons.gov.uk/employmentandlabourmarket/peopleinwork/earningsandworkinghours/articles/womenshoulder theresponsibilityof unpaid work/2016-11-10>.

11 An ONS study states that '. . . the average man would earn £166.63 more per week if his unpaid work was paid, whereas the average woman would earn £259.63.' £259.63 × 52 = £13,500.76 (when I say 'household work' here I also take that to include childcare, as the ONS does).

12 Claire Cain Miller, 'A "Generationally Perpetuated" Pattern: Daughters Do More Chores', *The New York Times*, 8 August 2018 <https://www.nytimes.com/2018/08/08/upshot/chores-girls-research-social-science.html>.

13 From feminist Judy Brady's satirical essay, *I Want A Wife*, published in *Ms.* magazine's inaugural issue, 1972 <http://www.columbia.edu/~sss31/rainbow/wife.html>.

14 Jennifer Petriglieri, 'What I Learned About Equal Partnership by Studying Dual-Income Couples', *The Atlantic*, 13 October, 2019 <https://www.theatlantic.com/family/archive/2019/10/how-dual-income-couples-find-balance-love-and-work/599938/>.

15 Kathryn J. Lively and, L. Steelman, B. Powell, 'Equity, Emotion, and Household Division of Labor Response', *Social Psychology Quarterly*, 2010 <https://www.semanticscholar.org/paper/Equity%2C-Emotion%2C-and-Household-Division-of-Labor-Lively-Steelman/6f65eb74f7709ce52e099cb1300d0d84759608c5?p2df>.

Death of the Girlboss

1 Yelena Shuster, 'NastyGal Founder Sophia Amoruso On How To Become A #GirlBoss', *Elle*, 5 May 2014 <https://www.elle.com/culture/career-politics/a12716/nastygal-sophia-amorusa-girl-boss/>.

2 Kate Clark, 'New media investment firm Attention Capital acquires Girlboss', *Tech Crunch*, 17 December 2017 <https://techcrunch.com/2019/12/17/new-media-investment-firm-attention-capital-acquires-girlboss/?guccounter=1>.

3 Chloe Jepps, 'Self-Employment in the Modern Economy in 2018', *IPSE*, 3 May 2019 <https://www.ipse.co.uk/resource/self-employment-in-the-modern-economy.html>.

4 Bärí A. Williams, 'The Tech Industry's Missed Opportunity: Funding Black Women Founders', *Fast Company*, 25 May 2017 <https://www.fastcompany.com/40422830/why-the-tech-industry-is-hurting-itself-by-not-funding-black-women-founders>.

5 *The Broad Experience*, Episode 27: Rise of the well-paid woman, 6 October 2013 <http://www.thebroadexperience.com/listen/2013/10/6/episode-27-rise-of-the-well-paid-woman.html>.

6 Erin Durkin, 'Michelle Obama on "leaning in": "Sometimes that shit doesn't work"', *Guardian*, 3 December 2018 <https://www.theguardian.com/us-news/2018/dec/03/michelle-obama-lean-in-sheryl-sandberg>.

7 Ann E. Cudd, *Capitalism, For and Against: A Feminist Debate*, 2011.

8 Andi Zeisler, *We Were Feminists Once*, 2016.

9 https://twitter.com/the_wing/status/1135534349238112257?s=20

10 https://www.crunchbase.com/organization/the-wing

11 Gillian Tan, 'WeWork Is Weighing the Sale of Its Stake in the Wing', *Bloomberg*, 1 October 2019 <https://www.bloomberg.com/news/articles/2019-10-01/wework-is-said-to-be-weighing-the-sale-of-its-stake-in-the-wing>.

12 https://www.instagram.com/p/BouKsOnlk6v/

13 Linda Kinstler, 'The Wing: how an exclusive women's club sparked a thousand arguments', *Guardian*, 18 October 2019 <https://www.theguardian.com/world/2019/oct/18/the-wing-how-an-exclusive-womens-club-sparked-a-thousand-arguments>.

14 Amanda Hess, 'The Wing Is a Women's Utopia. Unless You Work There', *The New York Times Magazine*, 17 March 2020 <https://www.nytimes.com/2020/03/17/magazine/the-wing.html>.

15 Ibid.

16 Ibid.

17 Chantal Fernandez, 'Transforming Condé Nast's Problem Child', *Business of Fashion*, 28 September 2017 <https://www.businessoffashion.com/articles/news-analysis/transforming-conde-nasts-problem-child>.

18 Anna Merlan, 'Lawsuit: Nasty Gal's #GIRLBOSS Fired Employees For Getting Pregnant', *Jezebel*, 9 June 2018 <https://jezebel.com/lawsuit-nastygals-girlboss-fired-all-her-pregnant-emp-1710042755>.

19 Rachel Zarrell and Stephanie McNeal, 'Nasty Gal Employees Describe The Company Environment As "Toxic" After New Lawsuit', *Buzzfeed*, 10 June 2015 <https://www.buzzfeednews.com/article/rachelzarrell/nasty-gal-a-horrible-place-to-work-if-youre-pregnant> and Anna Merlan, 'After Months of Reported Dysfunction, Nasty Gal Lays Off 19 Employees', *Jezebel*, 4 February 2015 <https://jezebel.com/after-months-of-reported-dysfunction-nasty-gal-lays-of-17571 69251>.

20 Noreen Malone, 'Sexual-Harassment Claims Against a "She-E.O."', *The CUT* <https://www.thecut.com/2017/03/thinx-employee-accuses-miki-agrawal-of-sexual-harassment.html>.

21 Zoe Schiffer, 'Emotional Damage', *The Verge*, 5 December 2019 <https://www.theverge.com/2019/12/5/20995453/away-luggage-ceo-steph-korey-toxic-work-environment-travel-inclusion>.

22 Rose Minutaglio, 'Audrey Gelman Resigned As CEO Of The Wing, But Employees Say It's "Not Enough"', *Elle*, 11 June 2020 <https://www.elle.com/culture/a32841010/audrey-gelman-wing-resigned/>.

23 Sam Levin, 'Uber's scandals, blunders and PR disasters: the full list', *Guardian*, 28 June 2017 <https://www.theguardian.com/technology/2017/jun/18/uber-travis-kalanick-scandal-pr-disaster-timeline>.

24 Gloria Steinem, 'Sex, Lies & Advertising', *Ms.* magazine, 1972 <http://www1.udel.edu/comm245/readings/advertising.pdf>.

Rumspringa

1 Journal of Financial Planning <https://www.financialplanning association.org/learn/journal>.

2 Mona Chalabi, 'Money dysmorphia: why I can't let myself have nice things', *Guardian*, 21 March 2019 <https://www.theguardian.com/money/2019/mar/21/money-dysmorphia-cant-let-myself-have-nice-things>.

3 Cara Feinberg, 'The Science of Scarcity', *Harvard Magazine*, May 2015 <https://harvardmagazine.com/2015/05/the-science-of-scarcity>.

4 Hua Hsu, 'How Can We Pay for Creativity in the Digital Age?', *The New Yorker*, 7 September 2020 <https://www.newyorker.com/magazine/2020/09/14/how-can-we-pay-for-creativity-in-the-digital-age>.

5 Tavi Gevinson, 'Editor's Letter', *Rookie*, 30 November 2018 <https://www.rookiemag.com/2018/11/editors-letter-86/>.

6 Naomi Klein, 'No Logo at 20: have we lost the battle against the total branding of our lives?', *Guardian*, 11 August 2019 <https://www.theguardian.com/books/2019/aug/11/no-logo-naomi-klein-20-years-on-interview>.

7 Allegra Hobbs and Josh Kramer, 'The Writer as Influencer', Study Hall, 10 October 2019 <https://www.patreon.com/posts/writer-as-306530 19>.

A Room of One's Own

1 Ellen Scott, 'Housing issues are making people's mental health worse', *Metro*, 2 May 2018 <https://metro.co.uk/2018/05/02/housing-issues-making-peoples-mental-health-worse-7514176/>.

2 John Bibby, 'What is "affordable housing?"', Shelter, 10 August 2015 <https://blog.shelter.org.uk/2015/08/what-is-affordable-housing/>.

3 Rob Merrick, 'Home ownership now out of reach for most young people, study finds', *Independent*, 27 March 2017 <https://www.independent.co.uk/news/uk/politics/home-ownership-young-people-study-alan-milburn-government-a7651126.html>.

4 https://www.yourmoney.com/mortgages/half-of-first-time-buyers-under-35-funded-by-bank-of-mum-and-dad/?ac=10&as=127&ag=131

5 'Bank of mum and dad "one of UK's biggest mortgage lenders"', *BBC News*, 27 August 2019 <https://www.bbc.co.uk/news/business-4947 7404>.

6 UK House Price Index: November 2020, Office for National Statistics <https://www.ons.gov.uk/economy/inflationandpriceindices/bulletins/housepriceindex/november2020>.

7 Eric J. Schoenberg, 'When too much is not enough: Inherited wealth and the psychological meaning of money', Columbia University <https://www0.gsb.columbia.edu/mygsb/faculty/research/pubfiles/2669/Too%20much%20not%20enough.pdf>.

8 English Housing Survey Headline Report, 2018–19 <https://assets.publishing.service.gov.uk/government/uploads/system/uploads/attachment_data/file/860076/2018-19_EHS_Headline_Report.pdf>.

9 Lisa Adkins and Martijn Konings, 'Inheritance, not work, has become the main route to middle-class home ownership', *Guardian*, 9 November 2020 <https://www.theguardian.com/commentisfree/2020/nov/09/inheritance-work-middle-class-home-ownership-cost-of-housing-wages>.

10 'Rise of the stay-at-home generation', *Financial Times* <https://www.ft.com/content/14c503b6-2a25-11e9-88a4-c32129756dd8>.

11 English Housing Survey Headline Report, 2018–19 <https://assets.publishing.service.gov.uk/government/uploads/system/uploads/attachment_data/file/860076/2018-19_EHS_Headline_Report.pdf>.

12 'Women "home alone"', *BBC News*, 29 November 2002 <http://news.bbc.co.uk/1/hi/business/2525561.stm>.

13 Sara Reis, 'A home of her own', Women's Budget Group, July 2019 <https://wbg.org.uk/wp-content/uploads/2019/07/WBG19-Housing-report-exec-sum-digital.pdf>.

14 'Up to a third of millennials face renting from cradle to grave', Resolution Foundation, 17 April 2018 <https://www.resolutionfoundation.org/press-releases/up-to-a-third-of-millennials-face-renting-from-cradle-to-grave/>.

15 Amelia Hill, 'UK's renting millennials face homelessness crisis when they retire', *Guardian*, 17 July 2019 <https://www.theguardian.com/society/2019/jul/17/renting-millennials-homelessness-crisis-retire>.

16 Home ownership, GOV.uk <https://www.ethnicity-facts-figures.service.gov.uk/housing/owning-and-renting/home-ownership/latest#by-ethnicity>.

Homecoming

1 See, for example: Hannes Schwandt, 'Recession Graduates: The Long-lasting Effects of an Unlucky Draw', Stanford Institute for Economic Policy Research, April 2019 <https://siepr.stanford.edu/research/publications/recession-graduates-effects-unlucky> and 'The Career Effects Of Graduating In A Recession', National Bureau of Economic Research, 11 November 2006 <https://www.nber.org/digest/nov06/career-effects-graduating-recession>.

2 Claudia Hupkau and Barbara Petrongolo, 'Work, care and gender during the Covid-19 crisis' <https://cep.lse.ac.uk/pubs/download/cepcovid-19-002.pdf>.

3 Robert Joyce and Xiaowei Xu, 'Sector shutdowns during the coronavirus crisis: which workers are most exposed?', Institute for Fiscal Studies, 6 April 2020 <https://www.ifs.org.uk/publications/14791>.

4 Laura Whateley, 'From furlough to tax relief: how women's pensions will be affected by coronavirus for decades to come', *i News*, 11 June 2020 <https://inews.co.uk/opinion/pensions-coronavirus-women-furlough-tax-relief-effects-explained-434486>.

5 Donna Ferguson, '"I feel like a 1950s housewife": how lockdown has exposed the gender divide', *The Guardian*, 3 May 2020 <https://www.theguardian.com/world/2020/may/03/i-feel-like-a-1950s- housewife-how-lockdown-has-exposed-the-gender-divide>.

6 Claire Cain Miller, 'Nearly Half of Men Say They Do Most of the Home Schooling. 3 Percent of Women Agree', *The New York Times*, 6 May 2020 <https://www.nytimes.com/2020/05/06/upshot/pandemic-chores-homeschooling-gender.html>.

7 Disparities in the risk and outcomes of COVID-19 <https://assets.publishing.service.gov.uk/government/uploads/system/uploads/attachment_data/file/908434/Disparities_in_the_risk_and_outcomes_of_COVID_August_2020_update.pdf>.

8 Rianna Croxford, 'Coronavirus: Black African deaths three times higher than white Britons – study', *BBC News*, 1 May 2020 <https://www.bbc.co.uk/news/uk-52492662>.

9 Marianna Hunt, 'In charts: how coronavirus is worsening Britain's racial wealth gap', *The Telegraph*, 18 June 2020 <https://www.telegraph.co.uk/money/consumer-affairs/charts-coronavirus-worsening-britains-racial-wealth-gap/>.

10 Lee Elliot Major and Stephen Machin, 'How to stop UK's declining social mobility amid COVID-19', LSE, 17 July 2020 <https://blogs.lse.ac.uk/covid19/2020/07/17/how-to-stop-uks-declining-social-mobility-amid-covid-19/>.